FROM THE LANDS
OF FIGS AND OLIVES

FROM THE LANDS OF FIGS AND OLIVES

OVER 300 DELICIOUS AND UNUSUAL RECIPES FROM
THE MIDDLE EAST AND NORTH AFRICA

Habeeb Salloum and James Peters

DRAWINGS BY LYNN PETERFREUND
PHOTOGRAPHS BY NEAL CASSIDY

INTERLINK BOOKS
An imprint of Interlink Publishing Group, Inc.
New York

First published in 1995 by

INTERLINK BOOKS
An imprint of Interlink Publishing Group, Inc.
99 Seventh Avenue • Brooklyn, New York 11215

Library of Congress Cataloging-in-Publication Data

Salloum, Habeeb.
From the lands of figs and olives: over 300 delicious and unusual recipes from
the Middle East and North Africa / Habeeb Salloum and James Peters; drawings
by Lynn Peterfreund; photographs by Neal Cassidy.
p.   cm.
Includes bibliographical references and index.
ISBN 1–56656–159–0 (HB)
1. Cookery, Arab. 2. Cookery, Middle Eastern. 3. Cookery, North African.
I. Peters, James. II. Title.
TX725.A7S23   1995
641.5956—dc20   94–12940
CIP

GENERAL EDITOR: RUTH LANE MOUSHABECK
Food Editor: Linda Sue Park
Photography: Neal Cassidy
Drawings: Lynn Peterfreund
Art Direction and Jacket Design: Rick Schneider
Food Preparation and Styling: Ruth Lane Moushabeck

Printed and bound in the United States of America
10 9 8 7 6 5 4 3 2 1

Contents

Acknowledgements

The authors wish to thank Fareeda Salloum, Muna Salloum, and Thelma Peters for their assistance in testing and tasting the recipes. They also wish to thank those authors whose books provided quotable material, especially Claudia Roden, whose *A Book of Middle Eastern Food* was particularly interesting and useful.

Interlink Publishing is grateful also to: Mary Wilson, Hala Moushabeck, Amy Kahn, Kathy Olson, Dede Wilson, and Samar Moushabeck for supplying props for the photography sessions; to Phyllis Bennis for her cheerful help and numerous trips to the supermarket during the frantic photo shoot; to Lynn Peterfreund for her striking illustrations; to Linda Sue Park for her intelligent editing; to Rick Schneider for his superb jacket design and for his art direction and advice; to Neal Cassidy for his wonderful photography and for eating his way constructively throughout the photo sessions.

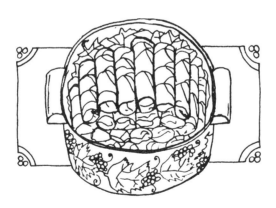

Introduction

For Arabs, hospitality is among the most admired of virtues. Families judge themselves and are judged by their peers by the degree of good-natured generosity they lavish when entertaining. Arabs feel that they are failing in their duty as hosts unless they cajole their guests into eating far more than is comfortable; likewise, a visitor who does not overeat has failed to show proper appreciation as a guest.

Such a meal always begins with *maza*, a bewildering variety of appetizers ranging from simply prepared vegetables and yogurt to highly flavored salads and dips. For a special occasion, it is not uncommon for the *maza* dishes to number in the dozens. After the *maza*, a main course of meat with bread or rice and yet more vegetables will arrive, followed by a fantastic array of Arabic sweet pastries and coffee or mint tea.

As in most cultures, the everyday meals are simpler. Most Arabs breakfast on bread and coffee, with perhaps a few olives or tomatoes to add savor. Egyptians like *fool mudammas*, a pottage of small fava beans; Syrians and Lebanese prefer cheese, of which the braided Syrian white string cheese is perhaps the best known. Another popular breakfast dish is *minoushee*, bread baked with a spicy sauce of olive oil and *za'tar*. In Arabic villages where the homes are not equipped with baking ovens, women and children with jars of *za'tar* gather at the local bakery in the morning. The baker spreads their *za'tar* on the unbaked bread dough, then pops it in the oven; in a few minutes, a freshly baked treat emerges.

The main meal is eaten at midday: a selection of *maza*, simpler than that offered to guests but a good variety nonetheless; meat and vegetables or a main-course vegetable dish; then perhaps a pastry or sweet with coffee. At supper-time, a family might dine on *maza* alone, or perhaps a simple meat or vegetable pie, the equivalent of the Western sandwich. Throughout the day in the larger towns and cities, open-air food vendors hawk their wares of skewered meats, pies, pastries, all kinds of portable Arabic goodies, to those wanting a quick snack or meal.

Wheat is the staple grain of Arabic cooking, although how it is used varies depending on the region. Moroccans like couscous, a rolled semolina cereal, while other Arabs prefer burghul, which is less refined. The staff of life is Arabic or pita bread, now easily found in most Western supermarkets. And wheat dough is exclusively used in the great family of sweet pastries. Most eastern Arabs also depend on rice as a staple.

Vegetables are accorded far more prominence in the daily diet than in Western cuisine. The various religious taboos—no pork for Jews or Muslims, meat abstinence for Christians at Lent—and the difficulty of storing meat in a hot climate have conspired to make Arabic cuisine a vegetarian's delight. For example, parsley is regarded as a vegetable in Arabic cui-

1

sine, and recipes calling for cupfuls of it are not uncommon. Rich in vitamin C and iron, easy to grow and refreshing in flavor, Arab cooks find uses for it far beyond the role it serves as a mere tired garnish in Western cuisine.

Important as vegetables are to everyday meals, Arabs still regard meat as a status symbol. Traditionally beyond the means of most rural Arabs, meat is reserved for special celebrations or honored guests. The stuffed whole lamb that forms the centerpiece of many Arab feasts is indeed a Lucullan treat, and traditionally, Arabs do not regard their tasty vegetarian dishes alone as suitable fare for guests. (We disagree.)

Arabic pastries are the food of the gods—rich, golden, dripping with butter and honey or syrup. Making the pastry dough requires a great deal of skill of the type handed down from mother to daughter over the years. The task has been made far easier with the increased availability of frozen filo or strudel dough. With this product, it is simple and enjoyable to make the sweet, flaky pastries so beloved of Arabs, the perfect dessert or luxurious snack.

* * * * *

For generations, many Westerners have entertained the belief that most Arabs are desert nomads, and that the highlight of their cuisine is sheep's eyeballs. These stereotypes have arisen from the incomplete picture given them by their limited contact with Arabic culture. It has been a relationship characterized by constant military, economic, and religious struggle, and popularized by a few grandiose but inaccurate novels and films.

As with any culture, however, Arabic culture cannot be easily encapsulated in a single image. The term "Arab" no longer denotes a particular race or nation; nor does it signify a single religious group. Arabs comprise Christians and Jews as well as Muslims, living in the eastern Mediterranean and adjacent lands.

The area is the cradle of civilization; some scholars believe even Chinese civilization was an early transplant from the Mediterranean. The region has seen a thousand cultures—from the ancient Sumerians to the present day—rise, flourish, and die.

The dishes featured here are those inherited and developed by the current occupants of this cradleland, who arrived from the Arabian peninsula around the middle of the seventh century. Every region and religion in the area has made its contribution to the vast culinary riches of the Arab world. Arabs from North Africa like their food highly spiced, making liberal use of the condiment *hreesa*, a red-pepper sauce. In the Middle East, you will find a preference for milder flavorings such as coriander and cumin. It is nearly always evident that the region was historically an important stop on the Spice Road between Europe and the Far East.

While a few of the spices and ingredients in this book may seem exotic, most of the foods in these recipes will be familiar—just used in different and exciting ways. And you need not partake of an entire feast to appreciate the spirit of Arabic hospitality. We hope this book will introduce you to a few dishes that can become part of that spirit in your own home.

Habeeb Salloum

James Peters

Spices, Herbs, and Other Delights

allspice (*bahar*): The dried berry of the pimento tree. The name derives from its taste, resembling a combination of cinnamon, cloves, and nutmeg.

aniseed (*yanisoon*): The seed of a small annual plant which has a liquorice taste. It is used to flavor pastries and drinks, especially the Arab brandy *arrack*.

baklawa or baklava dough: A fine, thin dough known in the West as *filo* (also *phylo* or *phyllo*) dough. Sold in all stores stocking Mediterranean foods, often as a frozen product.

bamia or bamya: See *okra*.

basil (*rayhan*): The dried or fresh leaf of an annual plant native to the Mediterranean, employed in flavoring soups and salads.

bay leaf (*ghar*): The aromatic leaf of the sweet bay or laurel tree. It gives flavor to soups and stews.

brochette: The French word for shish kababs.

burghul or bulghur: Whole wheat kernels which are boiled, then dried and broken into fragments. It is always soaked before using in a dish.

caraway (*karawya*): The fruit of a biennial plant used to flavor bread, pastries, and other types of dishes.

cardamom or cardamon (*hul*): An aromatic dried pod of the cardamom plant which is used to flavor Arabic coffee and pastries.

cayenne (*fulful ahmar*): The dried and powdered fruit of the hot red pepper belonging to the *capsicum* family.

chickpeas: See hummus.

chilli powder: A hot red pepper belonging to the *capsicum* family.

chives: A herb allied to the leek and the onion.

cinnamon (*qurfa*): The dried bark of the caccia tree, available in stick or in ground form. Widely used in foods and beverages.

clarified butter: Butter that is heated to a gentle boil so that the salt and other substances rise to be skimmed off.

cloves (*kurunful*): The dried unopened bud of an evergreen tree. It has an infinite variety of uses as a spice.

coriander (*kuzbura*): A herb whose seed and leaf are used in a variety of stews and salads. Also known as cilantro or Chinese parsley. A mixture of $^1/_2$ chives and $^1/_2$ fresh parsley can be substituted for coriander.

couscous: Strictly speaking, couscous is a cereal dish prepared by rolling moistened semolina into small pellets which are dried for storage. When served as a dish, it is steamed. However, the term couscous is applied to the cereal along with a great variety of accompanying *tajins* (stews) and desserts.

cumin (*kammoon*): A small, dried, slightly bitter fruit of the parsley family, used as a spice in many dishes.

dibs rumman: See *pomegranate concentrate.*

fava beans: see *fool.*

fennel (*shammar*): The dried fruit of a plant belonging to the parsley family.

filo dough: See *baklawa* above.

fool: The Arabic word for fava or broad beans, either dried or fresh.

ginger root (*zinjabeel*): A spice in root form, used when fresh, or preserved, or dried and powdered.

hareesa, hreesa or harisa: A Tunisian hot sauce.

hummus (*chickpeas*): A legume known in English as chickpeas. The element "chick" derives from the Latin *cicer.* Known as *garbanzo* in Spanish and *cecci* in Italian. Usually used split: place the chickpeas on one half of a towel, fold over the other half to cover; then roll with a rolling pin—the chickpeas will split into two and the skin will loosen. Discard the skins.

kishk: A type of powdered cheese. See Basic Recipes.

knafa: a shredded wheat-like dough used in making pastries. It is sold in Middle Eastern stores.

koosa: A green squash, known in English as vegetable marrow. Favored by the Arabs for stuffing with rice, meat, and tomato sauce. Zucchini can be substituted.

laban: Known commonly in the West as yogurt. This is the unversal sauce of the Arabs.

labana: The cheese-like paste derived from yogurt or *laban* when most of the water has been extracted by drainage through a fabric. Also known as yogurt spread.

leeks (*kurath*): A culinary green plant related to the onion and belonging to the lily family.

lentils (*'adis*): The edible seed of a plant belonging to the pea family. There are red, green, and brown lentils, used interchangeably in these recipes. Middle Eastern cooks usually use a greenish variety.

maza or mezze: An Arabic smorgesbord of appetizers served on small dishes, often accompanied by alcoholic drinks where permitted.

mazahar: Orange blossom water.

mint (*na'na'*): This fragrant herb comes in many varieties. Arabs prefer the spearmint. Used in many dishes and particularly favored as a tea.

molokhia or melkhia: Jew's mallow. An edible plant resembling spinach.

nutmeg: The dried seed or nut found inside the kernel of the tropical fruit of the nutmeg tree.

okra (*bamiya*): The edible pods of an annual belonging to the mallow family.

oregano (*anrar*): A fragrant herb whose leaf is a popular flavorant in a wide variety of dishes in Arabic and Italian Arabic cuisine.

orzo (*sha'ayriya*): Rice-shaped pasta.

paprika: A sweet, red pepper which is dried and powdered and used to flavor and color dishes.

peppercorns: The berries of the tropical vine *Piperna* which, when ground, are used as a spice.

pimento or **pimiento**: A sweet pepper whose fruit is used as a relish and for stuffing olives.

pine or **pineola nuts** (*sanawbar*): A white rice-shaped nut taken from the cones of certain pine trees which grow on the shores of the Mediterranean.

pomegranate concentrate (*dibs rumman*): A concentrated syrup distilled from the pomegranate fruit. Available in Middle Eastern groceries. To remove the seeds, press and roll the pomegranate on a hard surface, then remove the stem. With a sharp knife, score the outer skin from top to bottom at one inch intervals. After this, the fruit can be easily broken into pieces with the fingers and the seeds removed.

ricotta: A smooth, rich cottage cheese made from cream. Often used as a filling for a pastry.

rosemary (*ikleel al-jabal*): The leaf of an evergreen shrub used as a flavoring in a great variety of dishes.

saffron (*za'faran*): The dried stigma of the yellow crocus native to the Mediterranean. Its strong yellow color and delicate flavor are used for flavoring and coloring many dishes.

sage: A shrub of the mint family used for flavoring.

sauté: To fry quickly and superficially in fat or oil.

savory (*naghd*): A herb of the mint family. It is mild in flavor and is usually used dried.

scallions (*qufloot*): A type of green onion which is very mild in taste.

sesame seed (*simsim*): These seeds of the sesame plant are used whole, and also as a source of *taheena* oil. When finely ground, they are used in pastries.

soy bean (*fool al-suya*): A member of the bean family used in flour, oil, and other products. Best known for its use as a tasty sauce in Chinese cooking.

strudel dough: See *baklawa* dough above.

sumac (*summak*): The dried seeds of the fruit of the Mediterranean sumac. When ground to a powder, the seeds are used as a spice sprinkled on food.

Swiss chard: A vegetable of the beet family whose large leaves are used in salads and as a cooked vegetable.

taheena or **tahina**: A sauce and oil derived from sesame seeds. Best known when combined with a purée of chickpeas as *hummus*.

tajin: The name applied to North African stews often served with couscous. Tajin is also the name of the earthenware vessel in which they are cooked.

thyme (*za'tar*): A herb of the mint family. Very aromatic and widely used.

turmeric (*kurkum*): This yellow spice is often substituted for the very expensive saffron. It is much used in pickling, and for seasoning composite dishes.

vermicelli: A fine-gauge spaghetti-type pasta.

Special Equipment

None of the Arabic equipment on the following list is absolutely necessary; suggestions are included for appropriate substitutions.

blender: For pureeing food.

corer: For removing pulp from zucchini, small eggplants, etc.

couscousière: Two-compartment steamer pot used in cooking couscous. Substitute a colander over a saucepan.

falafel mold: A mold made especially for shaping falafel patties. They can also be shaped by hand.

garlic press: A small, hand-operated press for crushing garlic.

grater: For shredding and grating various ingredients.

ibreeq or *raqwa*: An open-topped metal pot with a long handle for making Arabic coffee. Substitute a small saucepan.

meat grinder or food processor: For chopping or grinding meat, vegetables, etc.

mortar and pestle: A wooden, metal, or porcelain bowl and rounded hammer for crushing garlic, spices, etc. A rolling pin or blender can sometimes be substituted, but a mortar and pestle can be purchased cheaply, and once you are accustomed to using them, you will find there is really no good substitute. By far the best tool for grinding and crushing spices.

sieve or strainer: Vessels with holes or mesh for draining foods.

skewers: Sharpened metal rods used in barbecuing meat, etc.

Basic Recipes

The following recipes comprise foods basic to Arabic cuisine. Some are eaten as dishes in their own right, but most are usually served as a supplement to other dishes, i.e. yogurt as a sauce, or rice as a base for meat or vegetables. A number of the recipes that follow will refer to these basic items.

Pita Bread
Khubz 'Arabee

Makes about 2 dozen loaves

Arabs eat bread with every meal, claiming that they cannot taste other foods without bread. It is used for picking up meat, vegetables, and salads, and serves as a scoop for sauces, dips, yogurt, and other semi-liquids. When the loaf is cut into two, the top and bottom of the loaf separate easily and the halves form pockets which can be filled with hot shish kababs, falafal, and/or salads. In tradition, and in daily life, bread is held to be a divine gift from God.

1 oz (2 cakes) fresh yeast or $^1/_2$ oz (2 packages) dried yeast	8 cups flour (white, whole wheat, or a half and half mixture of each)
3 cups warm water	2 teaspoons salt
1 teaspoon sugar	1 tablespoon oil

Dissolve the yeast and sugar in 1 cup of the warm water; then set aside for about five minutes.

Mix flour, salt, and oil in a large bowl, and add the yeast mixture; add remaining warm water and mix well. Knead for at least ten minutes until smooth and elastic; then place in a warm and oiled bowl, turning dough over to coat surface with oil. Cover bowl with a dry cloth and set in a warm place, allowing dough to rise until double in volume (about 2 to 3 hours).

Punch dough down, then knead for about 2 minutes. Form into smooth balls the size of small oranges, rolling them gently between your hands. Place balls on a dry cloth in a warm place; then cover with another cloth and let rise for about 30 minutes.

Preheat oven to 500°F. On lightly floured board, roll out balls into circles about $^1/_4$ inch thick. Bake the loaves 5–8 minutes on a preheated baking sheet with the oven rack at the center notch.

Note: The bread will puff up like a balloon while baking and will collapse when cooled. Loaves may be eaten immediately, or frozen for long-term storage. For short-term storage the loaves should be sealed in plastic wrap or a plastic bag. The loaves may be quickly warmed in the oven.

Arabic Plain Rice
Rizz Mufalfal

Serves 4

¹/₄ cup butter	2 cups boiling water
1 cup long grain rice, rinsed	salt to taste

Place the butter in a frying pan and melt; then add the rice and stir-fry on high heat for a few minutes until the rice is well coated with the butter.

Add the water and the salt; then reduce the heat to medium and bring to a boil. Lower the heat and cover; then cook for about 15 minutes or until all the water has been absorbed. Turn off the heat and allow the rice to finish cooking in its own steam.

Basic Dough for Pies
'Ajeenat al-Fatayar
Syria and Lebanon

This basic recipe is designed for meat, spinach, cheese, and leek pies. It will make about 18 pies.

1 tablespoon sugar	¹/₂ teaspoon salt
¹/₄ cup lukewarm water	¹/₈ teaspoon ground ginger
¹/₄ oz package dry yeast	³/₄ cup warm milk
3 cups flour	1 tablespoon olive oil
2 tablespoons butter	

Dissolve the sugar in the lukewarm water, then sprinkle the yeast in and stir. Allow to sit in a warm place until the yeast begins to froth.

Meanwhile, mix the flour, butter, salt, and ginger in a large mixing bowl. Make a well in the flour and add the milk and the yeast mix and knead well. Add more warm milk or flour if necessary. Do not allow the dough to become sticky.

Shape into a ball; then brush the entire outside of the ball with oil, and place on a floured sheet. Cover with a dampened cloth, then place in a warm spot and allow to rise until double in bulk. The dough may be frozen at this point; defrost thoroughly before using as directed in the pie recipes.

Powdered Cheese
Kishk

Kishk is a type of powdered cheese and is considered one of the oldest cheeses known to humankind. Perhaps only the bone-dry yogurt produced by the Bedouin of the desert goes back to remoter times. It is believed that *kishk* was discovered in the Fertile Crescent when humankind learned to make its own food instead of hunting it. *Kishk* can be bought from Middle Eastern specialty stores.

Makes about 4 lbs

2 quarts *laban* (yogurt–see p. 16)

3 lbs coarse burghul, rinsed, drained, and allowed to stand for $^1/_2$ hour

4 lbs *labana* (see p.17)

2 tablespoons salt

Mix the 2 quarts of *laban* with the burghul and let stand for 6 hours.

Add 2 lbs of the *labana* and the salt; then mix well and put in a warm place to ferment. Every day for the next 9 days, add a little of the remaining 2 lbs of *labana*, and stir. Make sure the *labana* lasts for the 9 days.

On the tenth day, form into small balls and spread on a white sheet in the sun to dry. (For fast drying, artificial heats such as an oven may be utilized, but the taste will not be the same.)

After drying to a consistency of half-wet, put through a grinder twice, then return to dry in the sun, spreading out thinly on a white sheet. Rub between the palms of the hands once in a while to break up the small balls; then stir the *kishk* by hand.

When the *kishk* is bone-dry, divide into fine and coarse by rubbing through a sieve.

Note: Kishk need not be refrigerated. However, it should be stored in a cool dry place.

Preserved Meat

Qawarma

Habeeb Salloum remembers his boyhood on a homestead in Saskatchewan during the 1920s and 30s. "One of my chores as a boy was to fetch water for our two sheep. Twice a day, I would walk down to the spring at the bottom of the hilll and lug two heavy pails of water back up to the sheep. On hot summer days, this was my least favorite job.

"One day, I had what I thought was a great idea. I proposed to my mother that, instead of hauling the buckets, I would walk the sheep down the hill, let them drink, then walk them back up again.

"She laughed at my idea. Didn't I know that those sheep were our winter's supply of fat? If I walked them up that steep hill every day, they would be sure to lose weight and not give enough fat to see us through to spring.

"I probably still grumbled from time to time, but I'm sure all the resentment faded when my mother served her homemade *qawarma*."

Qawarma, meat preserved in its own fat, may not seem a likely recipe for the Western kitchen, yet it is not far removed from the French *confit* of duck or English potted meats. Once a mainstay of the Syrian kitchen, it is now scorned by city dwellers as peasant food, and indeed, the countryside is the only place it continues to be made. *Qawarma* can be used in place of fresh meat in almost any stew or stuffed vegetable recipe.

Makes 4–6 quarts

$2^{1}/_{2}$ lbs melted beef fat (not suet), or margarine

5 lbs lean beef (any cut), cut into $^{1}/_{4}$ inch cubes. Mutton may be substituted for beef

5 teaspoons salt

$2^{1}/_{2}$ teaspoons pepper

Place the melted fat or margarine in a pot over medium heat and bring to a boil; then stir in the beef, salt, and pepper. With the heat at medium, cook uncovered, stirring once in a while to make sure the meat does not stick to the bottom of the pot, until the meat is well cooked.

Allow to cool; then pour into earthenware or glass jars, making sure the meat is covered with $^{1}/_{2}$ inch of fat. Discard the remaining fat, or store for use in the future.

Store the *qawarma* in a cool place. Before using, melt the *qawarma* and discard the fat. Always return to the same cool place after use.

Note: There is no need to refrigerate if the *qawarma* is well cooked. If the utensils or jars are well sealed, the *qawarma* will stay usable for one to two years.

Syrup
Qater

The divinely sweet taste of baklawa and other Arab pastries derives from the following:

2 cups sugar

1 cup water

2 tablespoons lemon juice

2 tablespoons orange blossom water (*mazahar*)

Place the sugar and the water in a pot over a medium heat. Stir constantly for 10 minutes or until the sugar is thoroughly dissolved.

Remove from the heat; then stir in the lemon juice. Return to the heat and bring to a boil. Remove from the heat and stir in the *mazahar* (orange blossom water), then allow to cool until the pastry is ready.

Note: If a less sweet syrup is desired, use only half the sugar.

Red Pepper Spice
Hreesa
Tunisia

Unlike most Middle Eastern and North African foods, the Tunisian kitchen is noted for its spicy hotness. It is said that a husband will judge his wife by the amount of *hreesa* with which she prepares his food. Some even believe that if a wife's cooking becomes bland, it means her love for her husband is fading. On the other hand, when food is prepared for visitors, the amount of *hreesa* is decreased to suit the more delicate palates of the guests.

2 tablespoons caraway seeds, ground

5 cloves garlic, crushed

1/2 cup ground fresh cayenne

1/4 cup cumin

2 tablespoons salt

1/2 cup olive oil

In a bowl, thoroughly mix all ingredients. Pour into a jar with a tight-fitting lid. Cover and store in a cool place to use as needed.

Rice Stuffing
Hashwat Rizz
Palestine and Jordan

4 tablespoons butter
$^1/_2$ lb lean beef or lamb, cut into
  $^1/_2$ inch cubes
2 teaspoons salt
1 teaspoon pepper
$^1/_4$ teaspoon cinnamon

$^1/_4$ teaspoon nutmeg
1 cup rice, rinsed
2 cups boiling water
1 tablespoon almonds, toasted
1 tablespoon pine nuts, toasted

In a frying pan, melt the butter; then sauté the meat over a medium heat until it turns light brown.

Stir in the salt, pepper, cinnamon, nutmeg, and rice. Add the boiling water; then bring to a boil. Lower the heat to a simmer, and cook for 15 minutes.

Remove from the heat; then stir in the almonds and pine nuts. Use as a stuffing for fowl, breast of lamb or veal.

Sumac and Thyme Seasoning
Za'tar

Sumac is an important ingredient in this dish, which is used to season other foods. As a flavorant, it gives bread, olives, and yogurt an exquisite taste. *Za'tar* can be found mixed and ready to use in almost all Middle Eastern markets located in every large city in North America. If it cannot be found, this simple recipe can be followed.

1 cup dried thyme, pulverized
1 cup sumac
$^1/_4$ cup cooked, dried unsalted chickpeas,
  finely pulverized

3 tablespoons sesame seed, toasted
1 tablespoon marjoram
2 tablespoons salt

Mix all the ingredients together; then store in a jar for future use.

Yemeni Hot Sauce

4 cloves garlic, crushed
6 chilli peppers
$^1/_2$ cup fresh coriander leaves (cilantro),
   finely chopped

4 cardamom seeds
1 tablespoon cumin
1 teaspoon salt
2 large tomatoes, chopped

Place all the ingredients in a food processor and process into a paste; then place in a saucepan and bring to a boil. Remove from the heat and place in a bowl for serving.

Note: This is a hot chilli sauce. It may be diluted by adding one or two tablespoons of *taheena* (see p. 18), and used a hot dip.

Yogurt
Laban

Makes about 1 quart

The history of yogurt goes back perhaps 8,000 years, to the dawn of civilization. It is believed to have been discovered by the Bedouins of the Arabian peninsula. The story goes that when a family of nomads had stored milk in bags made from goat stomachs in preparation for a long journey, the hot sun, the movements of the pack animal, and the bacteria from the goat's stomach combined to ferment and produce yogurt.

1 quart milk, preferably homogenized
   whole milk

2 tablespoons plain yogurt

Heat milk over a medium heat in a large heavy pot until it rises; then allow to cool enough to be able to insert the little finger and count to ten.
   Pour into an earthenware pot or pyrex bowl with a tight-fitting lid, and stir in the starter yogurt until thoroughly mixed; then place in a warm spot away from draughts. Cover with a woolen blanket to keep warm, or alternately, leave vessel in a 150°F oven for 5 minutes, then turn heat off, leaving vessel in the oven. Let sit for 6 hours undisturbed; then remove the blanket, or remove from the oven, and refrigerate till next day.
   Remove about 2 tablespoons of the yogurt and place in a small, covered glass jar, and keep in the refrigerator. This will be your starter (or *rawba*) for the next yogurt preparation.

Yogurt Cream Cheese
Labana

Pour a quart of yogurt (see preceding recipe) into a fine white cotton bag. Stir in 1 teaspoon of salt. Suspend the tied bag from a faucet over a sink overnight, or until contents are firm.

When firm, remove contents from the bag and place in a deep bowl; then taste to see if *labana* requires more salt. Stir, cover contents and refrigerate.

To serve, remove the required amount into a saucer; pour a little olive oil in the middle.

Note: Labana is widely available ready-made in Middle Eastern specialty stores. It is sometimes called yogurt spread.

Yogurt Cheese Balls
Zanakeel Laban

To preserve the *labana* or cream cheese for long periods, the following steps may be taken:

Place 1 heaping tablespoon of *labana* in the palm of the hand; then roll into balls and place on a tray.

Allow to stand overnight; then place in sterilized jars and cover with olive oil. Seal and store for future use.

Serve the balls with a little of the olive oil.

Note: In both forms, *labana* and *zanakeel laban*, this cheese is excellent for appetizers, sandwiches, and as a toast spread.

Yogurt Sauce
Labaniyya
Syria and Lebanon

Serves 6

Milk, both fresh and sour, and particularly in the form of *laban*, is a very ancient ingredient in the cooking of the Arabs. In certain soups, *laban* is added at the end of the cooking and just allowed to become hot, without boiling. In this case, there is little danger of it curdling. However, when *laban* is called for in the actual cooking, precautions must be taken in order that it does not curdle or separate. This is done by gently stirring over low heat till it comes to a gentle boil.

2 eggs, beaten

3 cups *laban* or plain yogurt

3 cups cold water

2 tablespoons butter

2 cloves garlic, crushed

salt to taste

2 tablespoons dried mint

In a deep pot, combine the eggs and yogurt and stir until well blended; then add the cold water and stir well. Place over medium heat and with a wooden spoon stir gently until the mixture comes to a boil; then reduce heat to very low.

In a small saucepan, melt the butter; then add the garlic, salt, and mint, and sauté over medium heat until the garlic turns golden brown. Stir the garlic mixture into the yogurt sauce and taste for seasoning; then remove from the heat and serve hot as a soup or as a sauce for other foods.

Sesame Sauce

Taheena

Palestine and Jordan

Makes about ³/₄ cup

Serve this sauce as an appetizer with pita bread. It also makes an excellent sauce for fish.

¹/₂ small head of garlic, peeled and crushed

salt to taste

¹/₂ cup *taheena* (sesame seed paste)

¹/₄ cup cold water

3 tablespoons lemon juice

1 tablespoon hot pepper, finely chopped

¹/₄ cup finely chopped parsley

1 tablespoon olive oil

In a blender, mix the garlic with the salt and *taheena*; then add the water, lemon juice, and hot pepper and blend further. Add more water a little at a time until sauce becomes light in color and the same consistency as mayonnaise.

Place the sauce on a serving platter and garnish with the parsley; then sprinkle with the olive oil. Refrigerate for at least half an hour before serving.

Variation: Add six chopped hard-boiled eggs and serve as an appetizer or a salad.

Garlic Sauce

Taratoor

Syria and Lebanon

Makes about ³/₄ cup

There is no place in the world where garlic is more used and enjoyed, especially in sauces, than in the Eastern Arab lands. This simple garlic sauce called *taratoor* is a common dish of the peasants in Syria and Lebanon. It is used as a condiment with fowl, meat, or vegetables.

2 heads of garlic, peeled	¹/₃ cup olive or vegetable oil
salt to taste	¹/₃ cup lemon juice

Place all the ingredients in a blender and purée until a creamy sauce is produced. Store in a jar or bottle with a tight-fitting lid, and refrigerate until ready to use.

Hot Spice Sauce

Shata

Sudan

Serves 4 to 6

In the Sudan, five dishes are usually served for each main meal: soup, salad, a meat or fish entrée, *shata*, and dessert, accompanied by cinnamon tea.

¹/₂ cup lemon juice	1 tablespoon ground chilli pepper
2 tablespoons olive oil	¹/₂ teaspoon pepper
4 cloves garlic, crushed	salt to taste

In a bowl, thoroughly mix all the ingredients; then place in tiny dishes and serve to each person with the entrées.

Appetizers

Appetizers, called *maza* in Arabic, constitute one of the glories of this ancient cuisine. They serve as a foretaste of the delights to come in the meal, and are served on small dishes in what can amount to an incredible number, depending on the formality and importance of the meal.

The impressive variety of these appetizers range from the simply presented olives or cheese to more complex preparations such as eggplant purée and *hummus*.

Not infrequently, guests cannot eat the main courses after sampling two or three dozen *mazas* out of a total of 60 or more. Moreover, the code of hospitality forbids the warning of the guests not to partake too much of the appetizers. Even experienced guests will have trouble confining themselves to a reasonable number of appetizers. Meals in which *mazas* play a large role usually last at least a couple of hours, and are often even longer.

The serving of these tidbits of food is believed to have been carried by the Arabs to the Iberian Peninsula during the 900 years the Arabs were in that part of Europe. The Spanish tradition of gathering before a meal for a drink and the sampling of endless appetizers called *tapas*, matches the Arab custom (but without the drinks for Muslims), and to a large extent this pleasant precursor to an elaborate meal is found only in the Middle East and in Spain.

Avocado Appetizer
Abakadoo ma' Taheena
Syria and Lebanon

Makes 1 cup

4 tablespoons lemon juice	1 clove garlic, crushed
3 tablespoons *taheena* (see p. 18)	$^1/_4$ teaspoon salt
1 large or 2 medium avocados	$^1/_4$ teaspoon pepper
$^1/_4$ cup finely chopped parsley	pinch cayenne
2 tablespoons olive oil	$^1/_2$ teaspoon paprika

Place the lemon juice and *taheena* in a blender and blend for a moment; then set aside.

Pit and peel the avocados and cut into pieces, then add them with the remaining ingredients—except the paprika—to the lemon juice/*taheena* mixture and blend into a smooth paste. Place on a flat serving platter and sprinkle with the paprika. Can be served as is, or chilled.

Chickpea Appetizer
Hummus Habb
Palestine and Jordan

Serves 4

This simple appetizer does not need any great effort to make; yet it is very tasty.

1 can chickpeas (19 oz or 540 ml), drained	1 teaspoon salt
	2 tablespoons finely chopped scallions
1/4 cup olive oil	2 tablespoons finely chopped fresh
1/4 cup lemon juice	coriander leaves (cilantro)
6 cloves of garlic, crushed	1 tablespoon finely chopped fresh mint

Thoroughly mix all the ingredients except the mint; then place in a serving bowl and refrigerate for 1 hour. Just before serving, decorate with the mint.

Note: Chives may be substituted for the coriander leaves and 1/2 teaspoon of dried mint for the fresh mint.

Chickpea Purée
Hummus bi-Taheena
Syria and Lebanon

Serves 4

In the Arab lands along the eastern Mediterranean, one usually starts the day by breakfasting on *hummus bi-taheena*. This delightful dish is also on the menu when appetizers are served, and nearly always accompanies a normal Middle Eastern family meal.

1 can chickpeas (19 oz or 540 ml), undrained	salt to taste
	pinch of cayenne
4 tablespoons *taheena* (see p. 18)	1 tablespoon finely chopped parsley
1/4 cup lemon juice	2 tablespoons olive oil
4 cloves garlic, crushed	

In a blender, place the chickpeas and their liquid, *taheena*, lemon juice, garlic, salt, and cayenne. Blend into a thick paste. (If a thinner consistency is desired, add more water). Place in a shallow platter and refrigerate for at least 1 hour. Just before serving, decorate with the parsley and sprinkle with oil.

Chickpea Dip
Hummus bi-Taheena Filasteeniya
Palestine and Jordan

Serves 4

Chickpeas are used extensively in Middle Eastern and North African cooking, and are credited with more than mere nutritional value. Many believe that chickpeas increase the energy and sexual desires of both men and women. Shaykh 'Umar Abu Muhammad, a 16th century North African Arab writer, in his book *The Perfumed Garden*, suggests chickpeas as a cure for impotence and as a first-rate sexual stimulant. In the eastern Arab lands, the peasants are convinced that chickpeas have qualities which give them the essential energy necessary for their lives of toil. As is often the case with folk wisdom, modern science supports such claims at least partially: chickpeas are a valuable source of both muscle-building proteins and energy-rich carbohydrates.

1 can chickpeas (19 oz or 540 ml), drained, with $1/4$ cup of the liquid reserved	6 tablespoons lemon juice
	salt to taste
$1/2$ cup *taheena* (see p. 18)	2 tablespoons olive oil
	1 tablespoon finely chopped fresh mint

In a blender, place the chickpeas with the $1/4$ cup of reserved water, *taheena*, lemon juice and salt. Blend until a smooth paste is formed. The paste should be of an easily spreadable consistency. If too thick, thin with water.

Spread on a serving plate; then sprinkle with the oil and decorate with the mint. Serve with raw vegetables, bread sticks or cut pieces of Arabic bread (pita).

Drained Yogurt with Za'tar
Labana ma' Za'tar
Syria and Lebanon

Makes 8 oz

$1/2$ lb *labana* (see p.17), or cream cheese	1 tablespoon olive oil
	1 teaspoon *za'tar* (see p. 15)

Spread the *labana* or cream cheese evenly in a serving dish; dribble the olive oil over the top. Sprinkle the *za'tar* over the olive oil and serve as a dip or as a spread for toast.

Chickpea and Olive Appetizer

Palestine and Jordan

Serves 4 to 6

1 cup dried chickpeas, washed and soaked overnight in 8 cups water	1 clove garlic, crushed
	salt to taste
1/2 cup black olives, chopped	1/2 teaspoon paprika
1/4 cup scallions, finely chopped	1/8 teaspoon chilli powder
2 tablespoons finely chopped fresh coriander leaves (cilantro)	1 tablespoon olive oil
	2 tablespoons lemon juice

Place the chickpeas with their water in a saucepan, and bring to a boil, then cook over a medium heat for about 2½ hours, or until the chickpeas are tender. Drain; then place the chickpeas in a salad bowl and allow to cool. (Or, substitute half a 19 oz can of chickpeas, drained.) Add the remaining ingredients and mix thoroughly. Serve immediately.

Eggplant Appetizer

Salatat Bathinjan
Palestine and Jordan

Serves 4 to 6

Eggplant, often called "the poor man's meat" or "the poor man's caviar," is one of the staple foods of the Middle East, valued for its great versatililty.

1 large eggplant, peeled and thickly sliced	4 cloves garlic
salt	1 medium hot pepper, finely chopped
8 tablespoons olive oil	3 tablespoons lemon juice

Sprinkle the eggplant slices with salt. Place in a strainer or colander, top with a weight, and allow to drain for 45 minutes.

Heat the oil in a frying pan, then add the eggplant slices and fry on both sides until they are golden brown. Remove the eggplant slices, dice them, then set aside in a bowl.

Mash the garlic cloves with salt. Add to the diced eggplant along with the hot pepper and lemon juice. Chill slightly and serve.

Eggplant Dip
Bathinjan Mfasakh
Syria and Lebanon

Serves 6 to 8

1 large eggplant, peeled and sliced $^1/_2$ inch thick	2 cloves garlic, crushed
salt	1 teaspoon crushed dry mint
$^1/_2$ cup olive oil	$^1/_2$ teaspoon pepper
2 cups yogurt (**laban**—see p. 16)	$^1/_2$ cup finely chopped tomatoes
	$^1/_2$ cup finely chopped parsley

Sprinkle the eggplant slices with salt, then place in a strainer, top with a weight, and allow to drain for 45 minutes.

In a frying pan, heat the oil; then sauté the eggplant slices on a moderately high heat until they turn golden brown. Add more oil if necessary.

Remove the eggplant pieces from the oil. Drain and mash them, then add salt to taste, *laban*, garlic, mint, and pepper and mix thoroughly. Place on a flat serving dish; then refrigerate until chilled.

Eggplant Pickles
Bathinjan Makboos
Syria and Lebanon

Makes one quart

1 large eggplant, unpeeled and cut in the middle lengthwise; then sliced across into $^1/_2$-inch-thick slices	1 teaspoon dried thyme
salt	1 teaspoon peppercorn
$^1/_2$ cup vinegar	1 teaspoon ginger
4 large cloves of garlic, finely chopped	1 teaspoon ground coriander
	1 cup olive oil

Sprinkle the eggplant slices with salt; then place in a strainer, top with a weight, and allow to drain for 45 minutes.

Place the eggplant slices and the vinegar in a pot; then cover with water and bring to a boil. Cook from 3 to 5 minutes; then remove, drain, and allow to cool.

Mix together the garlic, thyme, peppercorns, ginger, coriander, and salt to taste. Set aside. Pack the eggplant slices in a quart jar with the seasoning mixture sprinkled between each layer. Add the olive oil, and if needed, extra oil to cover the eggplant slices by $^1/_2$ inch; then store for two weeks before use.

On the brass plate clockwise from bottom front: cumin, za'tar (p. 15), cardamom, sumac, coriander seeds, allspice, and cinnamon sticks (in the center). From top left to bottom right: dates, whole almonds, small fava beans (fool), pine nuts, brown lentils, green lentils, vermicelli (above garlic), chickpeas, red lentils, and shelled pistachios.

FROM THE LANDS OF FIGS AND OLIVES

Eggplant Purée
Baba Ghannooj
Syria and Lebanon

Serves 4 to 6

Baba Ghannooj translates to "spoiled old daddy" because its inventor is said to have mashed the eggplant to a pulp in order to pamper her old and toothless father. When properly garnished, it is as pleasing to the eye as it is to the palate.

1 large eggplant	3 tablespoons olive oil
2 cloves garlic	a few parsley sprigs
salt to taste	1 tablespoon pine nuts, fried
¹/₃ cup lemon juice	¹/₂ small tomato, diced
¹/₃ cup *taheena* (see p. 18)	

Place the eggplant in a pan; then bake in a 425°F oven, turning frequently until tender. Allow to cool; then remove the skin and mash pulp well. Set aside. Mash the garlic with salt; then add 1 teaspoon of lemon juice and mix until smooth. Add to the eggplant. Place the remaining lemon juice and the *taheena* in the blender and mix for a few moments; then add to the eggplant. Add salt to taste; then spread on a platter.

Sprinkle with the oil and garnish with the parsley, pine nuts, and tomato pieces.

Instant Labana
Syria and Lebanon

Serves 4

1 lb dry cottage cheese, also known as farmer's cheese or baker's cheese	salt to taste
	1 tablespoon oil
6 tablespoons plain yogurt	

Place the cheese, yogurt, and salt in a blender and blend for a minute.

Place in a serving bowl and refrigerate for at least an hour. Remove and sprinkle with the olive oil before serving.

Maza plates clockwise from the front: turnip pickles (p. 30), black olives, pickled peppers, green olives, Arabic (pita) bread (p. 10), cucumber pickles, pickled eggplants, stuffed grape leaves (p. 203). In the center: chickpea purée (p. 23) and eggplant purée (p. 27).

Kishk Dip

Syria and Lebanon

Serves 4 to 6

In the 19th century, missionaries from the USA traveling through the Syrian mountains noted that although the peasants were poor, they were as healthy as American farmers. After a number of years of informal research, it was discovered that *kishk* was at least part of the answer. This ancient food, produced from two staples of the most basic—wheat and milk—contains most of the nourishment people need.

1 cup fine *kishk* (see p. 12)	1 large onion, finely chopped
cold water	2 small tomatoes, finely chopped
1/4 cup olive oil	a few sprigs of parsley

Place the *kishk* in a small bowl. Gradually stir in cold water until the *kishk* reaches the consistency of thick cream.

Transfer to a flat serving dish and sprinkle the olive oil on top; then spread the onions and tomatoes evenly over the oil and the *kishk*. Garnish with the parsley and serve.

Moroccan Bean Purée

Bissara

Serves 8

Although frozen or canned green fava beans are sometimes used, the beans are usually allowed to dry on the plant before harvesting. Dried fava beans are either sold in bulk or packaged in plastic bags.

2 cups large size dry fava beans, soaked overnight and drained	5 tablespoons lemon juice
3 cloves garlic, crushed	2 teaspoons cumin
salt to taste	1 teaspoon paprika
1/2 cup olive oil	1/2 teaspoon chilli powder
8 cups water	1/2 cup chopped parsley

Place the fava beans, garlic, salt, 4 tablespoons of the olive oil, and water in a pot; then cook over medium heat until the beans are tender.

Place the beans in a food processor and process until smooth, then return to the pot. Add the lemon juice and cumin, and cook for 5 minutes over low heat. Spoon onto a serving platter. Pour the remaining olive oil evenly over the top; then sprinkle with the paprika and chilli powder. Garnish with the parsley and serve.

Olive Dip

Palestine and Jordan

Serves 4 to 6

Olives are the fruit of an evergreen tree with small greenish-silvery leaves which bears clusters of fragrant white flowers. The plant, started from a cutting, grows in height from 10 to 40 feet and begins to bear fruit when 4 to 8 years old. It takes about 15 years to fully mature, but will bear fruit for hundreds of years. Some trees in the eastern Mediterranean are believed to be over 2,000 years old.

Table olives are usually picked by hand while the ones to be utilized for oil are beaten off the branches or allowed to fall on the ground, then gathered. An orchard will yield about two tons of olives per acre—a ton producing about 50 gallons of oil.

2 cups green olives, pitted and washed to remove the salt	1 tablespoon lemon juice
4 tablespoons *taheena* (see p. 18)	2 cloves garlic, crushed
2 tablespoons chopped fresh coriander leaves (cilantro)	¹/₈ teaspoon cayenne
	1 small tomato, finely chopped
	1 tablespoon olive oil

Place all the ingredients except the tomatoes and olive oil in a blender; blend until smooth.

Place in a flat serving dish and refrigerate for 1 hour; then spread the tomato pieces on top, and sprinkle with the oil just before serving.

Olives with Za'tar

Syria and Lebanon

Makes 1 lb

The people of the early civilizations in the Middle East believed that olive oil would cure every illness except the illness of death. A story is related that Adam was suffering with pain and complained to God. Gabriel descended from heaven with an olive tree and presented it to Adam, telling him to plant it, then pick the fruit and extract the oil to use whenever he had pain, assuring him that it would cure all sicknesses. In the Arab world, this story is still being told.

Some people in the Middle East believe that if they drink half a cup of olive oil before breakfast, it will clear their system and they will live a long life free from disease. Their cure for an infected ear is several doses of a little heated olive oil dropped into the ear. For sore muscles, the remedy is a massage of olive oil.

1 lb black olives, washed

½ cup olive oil

2 tablespoons za'tar (see p.15)

Mix all the ingredients and store in a covered jar, serving as needed. Stir the olive before each serving.

Taheena Mix
Salatat Taheena
Palestine and Jordan

Serves 4 to 6

5 medium sized tomatoes, finely diced
1 medium sized cucumber, finely diced
½ cup finely chopped parsley
3 tablespoons *taheena* (see p. 18)

¼ cup lemon juice
4 cloves garlic, crushed
salt to taste
1 tablespoon dried mint

Mix tomatoes, cucumber, and parsley; set aside.

In another bowl, mix the *taheena* with the lemon juice until combined well; then set aside. Mash the garlic with the salt. Add to the *taheena*-lemon juice mixture and mix thoroughly; then add the vegetables and toss. Garnish with the dried mint.

Turnip Pickles
Lift
Syria and Lebanon

Makes 6 quarts

4 medium sized beets for color
10–12 lbs (6 quarts) of small white
turnips, peeled and cut into quarters
garlic cloves, peeled

coarse pickling salt
10 cups of water
4 cups white vinegar

Boil beets until tender; then peel and cut into quarters.

Divide the turnips evenly between six sterilized quart jars. Add 1 beet quarter, 1 garlic clove, and 1 teaspoon of coarse salt to each jar.

Combine the water and the vinegar and bring to a boil; then lower the heat and simmer for 5 minutes.

Place a towel under the jars; then pour in enough hot vinegar solution to cover contents. Seal the jars immediately and allow to cool; store in a cool dry place. The pickles should be ready in 2 to 3 weeks.

Note: This measured quantity of vinegar and water, with the coarse salt added to each jar, is suitable for pickling many other vegetables. Some examples: cauliflower florets, carrots, small peppers, green tomatoes, gherkin-size cucumbers, etc.

Yemeni Eggplant Purée

Serves 4 to 6

2 medium sized eggplants	¹/₂ teaspoon pepper
1 medium Spanish onion, very finely chopped	2 tablespoons lemon juice
	¹/₄ cup olives, pitted and sliced
3 tablespoons olive oil	1 small tomato, finely chopped
1 clove garlic, crushed	¹/₄ cup finely chopped parsley
salt to taste	

Grill the eggplants over an open fire or bake in hot oven, turning often until they are tender.

Peel the eggplants while they are still hot; then mash the flesh to a pulp. Add the onion, olive oil, garlic, salt, pepper, and lemon juice. Mix well and place on a flat serving dish. Garnish with the olives, tomato, and parsley to serve.

Yogurt and Basil Appetizer

Laban ma' Habaq
Palestine and Jordan

Serves 6 to 8

4 cups yogurt, plain	2 cloves garlic, crushed
¹/₄ cup finely chopped fresh basil, or 2 teaspoons dried basil	salt to taste

Place all the ingredients in a blender; then blend for a few moments. Place in a serving bowl and chill. Serve as a dip with Arabic (pita) bread.

Zucchini and Yogurt Dip

Palestine and Jordan

Serves 4 to 6

For thousands of years, the peasants in Biblical lands have been nourished by the consumption of meatless foods such as this tasty and healthful combination.

1 lb zucchini	2 tablespoons lemon juice
1 cup yogurt	salt to taste
2 cloves garlic, crushed	¹/₂ teaspoon pepper
¹/₂ cup *taheena* (see p. 18)	2 tablespoons finely chopped parsley

Bake the zucchini in the oven until they become soft; then peel and mash. Add the remaining ingredients except the parsley and mix thoroughly; then place on a serving platter and chill for at least one hour.

Decorate with the parsley just before serving.

Soups

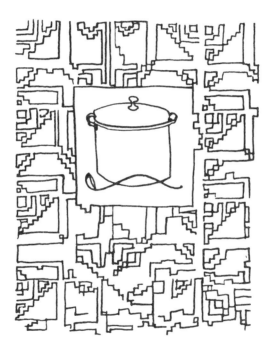

In the Arab world, legumes and cereals play a large and basic role in soups, and among the legumes, lentils stand at the top. They are moderately priced and universally available, as well as being an excellent source of basic nutrition.

Many spices and herbs are used to give these soups a rich variety of flavors. In many a humble household, soup comprises the main meal of the day. The pervasive aroma of a pot of soup simmering on the fire whets the appetite of all returning from their labors.

As a poet once wrote:

> Let Omar sing of wine and bread,
> But I prefer fine soup instead.

Aleppo Lentil Soup
Shawrbat 'Adas Halabiya
Syria and Lebanon

Serves 4 to 6

Lentils are among the most nutritious of legumes, rich in carbohydrates, iron, calcium, vitamins A and B, and, above all, protein. Dried lentils have more protein than an equal weight of choice lean sirloin steak. Few vegetables can equal their food value.

1 cup split red lentils, washed and drained	2 tablespoons oil
6 cups water	4 cloves garlic, crushed
¼ cup flour	¼ cup finely chopped fresh coriander leaves (cilantro)
¼ cup lemon juice	1 teaspoon cumin
salt to taste	pinch of cayenne

Place the lentils in a pot with 5 cups of the water. Bring to a boil, then lower the heat and simmer for approximately 5 minutes.

In the meantime, mix the flour with the remaining water to make a smooth paste. Add to the lentils. Stir in the lemon juice and salt and continue stirring over a high heat until the soup mixture returns to a boil. Lower the heat; then cover and cook for 15 minutes, stirring once in a while.

While the mixture is cooking, heat the oil in a frying pan. Add the garlic and the coriander and fry until the garlic is golden brown. Stir this mixture into the soup. Simmer for a few minutes, then add the cumin and cayenne pepper. Stir and serve hot.

Algerian Soup
Shawrba Jaza'iriya

Serves 6 to 8

Algerian soups can serve as meals in themselves. Although they are called soups, most of the soups in North Africa are indistinguishable from stews except for the fact that they have more liquid.

½ cup oil
1 lb stewing lamb or beef (with bones), cut into pieces
1 lb chicken wings and necks, cut in half
1 large onion, diced
  1 large potato, peeled and cubed
1 large zucchini, cut in large chunks
1 can chickpeas (19 oz or 540 ml), undrained

salt and pepper to taste
3 teaspoons dried mint, crushed
6 cups boiling water
½ cup fine egg noodles, broken into very small pieces
1 small can tomato paste (5 oz or 156 ml)
½ cup frozen or canned peas

In a saucepan, brown the meat and the chicken pieces in the oil, then add the onion, potato, zucchini, the chickpeas and their liquid, the salt, pepper, 1 teaspoon of the mint, and the boiling water. Bring to a boil; then lower the heat and simmer for 30 minutes.

Add the egg noodles; cook for a further 5 minutes. Stir in the tomato paste, peas, and the remaining 2 teaspoons of dried mint. Simmer for a further 10 minutes and serve hot.

Bean and Almond Soup
Asseeda
Morocco

Serves 4 to 6

In North Africa, soups are prepared somewhat differently than in the Middle East. Although the ingredients utilized are usually similar, North Africans omit the preliminary sautéeing.

½ cup navy beans, soaked overnight in 6 cups of water
¾ cup blanched almonds, ground
2 medium sized onions, chopped
¼ cup finely chopped fresh coriander leaves (cilantro)

3 cloves garlic, crushed
salt and pepper to taste
½ cup white grape juice
4 tablespoons slivered almonds, toasted

In a large saucepan, bring the beans and their water to a boil and cook over medium heat for 45 minutes.

Add the remaining ingredients except the toasted slivered almonds. Cook for another 45 minutes or until the beans are tender.

Purée in a blender; then place in a serving bowl, garnish with the toasted almonds and serve immediately.

Bean Soup
Shawrbat Fasoolya
Syria and Lebanon

Serves 6 to 8

1 1/2 cups dried navy beans, soaked
   overnight in 8 cups of water
3 tablespoons olive oil
2 medium onions, chopped
3 cloves garlic, crushed
1/2 cup finely chopped fresh coriander
   leaves (cilantro)

1 medium carrot, finely chopped
1 large potato, cut into 1/2 inch cubes
3 large tomatoes, chopped
1/2 cup finely chopped scallions
salt and pepper to taste
1/4 teaspoon allspice

Place the beans and their soaking water in a large pot and cover; then cook over a medium heat for about an hour or until the beans are cooked but still firm.

In a frying pan, sauté the onions, garlic, and coriander in the oil, stirring constantly until they begin to brown.

Add contents of the frying pan and the remaining ingredients to the beans. Simmer until the vegetables are tender.

Fava Bean Soup
Fool Nabed
Egypt

Serves 6 to 8

2 cups fava beans, washed and soaked in
   6 cups of water
salt and pepper to taste
1 teaspoon cumin
2 cloves garlic, crushed

1/4 cup olive oil
1/4 cup lemon juice
2 tablespoons finely chopped parsley
   or fresh coriander leaves

Drain the fava beans but reserve the water. Skin the beans and place in a saucepan. Measure the reserved water, and top up if necessary to make 6 cups; then bring to a boil. Cover the saucepan and cook over low heat for about 1 hour or until the fava beans are tender. Purée in a blender.

Return the purée to the saucepan and stir in the remaining ingredients except the parsley or coriander leaves. Bring to a boil and cook for about 5 minutes over low heat. Serve in individual bowls garnished with the parsley or coriander leaves.

Caraway Soup
Hareera Karawiya
Morocco

Serves 4 to 6

A simple and unusual soup.

6 cups water

2 tablespoons flour, dissolved in
   ½ cup water

2 cups very finely chopped fresh
   mint leaves

1 tablespoon ground caraway seeds

3 tablespoons butter

salt and pepper to taste

¼ cup lemon juice

In a saucepan, heat the water, but before it comes to the boil, slowly stir in the flour and water mixture.

Add the remaining ingredients except the lemon juice. Bring to a boil, stirring constantly.

Remove from the heat and stir in the lemon juice. Serve immediately; if the soup is not served at once, it will not be as tasty.

Chickpea and Fava Bean Soup
Shawrbat Hummus wa Fool
Palestine and Jordan

Serves 6 to 8

Fava beans, chickpeas and lentils formed the basis for endless soups eaten by the Arab families who settled in western Canada and the U.S.A. Eating these tasty soups relieved some of the hardships of the drought-ridden west.

Hot vegetarian country-style Arab soups not only satisfy hunger but also give warmth, pleasure and excitement with very little expense.

The skilled chef, Escoffier, could well have been talking about Arab soups when, according to K.S. Nelson, in *The Yogurt Cookbook*, he said: "Soup puts the heart at ease, calms down the violence of hunger, eliminates the tension of the day, and awakens and refines the appetite."

1 cup small fava beans, rinsed

8 cups of water

2 medium sized potatoes, peeled and diced

¼ cup olive or vegetable oil

2 medium sized onions, diced

4 cloves garlic, crushed

¼ cup finely chopped fresh
   coriander leaves (cilantro)

1 can stewed tomatoes (28 oz or 796 ml)

1 can chickpeas (19 oz or 540 ml),
   undrained

1 teaspoon oregano

salt and pepper to taste

pinch of cayenne

Bring the fava beans and water to a boil in a large pot. Cover and cook over medium heat for an hour and a half, then add the potatoes and cook for a further 25 minutes.

In the meantime, heat the oil in a frying pan and sauté the onions until they begin to brown. Add the garlic and coriander and stir-fry for 3 minutes.

Add the contents of the frying pan with the remaining ingredients to the fava beans and bring to a boil. Simmer over a medium heat for 30 minutes. Serve piping hot.

Note: The fava beans should be the small Egyptian type about the size of a pea. They can be found in Middle Eastern stores in the large cities of North America. Navy beans may be substituted; in fact, though not traditional, they make an equally delicious soup.

Chickpea Soup
Leblabi
Tunisia

Serves 6 to 8

The Arabs extolled both chickpeas and lentils for their aphrodisiacal values. R. Hentrickson, in his book *Lewd Foods*, quotes these lines by Shaykh Nefzawi in *The Perfumed Garden*:

> Abu el-Heidja has deflowered in one night
> Once eighty virgins, and he did not eat or drink between,
> Because he surfeited himself with chickpeas,
> And had drunk camel's milk with honey mixed.

1½ cups dried chickpeas, washed and soaked overnight in 10 cups water	1 teaspoon ground caraway seeds
	1 teaspoon oregano
4 cloves garlic, crushed	salt and pepper to taste
1 hot pepper, finely chopped	2 tablespoons lemon juice
¼ cup finely chopped fresh coriander leaves (cilantro)	3 tablespoons olive oil
	2 cups croutons

In a large saucepan, bring the chickpeas and their water to a boil, then cover and cook over medium heat for 2 hours.

Add the remaining ingredients, except the lemon juice, olive oil, and croutons; then cook over a medium heat for a further 30 minutes or until the chickpeas are tender. Remove from the heat and stir in the lemon juice and olive oil. Garnish each serving with croutons.

Cold Yogurt and Tomato Soup
Hasa Laban ma' Tomata
Iraq

Serves 6 to 8

Cold soups provide a refreshing midday meal or snack in the hot lands of the Middle East and North Africa. They are simple to prepare and in many cases turn out to be a gourmet's delight.

4 cups tomato juice
2 cups unsweetened yogurt
$^1/_4$ cup lemon juice
2 tablespoons olive oil

salt and pepper to taste
$^1/_8$ teaspoon chilli powder
2 tablespoons finely chopped fresh coriander leaves (cilantro)

Thoroughly mix all ingredients except the coriander leaves. Chill in a refrigerator for at least two hours.

Place in serving bowls and garnish with the chopped coriander leaves.

Cold Yogurt Soup
Shawrbat Laban Barida
Iraq

Serves 6 to 8

5 cups yogurt
1 small cucumber, peeled and finely chopped
2 cups water
$^1/_4$ cup finely chopped fresh coriander leaves (cilantro)

1 clove garlic, crushed
$^1/_2$ cup almonds, pulverized
salt and pepper to taste
pinch of cayenne

In a serving bowl, thoroughly mix all the ingredients. Chill for at least two hours before serving.

Couscous Soup
Hareera Kuskus
Morocco

Serves 6 to 8

6 cups warm water
³/₄ cup couscous
5 tablespoons butter
salt and pepper to taste

pinch of saffron
1¹/₂ teaspoons ground aniseed
¹/₄ cup finely chopped fresh coriander
    leaves (cilantro)

    In a saucepan, place all the ingredients except the aniseed and coriander leaves and bring to a boil. Cook over a medium heat for 3 minutes. Stir in the aniseed and the coriander leaves and serve immediately. If the soup is not served immediately, the texture and taste will change.

Egg and Meatball Soup
Shawrbat Bayd bil-Kufta
Algeria

Serves 6 to 8

    In the medinas, or the older parts of the cities in North Africa, the aromas of soups that impregnate the narrow streets make one ache with hunger.

3 tablespoons oil
2 medium onions, chopped
¹/₂ cup almonds
1 tablespoon butter
salt and pepper to taste
¹/₂ teaspoon cinnamon
¹/₈ teaspoon saffron
7¹/₂ cups boiling water

1 lb ground lamb or beef
2 tablespoons chopped fresh coriander
    leaves (cilantro)
2 eggs
1 cup fine vermicelli
1 tablespoon parsley, finely chopped
2 tablespoons lemon juice

    In a saucepan, heat the oil over low heat; then add half the onions and sauté until golden brown.

    Add the almonds, butter, salt, pepper, cinnamon, saffron, and 1¹/₂ cups boiling water. Cover and cook over low heat for 5 minutes.

    In the meantime, mix the meat, coriander leaves, one of the eggs, and the remaining onions, salt, and pepper. Form into balls the size of marbles and add to the mixture with the remaining boiling water. Cook over medium heat until the meatballs are well done.

    Add the vermicelli and cook for a further 5 minutes.

    Make a sauce by mixing the remaining egg, the chopped parsley, and the lemon juice. Add to the pot one minute before the soup is served. Stir well, but do not allow to boil.

Egyptian Lentil Soup
Shawrbat 'Adas Misriya
Egypt

Serves 4

In Egypt, from the days of the Pharaohs until the present time, lentil soup has been on the menu. Further, the Qur'an mentions that one of the foods which the Jews in Sinai asked Moses to provide was lentils. The following lentil soup recipe could possibly have been made, with the exception of the tomato – a New World discovery – in the same fashion at the time of Moses and the Pharaohs.

5 cups vegetable stock	4 cloves garlic, minced
1 cup split brown lentils, washed and drained	4 tablespoons butter
	2 teaspoons cumin
2 large onions, diced	salt and pepper to taste
2 medium tomatoes, diced	4 teaspoons lemon juice

Bring the stock to a boil. Add the lentils, two-thirds of the onions, the tomatoes, and garlic and return to a boil. Reduce the heat and simmer until the lentils are tender.

While the lentils are cooking, melt 1 tablespoon of butter in a frying pan. Fry the remaining onions over medium heat, stirring frequently until golden brown. Set aside.

Purée the lentil mixture in a blender, then return to the pot and reheat, stirring constantly. Add the cumin, salt, and pepper; season to taste.

Just before serving, stir in the remaining 3 tablespoons of butter. Place the soup into 4 soup bowls and add 1 teaspoon of lemon juice to each bowl; stir, then top with the reserved fried onions.

Note: For a Bahraini version, omit the fried onion garnish and do not purée the lentils. Add $^1/_4$ cup broken vermicelli, $^1/_2$ teaspoon ground coriander, and a pinch of cayenne toward the end of the cooking time and cook until the noodles are done.

Fish Soup

Morocco

Serves 8 to 10

The association of fish with aphrodisiac powers has a long history. A fair number of ancient religions forbade the eating of fish among their priests. It was believed that the consumption of sea animals made one ardent in love. The Greek poet Asclepiades advocated a meal of fish for anyone planning to spend an evening with a willing woman. In Roman times, a fish sauce was made to arouse sexual feelings.

Madame Pompadour, the greatest of French mistresses, often dined on seafood as a prelude to *l'amour*. Casanova, who usually ate 50 oysters for breakfast, believed that fish would increase his sexual powers.

This soup gives great pleasure to the palate, but we make no other guarantees!

6 tablespoons olive or vegetable oil
1 lb fish fillet (any kind), cut into
   1 inch cubes
2 medium onions, chopped
4 cloves garlic, crushed
$^1/_2$ small hot pepper, seeded and
   finely chopped
1 teaspoon oregano

salt and pepper to taste
$^1/_2$ teaspoon cumin
1 can tomato paste (5.5 oz or 156 ml)
8 cups water
$^1/_2$ cup rice, rinsed
3 tablespoons finely chopped fresh
   coriander leaves (cilantro)

In a large saucepan, sauté the fish in the oil over medium-high heat for 10 minutes, turning the pieces over once. Remove the fish with a slotted spoon and set aside. Add more oil to the pan if necessary, then sauté the onions, garlic, and hot pepper over medium heat for 15 minutes. Stir in the remaining ingredients except the coriander leaves and fish and bring to a boil. Cover and cook over medium heat for 20 minutes.

Add the fish and cook for a further 15 minutes. Remove from the heat, stir in the coriander leaves, and serve.

Iraqi Chickpea Soup
Hasa al-Hummus

Serves 4 to 6

1 cup dried chickpeas, washed and soaked overnight in 9 cups of water	$^1/_2$ cup finely chopped fresh coriander leaves (cilantro)
2 tablespoons butter	salt and pepper to taste
2 medium sized onions, diced	$^1/_2$ teaspoon mustard powder
4 cloves garlic, crushed	pinch of cayenne

In a saucepan, bring the chickpeas and their soaking water to a boil, then cook over medium heat for $1^1/_2$ hours.

In a separate pan, stir-fry the onions and garlic in the butter until they begin to brown. Add the coriander leaves and stir-fry for a few moments longer, then add the contents of the frying pan and the remaining ingredients to the chickpeas. Cover and cook over medium heat for 1 hour or until the chickpeas are tender.

Iraqi Yogurt Soup
Hasa Laban ma' Rizz

Serves 6 to 8

In the Middle East, countless varieties of yogurt soups are prepared. Hot, cold, spicy or sweet, they are all exotic and delectable.

$^1/_2$ cup rice, rinsed	2 cloves garlic, crushed
2 cups of water	1 cup finely chopped fresh mint
5 cups yogurt	salt and pepper to taste

Place the rice and water in a saucepan and cook over a medium heat until the rice is cooked, but still firm.

Remove the saucepan from the heat. Gradually add the yogurt, garlic, salt, and pepper, stirring constantly. Return to the heat and continue to stir until the soup comes to a boil, then remove and stir in the mint just before serving.

Kishk Soup

Syria and Lebanon

Serves 4

Omit the meat for an equally appetizing vegetarian version.

2 tablespoons butter
1 medium sized onion, finely chopped
2 cloves garlic, crushed
³/₄ cup *kishk* (see p. 12), dissolved in
  ¹/₂ cup of water

¹/₂ cup *qawarma* (see p. 13), fat removed
  (or, substitute lean lamb or beef,
  cubed and sautéed)
4 cups boiling water
salt and pepper to taste

Melt the butter in a saucepan. Add the onions and garlic and sauté until the onions turn golden brown.

Stir in the *kishk* and *qawarma* or meat and sauté for a moment; then add the rest of the ingredients and bring to a boil over medium heat. Cover and simmer over low heat for 10 minutes. Serve hot with toast.

Note: Makes an excellent breakfast dish, especially on cold winter mornings.

Lentil and Noodle Soup

Shawrbat 'Adas ma' Sha'iriya
Syria and Lebanon

Serves 6 to 8

8 cups of water
salt and pepper to taste
1 cup brown lentils, rinsed and drained
¹/₄ cup olive oil
2 medium onions, chopped

4 cloves garlic, crushed
¹/₂ cup finely chopped fresh coriander
  leaves (cilantro)
¹/₂ cup vermicelli, broken into small
  pieces

In a pot, bring the water, salt, pepper, and lentils to a boil; then cook for about 30 minutes over medium heat, until the lentils are tender but still intact and slightly firm.

In the meantime, place the oil, onions, and garlic in a frying pan and sauté over medium heat until the onions are slightly brown. Add the coriander leaves and stir-fry for a few more minutes.

Add the contents of the frying pan to the lentils; then stir in the vermicelli and bring to a boil. Lower the heat and simmer for about 20 minutes, or until the vermicelli is done.

Lentil Soup with Spinach
Shawrbat 'Adas ma' Sabanikh
Syria and Lebanon

Serves 6 to 8

Cooked, lentils can be served as a vegetable with other food or in salads, but they are most often used as the main ingredient in soups and stews.

Dry lentils do not require soaking and are usually only washed before cooking, but they may be soaked, and if soaked they require only half the time for cooking.

1 cup brown lentils, rinsed and drained	4 cloves garlic, crushed
8 cups water	$^1/_4$ cup olive oil
salt to taste	$^1/_2$ package spinach (10 oz or 184 g),
$^1/_4$ cup finely chopped fresh coriander leaves (cilantro)	washed and chopped
	1 cup finely chopped parsley
2 large onions, finely chopped	$^1/_2$ cup lemon juice

Place lentils, water, and salt in a pot and cook over a medium heat until the lentils are tender but still intact and slightly firm.

Meanwhile, fry the coriander leaves, onions, and garlic in the oil, stirring until the onions are golden brown. Add the fried mixture with its oil to the lentils, then stir in spinach, parsley, and lemon juice. Simmer until the spinach is cooked.

Note: Swiss chard may be substituted for the spinach.

Marrakesh Rice and Lentil Soup
Hareera Marrakashee
Morocco

Serves 6 to 8

The ancients in the Middle East and North Africa believed that the herbs and spices in the broth, besides enriching the soup, stimulated the appetite, helped in the circulation of the blood, alleviated rheumatic disorders, and eased diabetic problems. Even if these claims were only myths, these hearty and nourishing concoctions make an appetizing and gratifying meal.

$^3/_4$ cup lentils, washed and soaked overnight in 7 cups of water	salt and pepper to taste
	$^1/_2$ teaspoon cumin
2 tablespoons olive oil	pinch of chilli powder
$^1/_2$ cup finely chopped fresh coriander leaves (cilantro)	2 tablespoons flour, dissolved in $^1/_2$ cup of water

1 teaspoon paprika
'/2 cup rice, rinsed

'/4 cup lemon juice

In a saucepan, place the lentils and their soaking water, olive oil, coriander leaves, and paprika. Bring to a boil over high heat. Cover and cook over medium heat for 25 minutes; then add the remaining ingredients except the flour and lemon juice and cook for a further 20 minutes or until the rice grains are tender but still whole.

Remove from the heat and slowly stir in the flour paste and lemon juice. Return to the heat and bring to a boil. Serve immediately.

Meat Soup
Fatta
Egypt

Serves 6

This soup is traditionally served by Egyptian Christians as the first meal after the Lenten fast.

1 lb lean beef or lamb, cut into small
   pieces
6 cups water
salt and pepper to taste
1 medium onion
3 tablespoons butter

5 cloves garlic, crushed
1 teaspoon vinegar
1 loaf Arabic pita bread, dried in the
   oven until crisp
2 cups cooked rice

Simmer the meat in the water, with the salt, pepper, and the whole onion, until the meat is tender; then skim off the scum and discard the onion. Remove the meat from the broth with a slotted spoon, and drain on paper towels. Set aside.

Melt 2 tablespoons of the butter in a frying pan. Fry the meat over high heat until well browned; then remove to a serving bowl and keep warm.

Fry the garlic in the remaining butter until golden brown. Stir the contents of the frying pan and the vinegar into broth; then bring to a boil.

Just before serving, break up the bread into the soup; then divide into individual bowls. Present the meat and rice separately, allowing each person to serve themselves.

Moroccan Eggplant and Vegetable Marrow Soup

Serves 6 to 8

salt
1 medium sized eggplant, peeled and
    cut into ¹/₂ inch cubes
¹/₂ cup olive oil
1 medium sized vegetable marrow, cut
    into ¹/₂ inch cubes (marrow should
    be about 7 to 8 inches long, or
    substitute 1 large zucchini)

1 small onion, finely chopped
2 cloves garlic, crushed
3 tablespoons finely chopped fresh
    coriander leaves (cilantro)
2 large tomatoes, finely chopped
1 teaspoon cumin
¹/₄ teaspoon pepper
5¹/₂ cups water

Sprinkle salt on the eggplant cubes; then place in a strainer, top with a weight, and allow to drain for 45 minutes.

In a large saucepan, heat the oil; then add the vegetable marrow and sauté over medium heat for 3 minutes. Stir in the eggplant, onion, garlic, and coriander leaves; then sauté further, stirring constantly until the eggplant begins to brown.

Add the rest of the ingredients, including salt to taste, and bring to a boil; then lower the heat, cover, and simmer for 30 minutes.

Palestinian Lentil Soup
Shawrbat 'Adas Filasteeniya
Palestine and Jordan

Serves 4 to 6

The ancient Egyptians and Greeks believed that lentils would enlighten the mind, open the heart, and render people cheerful. Thus it was a favorite food among both rich and poor. The Romans, on the other hand, believed that lentils made men reserved, indolent, and lazy. A story is told that in one of the many Roman-Parthian wars, a Roman general was convinced that the Romans were going to lose the war because the supply of grain was exhausted and his men had been obliged to eat lentils. Some writers have indicated that because of these ancient beliefs, lentils flourished in Asia, Africa, Greece, and in Spain, which was once under the control of the Arabs, but not in many other European countries.

2 large onions, diced
¹/₄ cup olive oil
1 cup split lentils
salt and pepper to taste
¹/₂ teaspon cumin

pinch saffron
7 cups boiling water
2 tablespoons rice
4 to 6 teaspoons lemon juice

In a pot, sauté the onions in the oil until they turn golden brown. Add the lentils, salt, pepper, cumin, and finally the boiling water. Simmer over low heat until the lentils are nearly cooked; then add rice and cook a further 15 minutes.

Serve in individual bowls, adding lemon juice to each dish.

Note: The soup can also be puréed if a smoother texture is desired. A Syrian/Lebanese version of this soup uses paprika and fresh coriander leaves instead of saffron and cumin, demonstrating how a basic recipe can be varied by the use of spices.

Pomegranate Soup
Shawrbat Rumman
Iraq

Serves 6 to 8

Among the ancient civilizations of the Middle East, the pomegranate was a symbol of fertility. The Romans believed its ovules to be an aphrodisiac—a belief which in later centuries spread to all parts of Europe. Hence, many labeled it the "love fruit." In Arabic folklore and poetry, the pomegranate is also a symbol for the female breast.

1 cup ground beef or lamb (lean)
1 medium sized onion, finely chopped
¼ cup breadcrumbs
salt and pepper to taste
¼ teaspoon cumin
pinch cayenne
¼ cup olive oil
½ cup finely chopped fresh coriander
  leaves (cilantro)
4 cloves garlic, crushed

½ cup finely chopped scallions
¼ cup finely chopped fresh mint
½ cup lentils, washed and soaked
  overnight
1 teaspoon tarragon
¼ teaspoon chilli powder
3 tablespoons pomegranate concentrate
  (*dibs rumman*—see Glossary, p. 6)
8 cups water

Mix thoroughly the meat, onion, breadcrumbs, salt, pepper, cumin, and cayenne. Form into small balls. In a saucepan, sauté the meatballs in the oil over medium heat, gently turning them over until they begin to brown.

Stir in the coriander leaves and garlic and sauté for a further few minutes; then add the remaining ingredients and bring to a boil. Cover the saucepan, and cook over medium heat for about 1 hour. Serve immediately.

Red Lentil Soup with Rice
Shawrbat 'Adas Ahmar ma' Rizz
Syria and Lebanon

Serves 6 to 8

The Spanish missionaries were the first to bring the lentil to the Americas, but it took many years before people began to appreciate its value. Slowly its cultivation spread, until now it is grown in parts of South America, the north-west U.S.A., and parts of western Canada. Although now cultivated to some extent in both North and South America, it is only lately that it has been used as a food in some of the countries in the western hemisphere; but in its native habitat, the Arab world, it has been used as a food for at least 4,500 years and perhaps longer.

$^3/_4$ cup red lentils, rinsed and drained
salt to taste
$^1/_2$ teaspoon pepper
1 teaspoon paprika
8 cups water
6 tablespoons butter

$1^1/_2$ cups chopped onions
4 cloves garlic, crushed
$^1/_2$ cup finely chopped fresh
    coriander leaves (cilantro)
$^1/_4$ cup rice, rinsed and drained

Place the lentils, salt, pepper, paprika, and water in a pot; then cook over a medium heat for about 30 minutes or until the lentils are tender, but still intact and slightly firm. While the lentils are cooking, heat the butter in a frying pan; then add the onions and garlic and fry until the onions begin to brown. Add the coriander leaves and sauté for a further 3 minutes; then stir the contents of the frying pan into the lentils.

Stir in the rice and bring to a boil; then reduce the heat to low, and simmer until the rice is tender but still intact and slightly firm.

Soup of Khartoum
Shawrbat al-Khartoom
Sudan

Serves 4 to 6

2 lbs lamb or beef bones
8 cups water
salt and pepper to taste
2 medium onions, diced
3 carrots, peeled and chopped into
    small pieces
$^1/_2$ head of small cabbage, chopped

$^1/_4$ cup finely chopped fresh coriander
    leaves (cilantro)
3 cloves garlic, finely chopped
1 cup frozen or fresh peas
$^1/_4$ cup rice, rinsed
3 tablespoons peanut butter, thinned
    with 2 tablespoons lemon juice

In a saucepan, cover the bones with the water. Add salt and pepper, bring to a boil, lower the heat and simmer for 1 hour. Add the onions, carrots, cabbage, coriander, and garlic. Simmer for 1 hour or until vegetables are thoroughly cooked.

Remove the bones, then add the peas and rice and cook for 20 minutes. Add the peanut butter with the lemon juice; then stir and serve hot.

Thick Chicken and Vegetable Soup

Saudi Arabia

Serves 4 to 6

$^1/_2$ lb chicken, cubed
4 cups chicken broth
salt and pepper to taste
$^1/_2$ teaspoon cumin
2 bay leaves
4 cups mixed shredded root vegetables

choose some or all of the following:
   carrots, potatoes, parsnips, turnips
$^1/_4$ cup finely chopped coriander
   leaves (cilantro)
2 medium onions, coarsely chopped
2 cups milk

In a large pot, bring the chicken, chicken broth, salt, pepper, cumin, and bay leaves to a boil. Cook over a medium heat until chicken is well done.

Add the remaining ingredients—except for the milk—and return to a boil, then cover the pot and reduce the heat. Simmer for about 30 minutes or until the vegetables are cooked. Slowly stir in the milk. Simmer for a further 3 minutes, stirring gently.

Note: Other lean meats may be substituted for the chicken.

Thick Chickpea and Meat Soup

Hareera

Morocco

Serves 12

Hareera is one of Morocco's oldest and by far the most popular of its soups. It plays an important role in Ramadan, Islam's annual fast which lasts 28 days. The end of each day's fast is announced by the firing of a cannon. At that instant, the first taste of food is always a mouthful of *hareera*.

$^1/_4$ lb chickpeas, soaked overnight
$^1/_2$ cup butter
2 cups chopped onion

3 quarts water
$^1/_2$ cup finely chopped fresh coriander
   leaves (cilantro)

salt and pepper to taste

$1/2$ lb lamb or beef with bones (any type of meat, diced, may be used)

pinch cinnamon

pinch saffron

2 cups tomato juice

1 cup rice

3 tablespoons flour

$1/2$ cup finely chopped parsley

$1/4$ cup lemon juice (optional)

Split the chickpeas and remove the skins. Set aside.

Melt the butter in a saucepan, then add 1 cup of the onions, salt and pepper. Sauté over medium heat until the onions turn light brown. Cut the meat from the bones and dice it. Stir the diced meat and the bones into the pan and sauté further until the meat turns light brown. Add the remaining cup of onions, the chickpeas, the cinnamon, the saffron, and 1 quart of the water, and cook until the chickpeas are done. Stir in 1 tablespoon of the coriander leaves and cook for a further 5 minutes. Set aside.

In another pot, boil the remaining two quarts of water, the tomato juice, salt, and pepper for 5 minutes. Add the rice and return to a boil; then lower the heat and simmer until the rice is done.

Mix the flour with 3 tablespoons cold water to make a thin paste. Slowly stir the paste into the rice mixture. Add the rest of the coriander and parsley. Cook for a further 5 minutes. Combine the meat and rice mixtures and serve.

Note: 1 teaspoon lemon juice may be added to each individual serving if desired.

Tomato and Chickpea Soup

Hasa Tamatat ma' Hummus

Iraq

Serves 8 to 10

2 tablespoons butter

2 medium onions, chopped

2 cloves garlic, crushed

$1/4$ cup finely chopped fresh coriander leaves (cilantro)

1 can chickpeas (19 oz or 540 ml), undrained

3 cups tomato juice

4 cups water

$1/2$ cup rice, rinsed

salt and pepper to taste

$1/4$ teaspoon cumin

$1/4$ teaspoon allspice

Melt the butter in a saucepan over medium heat. Add the onions and garlic and sauté until they turn golden brown.

Add the coriander leaves and stir-fry for a further few minutes; then stir in the remaining ingredients and bring to a boil. Cook over medium heat for about 20 minutes, or until the rice is cooked.

Vegetable and Meat Soup

Syria and Lebanon

Serves 6 to 8

Among the peasants of the Middle East, many of the soups are enriched by first sautéing some of the vegetables with herbs, especially fresh coriander. This exotic condiment gives the soup a characteristic flavor and aroma. However, people who are not familiar with fresh coriander sometimes dislike its smell and taste at first. For these reluctants, a mixture of chives and parsley may be substituted.

¹/₄ cup olive oil	6 cups water
1 lb beef, cut into ¹/₂ inch cubes	5 medium tomatoes, diced
2 medium onions, diced	2 medium potatoes, peeled and cubed
2 cloves garlic, crushed	¹/₂ teaspoon allspice
¹/₂ cup finely chopped fresh coriander leaves (cilantro)	2 small carrots, diced
	salt and pepper to taste

Heat the oil in a large saucepan, and sauté the meat over medium heat until it begins to brown. Stir in the onions, garlic, and coriander leaves and sauté further until the onions begin to brown. Add the remaining ingredients; then cover and bring to the boil. Lower the heat and simmer for 45 minutes over medium heat or until the vegetables are tender.

Vegetable Soup

Hasa al-Khadr

Iraq

Serves 6 to 8

Many of the easy-to-make vegetarian Arab soups are served as one-dish meals. All that is needed to complete the repast are Arabic bread (pita), *labana*, and perhaps a salad.

¹/₄ cup olive oil	1 cup finely chopped fresh coriander leaves (cilantro)
2 medium carrots, peeled and finely diced	5 cups water
2 medium potatoes, peeled and finely diced	1 can stewed tomatoes (19 oz or 540 ml)
1 medium onion, diced	¹/₄ teaspoon allspice
2 cloves garlic, crushed	¹/₄ teaspoon cumin
	salt and pepper to taste

Heat the oil in a saucepan, then add the carrots, potatoes, onion, garlic, and coriander. Sauté over medium heat for 8 minutes, stirring constantly, then add the remaining ingredients and bring to a boil. Lower the heat, then cover and simmer until the vegetables are tender.

Yemeni Lentil Soup
Shawrbat 'Adas Yamani

Serves 6 to 8

1 cup lentils, rinsed
6 cups water
5 tablespoons olive oil
$^1/_2$ lb beef or lamb, cut into very small pieces
2 medium onions, finely chopped
4 cloves garlic, crushed

$^1/_2$ cup finely chopped fresh coriander leaves (cilantro)
2 large tomatoes, finely chopped
$^1/_4$ teaspoon allspice
$^1/_4$ teaspoon cayenne
salt and pepper to taste

Place the lentils and water in a pot and bring to a boil; cook over a medium heat for 15 minutes.

In the meantime, heat the oil in a frying pan and sauté the meat until it begins to brown. Stir in the onions, garlic, and coriander leaves; sauté until the onions begin to brown. Add the tomatoes and cook for a further 3 to 5 minutes.

Stir the contents of the frying pan and the remaining ingredients into the lentils. Cover the pot and simmer over low heat for 20–30 minutes. Do not overcook; the lentils should still be whole.

Salads

In Europe, and later North America, many types of salad dressings have been developed—Caesar, French, Italian, Thousand Island, etc. However, in the lands of the Middle East and North Africa, the ancient dressing of lemon juice and olive oil has stood the test of centuries. The idea has always been to enhance, not mask, the flavor of the main ingredients.

In the countries of the Middle East and North Africa, the types of salads enjoyed by both rich and poor are without number. Simple salads have graced the Arabic table since the days of Summer and the Pharaohs. The inheritors of these civilizations documented a number of their dishes; some of their recipes were first recorded in the 10th century.

As is true of all salads, those offered here can be appetizers to start a meal or accompaniments to the main courses. Many can also serve as main dishes. Unlike the ubiquitous lettuce and tomato salad of North America, Arab salads are usually a combination of many vegetables and spices. They are never monotonous, for they can be altered in many ways. In this chapter, we have only included samples of a salad cuisine with a rich heritage.

Algerian Salad
Salata Jaza'iriya
Algeria

Serves 4 to 6

Olives are said to be an acquired taste — and one well worth acquiring. In the Mediterranean basin, however, people seem to be born with a taste for them. The oil- or salt-cured olives used in Arabic cooking are far more flavorful than the bland canned types common in North America. Use canned olives as an introduction for the uninitiated, but it is well worth seeking out the genuine article, readily available in Greek or Middle Eastern specialty stores.

2 sweet peppers, seeded and finely chopped	2 hard-boiled eggs, quartered
4 medium tomatoes	1 teaspoon chopped fresh basil or 1 tablespoon chopped fresh coriander leaves (cilantro)
½ cup sliced cucumber	
2 small onions, thinly sliced	3 tablespoons olive oil
½ cup black olives, pitted and halved	1 tablespoon vinegar
6 anchovy fillets, chopped	salt and pepper to taste

Place all the ingredients in a salad bowl and toss gently. Serve with pita bread if desired.

Artichoke Salad
Salatat Khurshoof
Syria and Lebanon

Serves 4 to 6

1 can artichoke hearts, drained and cut into quarters
1/2 head lettuce, chopped
1 large tomato, chopped into large pieces
1 small onion, finely chopped

11/2 cups finely chopped celery
2 cloves garlic, crushed
1/4 cup lemon juice
1/4 cup olive oil
salt and pepper to taste

Mix the artichoke, lettuce, tomato, onion, celery, and garlic in a salad bowl. Add the salt, pepper, lemon juice, and olive oil. Toss and serve.

Note: Frozen artichoke hearts may be used after being cooked according to directions on the package.

Avocado Salad
Palestine and Jordan

Serves 4

1 large avocado, cubed into small pieces
1 large tomato, diced
1 medium onion, finely chopped
1 small hot pepper, very finely chopped

2 tablespoons finely chopped fresh coriander leaves (cilantro)
3 tablespoons olive oil
2 tablespoons lemon juice
salt and pepper to taste

Toss all the ingredients together in a salad bowl just before serving.

Beet Salad
Salatat Shamandar
Syria and Lebanon

Serves 4 to 6

5 large beets
2 cloves garlic
2 tablespoons finely chopped fresh coriander leaves (cilantro)
1/4 cup finely chopped fresh chives

1/4 cup olive oil
1/4 cup lemon juice
1/4 cup chopped parsley
salt and pepper to taste

Boil the beets until tender. Peel, dice, and place in a salad bowl.
Mash the garlic with the salt. Add the garlic, pepper, coriander, chives, olive oil, and lemon juice to the beets and mix gently. Sprinkle with the parsley. Chill for at least one hour before serving.

Black Olive and Orange Salad

Salatat Zaytoon

Morocco

Serves 4

Olives come in dozens of shapes, sizes, and colors. They vary in size from half an inch to two inches. About 40% are picked green before they ripen, the remainder are harvested when ripe in various shades ranging from purple-blue to black.

Whatever the color, olives are bitter when picked and must be processed before they become palatable. In the Mediterranean countries, all types are usually slit or bruised and soaked in a lye solution to remove their bitterness. They are then washed and preserved in brine or oil. The pits of green olives are sometimes removed and the cavities stuffed with almonds, anchovies, or pimentos. More often, they are marinated in coriander, ginger, hot pepper, lemon juice, thyme, and other herbs or spices.

These are usually retailed in bulk, even in North America. The enticing pungent odors emanating from the barrels of ripe preserved olives are a recognizable feature of Mediterranean markets.

The following salad makes an unusual and vividly colored appetizer.

$^1/_2$ cup black olives, pitted and halved

4 large oranges, peeled, sectioned, and cut into small pieces

$^1/_2$ teaspoon cumin

pinch cayenne

Mix the olives and oranges in a salad bowl. Cover and refrigerate for at least one hour.

Mix the cumin and the cayenne in a separate dish. Just before serving, sprinkle over the olive-orange mixture and toss.

Note: Saudi Arabians serve an equally delicious version of this salad. Omit the cumin and cayenne. Add 2 small onions, thinly sliced, and a little olive oil and lemon juice. Season to taste and serve on lettuce leaves.

Clockwise from the top: red lentil soup with rice (p. 49), cold yogurt soup (p. 39), lentil soup with spinach (p. 45).

Bread Salad
Fattoosh
Syria and Lebanon

Serves 4 to 6

This salad can serve as a main course — perfect for a summer lunch.

1 loaf pita bread or 4 thin slices
   white bread, toasted until evenly
   brown, then broken into small pieces
juice of 1 large lemon
1 large English seedless cucumber,
   chopped, or ½ head of lettuce,
   chopped
1 small sweet red pepper, chopped
4 firm ripe tomatoes, chopped
1 bunch scallions, finely chopped

2 tablespoons finely chopped parsley
2 tablespoons finely chopped fresh mint
   or 1 teaspoon of dried crushed mint
2 cloves garlic, crushed
5 tablespoons olive oil
1 teaspoon sumac (see Glossary, p. 6)
3 tablespoons finely chopped fresh
   coriander leaves (cilantro)
salt and pepper to taste

Toss all the ingredients together. Taste and add more seasoning if desired. Serve immediately, before the bread becomes soft.

Fava Bean Salad
Salatat Fool
Syria and Lebanon

Serves 4

1 can green fava beans, drained
   (19 oz or 540 ml).
¼ cup finely chopped scallions
½ cup finely chopped parsley

2 cloves garlic, crushed
2 tablespoons lemon juice
¼ cup olive oil
salt and pepper to taste

In a serving dish, mix all the ingredients well. Serve with pita bread, if desired.

Note: Add three hard-boiled eggs, chopped, to make a main-course version; dust with paprika.

In the foreground: Algerian salad (p. 56). Top right: tabboola (p. 68). Top left: black olive and orange salad (p. 58).

Fava Beans with Yogurt
Fool ma' Laban
Syria and Lebanon

Serves 6

Fava beans are delicious when picked green and still tender. Harvested at this stage, the whole pod is tasty and enjoyable and the beans themselves can be eaten raw. In the Arab East, where the fava bean is known as *fool*, rare is the evening banquet or the gourmet meal where *fool* is not served as an hors d'oeuvre.

2 lbs fresh fava beans	1 teaspoon finely chopped fresh mint
1 teaspoon brown sugar	1/2 teaspoon freshly ground pepper
1 teaspoon lemon juice	1 cup yogurt
1 teaspoon mustard powder	1 egg, beaten
pinch nutmeg	salt to taste
1 clove garlic, crushed	

Shell the beans and cook in boiling, salted water until tender. Drain, return to the pot, and set aside.

Mix the yogurt with all the other ingredients except the egg. Pour the yogurt mixture over the beans and heat gently; then stir in the egg. Let the mixture thicken, but do not boil. Serve at once.

Carrot and Olive Salad
Salatat Jazar wa Zaytoon
Sudan

Serves 4 to 6

2 medium carrots, peeled and sliced into thin rounds	1/2 cup pitted black olives, halved
1/2 medium-sized head of lettuce, coarsely chopped	2 tablespoons lemon juice
1 tablespoon finely chopped fresh coriander leaves (cilantro)	2 tablespoons olive oil
	salt and pepper to taste

Place all the ingredients into a salad bowl. Toss gently just before serving.

Carrot Salad
Khissoo
Morocco

Serves 4

If your children like raw carrots, they will love this salad.

6 large carrots, grated
¼ cup sugar
4 tablespoons lemon juice

4 tablespoons olive oil
1 teaspoon orange blossom water
(*mazahar*)

In a salad bowl, mix all the ingredients together; chill for at least one hour before serving.

Cheese Salad
Salatat Jibna
Sudan

Serves 6

1½ cups onion, finely sliced
1½ cups cabbage, finely sliced
1 cup carrots, grated
1½ cups tomatoes, cubed
¼ cup olive oil

¼ cup lemon juice
1 clove garlic, crushed
½ cup grated white cheese
salt and pepper to taste

In a large bowl, mix together the onion, cabbage, carrots, and tomatoes, then mix well. Combine the olive oil, lemon juice, salt, pepper and garlic. Pour over the vegetables and toss. Sprinkle the cheese over the salad and serve.

Cooked Spinach Salad
'Assoora
Syria and Lebanon

Serves 4 to 6

¼ cup olive or vegetable oil
2 large onions, sliced
3 lbs fresh spinach, thoroughly
  washed and chopped

salt and pepper to taste
2 tablespoons lemon juice

In a saucepan, sauté the onions in the oil over medium heat until the onions turn a golden brown. Add the spinach to the sautéed onions. Cover and continue cooking for 20 minutes.

nove the pan lid but leave on the heat until the water has evaporated
: spinach becomes tender. Add the salt, pepper, and lemon juice and
_ well. Leave to cool and serve at room temperature.

Note: Never add water to the spinach; its own water moisture is sufficient.

Cucumber Salad
Salatat Khiyar
Kuwait

Serves 4 to 6

The oil-rich lands of the Arabian Peninsula have a cuisine which has been influenced in recent years by the thousands of workers from the Indian subcontinent. This Kuwaiti salad has a touch of India and Pakistan.

¹/₄ cup olive oil	salt to taste
1 large onion, finely chopped	2 cups yogurt
1 medium sweet pepper, finely chopped	2 medium cucumbers, peeled and chopped
1 teaspoon ginger	

In a frying pan, sauté the onion, sweet pepper, ginger and salt in the oil. Fry over low heat until the onion is limp, but not brown; then remove from the heat and stir in the yogurt and cucumber. Place in a refrigerator for at least one hour; serve well chilled.

Cucumber and Yogurt Salad
Khiyar bi-Laban
Syria and Lebanon

Serves 4

3 cloves of garlic	2 medium cucumbers, peeled and diced
salt to taste	2 tablespoons dried mint
1 quart plain yogurt	

Crush the garlic with the salt in a bowl. Add the yogurt and mix well. Stir in the cucumbers and, finally, the mint.

Salad of Dandelion Greens
Salatat Hindba
Syria and Lebanon

Serves 4 to 6

Dandelion greens, a vegetable utilized in the salads of the Mediterranean lands, is usually considered just a weed in North America. Although cultivated dandelion greens are now available, the wild species is much tastier, especially when the plants are at their tenderest before flowering. Their refreshing bitterness may take some getting used to for those accustomed to blander greens.

1 bunch dandelion greens, thoroughly washed and chopped into medium pieces
1 large tomato, diced into medium
1 medium Spanish onion, finely chopped

1 clove garlic, crushed
1/4 cup lemon juice
1/4 cup olive oil
salt and pepper to taste

Toss all ingredients in a salad bowl just before serving.

Note: A bunch of spinach may be substituted for the dandelion.

Eggplant and Cucumber Salad
Salatat Bathinjan wa Khiyar
Syria and Lebanon

Serves 6 to 8

1 large eggplant, peeled and cut into 1/2 inch cubes
1/2 cup plus 2 tablespoons olive oil
2 large tomatoes, diced
1 medium cucumber, peeled and diced
1 clove garlic, crushed

1 bunch scallions, finely chopped
1/2 cup finely chopped parsley
2 tablespoons lemon juice
1 teaspoon sumac (see Glossary, p. 6)
1/4 cup olives, pitted and quartered
salt and pepper to taste

Sprinkle the eggplant cubes with salt. Place in a strainer, top with a weight, and leave to drain for 45 minutes.

Heat the 1/2 cup of olive oil in a frying pan. Sauté the eggplant cubes over moderately high heat until they turn golden brown. Remove from the oil and place in a strainer. Set aside to drain and cool.

In a salad bowl, gently toss the eggplant with the rest of the ingredients, including salt to taste and 2 tablespoons of oil. Serve immediately.

Eggplant and Pepper Salad
Salatat Bathinjan wa Fulful
Morocco

Serves 4 to 6

1 large eggplant
2 cloves garlic, crushed
2 tablespoons finely chopped parsley
2 tablespoons finely chopped fresh
 coriander leaves (cilantro)
$^1/_2$ teaspoon cumin

$^1/_2$ teaspoon paprika
1 medium onion, chopped
2 tablespoons olive oil
1 large sweet red pepper, chopped
2 tablespoons lemon juice
salt to taste

Bake the eggplant in a 425°F oven, for about 1 hour, turning frequently. Cool, peel, and mash to a smooth pulp. Add the garlic, parsley, coriander, cumin, and paprika. Mix well and set aside.

In a frying pan, sauté the onion in the olive oil until the onion turns golden brown. Add the red pepper and fry a few minutes longer. Stir in the eggplant mixture, lemon juice, and salt. Mix well, place on a serving dish, and chill for at least one hour before serving.

Fried Pepper Salad
Salatat Fulful
Morocco

Serves 4 to 6

The salads in Morocco are for the most part different from those in the Eastern Arab world, in that vegetables are cooked rather than raw.

$^1/_2$ cup olive oil
4 large sweet peppers
3 medium tomatoes, diced
1 teaspoon paprika
salt and pepper to taste

$^1/_2$ teaspoon cumin
2 cloves garlic, crushed
1 teaspoon lemon juice
$^1/_4$ cup finely chopped parsley

Fry the whole peppers in the olive oil over medium-high heat, turning, them until they are soft. Remove and set aside.

In the same pan, sauté the tomatoes with the salt, paprika, pepper, cumin, and garlic until the tomatoes are cooked but still a little firm.

Peel the peppers, remove the seeds, and dice the flesh. Combine the peppers and the lemon juice with the tomatoes. Place in serving bowl, garnish with the parsley, and serve hot.

Grilled Vegetable Salad
Mechouia
Tunisia

Serves 6 to 8

2 large red sweet peppers
4 firm medium tomatoes
3 medium onions
1 small hot pepper
3 tablespoons lemon juice
3 tablespoons olive oil

1 teaspoon oregano
1 can tuna (7 oz or 198 g)
2 oz feta cheese, crumbled
2 hard boiled eggs, chopped
salt and pepper to taste

Grill the red peppers, tomatoes, onions, and hot pepper in the oven, turning them over once or twice until they are soft. (The onions will take longer than the other vegetables.) Leave to cool.

Remove the seeds from the peppers. Chop all the vegetables into small pieces, then place on a flat serving dish and stir in the lemon juice, oil, salt, oregano, and pepper.

Spread the tuna, cheese, and egg pieces evenly over the top and serve.

Kishk Salad
Salatat Kishk
Syria and Lebanon

Serves 4 to 6

Considered a peasant food, *kishk* is rejected by almost all the urban Arabs of today. As they trip over one another trying to tailor their menus to Western processed foods, they have forgotten this wholesome staff of life which kept their ancestors healthy. Only the farmers and the villagers of Syria and Lebanon, and the sons and daughters of Arab peasant immigrants in the Americas, appreciate the taste and food value of *kishk*.

1 bunch of dandelion greens, or a 10 oz
    package of spinach, coarsely chopped
1 bunch scallions, finely chopped
1 large tomato, finely chopped

$^1/_2$ cup *kishk* (see p. 12)
$^1/_4$ cup olive oil
2 tablespoons lemon juice
salt and pepper to taste

In a salad bowl, thoroughly mix the dandelion greens or spinach, and the onions, tomatoes, *kishk*, salt, and pepper. Add the oil and lemon juice, toss, and serve immediately.

Lentil Salad
Salatat 'Adas
Syria and Lebanon

Serves 6 to 8

In some parts of Spain, Don Quixote's Friday meal of lentils is still the mainstay of many peasants and city poor. This recipe could well have been Quixote's repast.

1 cup lentils, cleaned and washed	$1/2$ a 19 oz or 540 ml can of chickpeas,
6 cups water	drained
6 tablespoons olive oil	$1/2$ cup finely chopped parsley
$1/2$ cup lemon juice	1 large sweet red pepper, finely
1 bunch scallions, finely chopped	chopped
3 large tomatoes, diced	salt and pepper to taste

Cook the lentils in the water until tender but still intact and slightly firm. Allow to cool.

Drain the lentils; then mix thoroughly with the remaining ingredients just before serving.

Moroccan Eggplant Salad
Salatat Bathinjan

Serves 4 to 6

An Arab bride learns quickly to master the art of making succulent eggplant meals. There is an Arab proverb which says: "A woman, after marriage, controls her husband with her beauty; then in his middle age by feeding him delicious eggplant stews; and in his old age by beating him with her bathroom clogs."

1 large unpeeled eggplant, cut into	1 teaspoon cumin
1 inch cubes	1 teaspoon paprika
3 cloves garlic, finely chopped	$1/4$ cup lemon juice
5 cups water	$1/4$ cup olive oil
salt	

In a pot, place the eggplant cubes, garlic, water, and salt. Cover and boil for about ten minutes until the eggplant is cooked but still firm. Place the eggplant cubes in a strainer and allow to cool; then transfer to a salad bowl, sprinkle with salt, cumin, and paprika, and toss gently. Just before serving, add the lemon juice and olive oil. Toss gently again and serve immediately.

Onion and Sumac Salad
Salatat Basal wa Summaq
Syria and Lebanon

Serves 4 to 6

According to R. Landry, in his book *The Gentle Art of Cooking*, some historians believe that the dish of lentils that Jacob gave Esau was seasoned with berries of the *Rhus coriaria,* or sumac. Sumac—also spelled sumach or sumak, derived from the Arabic *summāq*—may be the last of the great condiments still to be introduced into the West. This sourish seasoning has been employed for thousands of years by Middle Eastern cooks, often as a replacement for lemon juice and vinegar.

3 large Spanish onions, thinly sliced	salt to taste
1 cup water	2 tablespoons sumac (see Glossary, p. 6)
1/2 cup vinegar	

In a salad bowl, place the onions, water, vinegar, and salt. Let stand for 2 hours, gently tossing two or three times.

Drain well, then sprinkle with the sumac and toss gently just before serving.

Orange Salad
Salatat Latsheen
Morocco

Serves 4

A simple salad or dessert.

5 large oranges	1/2 teaspoon ground cinnamon
2 teaspoons *mazahar* (orange blossom water)	

Slice the oranges thinly and arrange the slices on a serving plate. Sprinkle the *mazahar* evenly over the slices; then chill for at least one hour.

Just before serving, sprinkle the cinnamon evenly on the orange slices.

Parsley and Burghul Salad

Tabboola

Syria and Lebanon

Serves 6 to 8

In the Middle East, *tabboola* is believed to be the epitome of all salads. It is different from the salads familiar to the Western palate, and more difficult to prepare since its main ingredients are very finely chopped. It may be utilized as an appetizer or as a side dish with the entrée.

$^1/_4$ cup medium grind *burghul* (cracked wheat)	2 tablespoons finely chopped fresh mint leaves
2 medium ripe but firm tomatoes, diced finely	$^1/_4$ cup olive oil
1 cup finely chopped fresh scallions	$^1/_4$ cup lemon juice
2 large bunches of parsley, stems removed and leaves finely chopped	about a dozen romaine lettuce leaves, washed
1 clove garlic, crushed	salt and pepper to taste

Place the *burghul* in a bowl and cover with water. Let stand for 15 minutes. Drain, pressing well, in a colander, then place in a mixing bowl.

Add the remaining ingredients except the lettuce leaves; mix thoroughly.

Line a salad bowl with the lettuce leaves, place the *tabboola* on top, and serve.

Note: This salad keeps very well, and any left over may be used the next day, as it does not become soggy or lose its taste.

Peanut Salad

Sudan

Serves 4 to 6

An unusual way to use what most Westerners think of as just a snack food.

2 cups unsalted peanuts	pinch of cayenne
$^1/_4$ cup water	juice of 1 lemon
2 large tomatoes, diced	$^1/_4$ cup chopped parsley
1 medium onion, finely chopped	salt
$^1/_4$ cup olive oil	

Grind or pulverize the peanuts until they are as fine as cornmeal; then add the water and stir.

Add the tomatoes, onion, olive oil, salt, cayenne, and lemon juice. Mix well and adjust the seasoning to taste. Garnish with the parsley. Chill before serving.

Potato Salad
Batata Mutabbala
Syria and Lebanon

Serves 4 to 6

Although the potato is not native to the Arab countries, it has thrived in these lands since its discovery in America. This Arabic version of potato salad makes a refreshing change from the usual mayonnaise type and is perfect for picnics and barbecues.

5 large potatoes, cooked, peeled, and diced into ¹/₂ inch cubes	2 tablespoons finely chopped fresh mint
2 eggs, hard boiled, peeled, and chopped	¹/₄ cup olive oil
¹/₄ cup finely chopped scallions	2 cloves garlic
¹/₄ cup finely chopped parsley	¹/₄ cup lemon juice
	salt and pepper to taste

Place all the ingredients, except the garlic, salt, and lemon juice, in a salad bowl.

Mash the garlic with salt; then add the lemon juice and stir well. Add to the rest of the ingredients and toss gently, making sure the potatoes and eggs do not crumble too much. Serve well chilled.

Note: For an even more savory Tunisian salad, substitute ¹/₄ cup fresh chopped coriander leaves for the parsley, mint, and green onions. Add 1 2 oz or 50 g can of anchovies, finely chopped, and garnish with green olives.

Potato Salad with Caraway
Salatat Batata
Tunisia

Serves 4 to 6

¹/₄ cup olive oil	5 large potatoes, cooked, peeled, and cubed
3 tablespoons lemon juice	
1 teaspoon ground caraway	2 tablespoons finely chopped fresh mint
¹/₄ teaspoon cayenne	2 tablespoons finely chopped coriander leaves (cilantro)
salt	¹/₄ cup finely chopped parsley

In a frying pan, heat the olive oil over moderate heat; then add the lemon juice, caraway, cayenne, and salt, stirring constantly. Cook for 3–5 minutes, until some of the liquid in the frying pan evaporates.

Remove from the heat; then add the potatoes and turn gently with a fork until they are coated with the seasoned oil. Place in a salad bowl; then add the mint, coriander, parsley, and toss. Taste for seasoning; serve chilled.

Radish and Orange Salad
Salatat Fijl wa Latsheen
Morocco

Serves 4 to 6

6 seedless oranges, peeled
1/2 cup lemon juice
few drops orange blossom water
  (mazahar)
3 tablespoons sugar

1 bunch red radishes, soaked in cold
  water for 1 hour
1/4 tablespoon cinnamon
salt

Section the oranges into a salad bowl. Set aside.

In another bowl, stir the lemon juice, orange blossom water, sugar, and salt together until the sugar and salt are dissolved.

Grate the radishes coarsely. Add the lemon dressing and the radishes to the oranges and toss gently; then sprinkle with the cinnamon and serve.

Note: The salad must be served immediately. If allowed to stand for a long period of time, the taste will not be as fresh and sharp.

Spinach and Coriander Salad
Salatat Sabanakh wa Kuzbara
Syria and Lebanon

Serves 4 to 6

1/4 cup lemon juice
2 tablespoons olive oil
1 tablespoon dried oregano leaves
1 package spinach (10 oz or 284 g),
  chopped

3 medium tomatoes, diced into 1/2 inch
  cubes
1/2 cup finely chopped fresh coriander
  leaves (cilantro)
salt and pepper to taste

Make a dressing by mixing the lemon juice, oil, salt, oregano, and pepper. Set aside.

Combine all the remaining ingredients in a salad bowl. Add the dressing just before serving and toss.

Note: Young, tender dandelion leaves may be substituted for the spinach.

Tomato and Coriander Salad
Salatat Tamatim wa Kuzbara
Yemen

Serves 4 to 6

Coriander has been known to almost every Asian, African, and European civilization. In ancient China, it was believed that coriander bestowed immortality on those who constantly used it in their cooking. In the Egypt of the Pharaohs, it was thought that this herb was a food fit for the gods. Coriander seeds have been found in ancient Egyptian tombs, apparently as a food offering to the next world. The Bible (Exodus 16:31) compares coriander to the manna which fell from Paradise. On the other hand, the Romans, who employed it extensively, were not all agreed on its qualities. Pliny labeled coriander "a very stinking herb." In later centuries, Charlemagne, who loved its taste, ordered that it be grown in all his imperial gardens. In the same era, the gourmet Arabs used this herb on a massive scale, not only enjoying its exotic tang but also believing it stimulated sexual desire. The well-known Arabian classic, *A Thousand and One Nights*, mentions it as an aphrodisiac. This simple salad demonstrates its ability to enhance other ingredients while maintaining its own definite taste.

5 medium tomatoes, diced
³/₄ cup fresh coriander leaves
   (cilantro), chopped
¹/₈ teaspoon cayenne

3 tablespoons lemon juice
2 tablespoons olive oil
salt and pepper to taste

Combine the tomatoes and coriander leaves in a salad bowl. In a separate bowl, mix thoroughly the remaining ingredients. Pour over the tomatoes and toss just before serving.

Tomato and Vegetable Salad
Salatat Tomatim
Palestine and Jordan

Serves 4 to 6

3 medium tomatoes, diced
1 large sweet pepper, diced
1 medium cucumber, diced
¹/₂ bunch parsley, finely chopped
2 tablespoons finely chopped fresh mint
¹/₂ bunch scallions, finely chopped
1 clove garlic, crushed

¹/₄ cup olive oil
juice of two lemons
6 red radishes, chopped
10 pitted olives, diced
¹/₄ cup feta cheese, crumbled
salt and pepper to taste

Mix all the ingredients except the cheese and allow to marinate for 10 minutes. Sprinkle evenly with the cheese pieces and serve.

Tomato Salad
Salatat Banadoora
Syria and Lebanon

Serves 4 to 6

6 large firm tomatoes
1 medium Spanish onion
¹/₂ cup finely chopped scallions
3 cloves garlic, crushed
¹/₄ teaspoon thyme

1 teaspoon dried mint
¹/₄ cup lemon juice
¹/₄ cup olive oil
salt and pepper to taste

Cut the tomatoes into thin slices; then place in a salad bowl. Slice the onion very thin; then add to the tomatoes. Add the remaining ingredients and gently mix; then chill until ready to serve. Toss lightly again just before serving.

Tossed Salad
Salata
Syria and Lebanon

Serves 4

Eastern Arab dressing for salads are mixtures of olive oil and lemon juice or vinegar; crushed garlic is usually added with the salt and pepper. These lemon dressings are sharper than in the West because more lemon is used in proportion to the oil. Occasionally, the Middle Eastern cook uses as much lemon as oil, or more, in dressing vegetable salads; you can, of course, adjust these dressings to taste. Salads are never served without having been tossed in their dressing.

1 small head lettuce, cut or torn into large pieces
3 medium to large tomatoes, cut into large pieces
¹/₂ bunch scallions, finely chopped
¹/₄ cup of fresh finely chopped mint leaves, or 1 teaspoon dried mint

¹/₄ cup of fresh chopped parsley leaves
2 cloves garlic, crushed
salt
black pepper
¹/₃ cup olive oil
¹/₄ cup lemon juice

Place all the ingredients in a salad bowl. Toss lightly and season to taste.

Vegetable Salad
Salatat Khudr
Egypt

Serves 4 to 6

1 cup fresh green peas, cooked
1 cup fresh green beans, cooked
3 tomatoes, diced
1/2 cup pickled white onions, halved
3 tablespoons lemon juice
1/4 cup olive oil

1/4 cup sour cream
salt and pepper to taste
1 large beet, cooked, peeled and sliced
   thin
3 tablespoons chopped parsley

Combine the peas, beans, tomatoes, onions, lemon juice, olive oil, and sour cream in a salad bowl. Sprinkle on the salt and pepper, then toss. Decorate with the beets and parsley; serve chilled.

Yogurt and Dandelion Green Salad
Salatat Laban ma' Hindba
Iraq

Serves 4 to 6

Three times as easy to digest as milk, yogurt is rich in vitamin B and calcium, and high in protein. Plain yogurt contains few calories and is useful for low-calorie diets.

In the Middle East and the Balkans, millions rely on yogurt as a remedy for numerous types of illnesses, especially digestive problems.

1 small bunch of dandelion greens,
   washed and finely chopped
1/2 cup finely chopped fresh coriander
   leaves (cilantro)
1 clove garlic, crushed

2 tablespoons lemon juice
2 tablespoons olive oil
2 1/2 cups yogurt
salt and pepper to taste

In a serving bowl, thoroughly mix all the ingredients except the yogurt. Gradually stir in the yogurt and mix well. Serve chilled.

Yogurt and Vegetable Salad

Salatat Laban
Sudan

Serves 6

1 cup plain yogurt	1 clove garlic, crushed
1 tablespoon vinegar	1 head lettuce, chopped
1/4 cup olive oil	2 medium tomatoes, diced
1 teaspoon chilli powder	1/2 bunch scallions, finely chopped
salt	

In a large salad bowl, combine the yogurt, vinegar, oil, chilli power, salt, and garlic. Add the remaining ingredients, mix thoroughly and serve.

Meat Dishes

Like other peoples, the Arabs consider meat a token of wealth, and hence it is the regular food of the wealthy. However, on festive and religious occasions, even the poorest peasants will try to make a meal which includes the flesh of animals.

The most common meats used throughout the Arab world are lamb and mutton. In the last few decades, beef has gained some popularity and is usually cheaper in price. In some Arab lands, buffalo, camel, goat, and veal are at times part of the daily menu. Pork is never eaten by Muslims and Jews and rarely by the Christian Arabs.

In Syria and Lebanon, tender lamb or baby beef is eaten uncooked as a delicious dish called "*kibbeh nayyeh.*" Raw lamb liver with salt and pepper is often eaten for breakfast or as an appetizer. However, in the other Arab countries, raw meat is rarely served.

For festive gatherings, especially in rural regions, whole lambs are often barbecued and served with rice. At other times, lamb or beef are grilled, fried, or used in pies and stews, but always with herbs and spices to enrich the flavor.

Arabs, historically, have waxed poetic when talking or writing about dishes made with meat. We have taken the liberty of quoting a poem in Mas'udi's *Meadows of Gold*, translated by A.J. Arberry, and cited in *A Book of Middle Eastern Food* by Claudia Roden. At a banquet given by the Caliph Mustakfi of Baghdad in the tenth century, a member of the company recited a poem by Ishaq ibn Ibrahim of Mosul, describing a meat dish as follows:

> If thou wouldst know what food gives most delight,
> Best let me tell, for none hath subtler sight.
> Take first the finest meat, red, soft to touch,
> And mince it with the fat, not overmuch;
> Then add an onion, cut in circles clean,
> A cabbage, very fresh, exceeding green,
> And season well with cinnamon and rue;
> Of coriander add a handful, too,
> and after that of cloves the very least,
> Of finest ginger, and of pepper best,
> A hand of cumin, murri just to taste,
> Two handfuls of Palmyra salt; but haste,
> Good master haste to grind them small and strong.
> Then lay and light a blazing fire along;
> Put all in the pot, and water pour
> Upon it from above, and cover o'er.
> But, when the water vanished is from sight
> And when the burning flames have dried it quite,
> Then, as thou wilt, in pastry wrap it round,
> Fasten well the edges, firm and sound;
> Of, if it please thee better, take some dough,

Conveniently soft, and rubbed just so,
Then with the rolling pin let it be spread
And with the nails its edges docketed,
Pour in the frying pan the choicest oil
And in that liquor let it finely broil.
Last, ladle out into a thin tureen
Where appetizing mustard smeared hath been,
And eat with pleasure, mustarded about,
This tastiest food for hurried diner-out.

Stuffed Whole Lamb
Kharoof Mahshee
Palestine and Jordan

Serves 30

Kharoof mahshee or stuffed lamb is a repast which Arabs have served their most honored guests for hundreds of years. Indeed, T.E. Lawrence, the Briton famed as "Lawrence of Arabia," gives a detailed and riveting description of such a feast in his *Seven Pillars of Wisdom*.

The Bedouins and the villagers of Jordan cook the stuffed lamb, which they call "*zarb*," in an oven of underground rocks covered with leaves and stones, as they have done throughout the centuries. This tradition of the Bedouins has not been lost in the towns and cities. Today, *kharoof mahshee*, which is common all over the Arab world, is a feast dish designed to be served at a party or a meeting where there are a large number of guests.

It is always accompanied by side dishes of *kuzbara bi-laban* (coriander in yogurt; see p. 78) and *salatat tomatim* (tomato salad; see p. 71).

6 tablespoons salt	2 teaspoons pepper
a spring lamb weighing between 20 and 25 lbs	2 teaspoons allspice

Take 5 tablespoons of the salt and rub the lamb inside and out. Wash the lamb in cold water; then dry with paper towels. Mix the remaining salt, pepper, and allspice; then sprinkle the mixture inside and outside the lamb. Set the lamb aside and prepare the stuffing.

The Stuffing

3 lbs lamb, diced into very small pieces	$^1/_2$ teaspoon nutmeg
1 cup butter	1 teaspoon cinnamon
5 cups rice	6 cardamom seeds, crushed
salt to taste	8 cups water

| 1 tablespoon pepper | 1 cup pine nuts |
| 1 tablespoon allspice | 1 cup blanched almonds |

Brown the meat lightly in $1/2$ cup of butter; then add the rice and sprinkle with the salt, pepper, allspice, nutmeg, cinnamon, and cardamom. Stir until the spices are well mixed; then add the water. Cover and simmer over low heat for 30 minutes.

While the rice is cooking, sauté the pine nuts and almonds in the remaining butter until they turn light golden brown. Remove the rice from the heat and add the pine nuts and almonds; then mix well and set aside.

Stuffing and Cooking the Lamb

Sew the cavity of the lamb closed with thick white linen thread, leaving an opening large enough for stuffing the animal. Stuff the lamb with the prepared stuffing; then sew up the opening, closing it completely. Place the lamb in a large deep pan and set aside.

Preheat the oven to 450°F; then place the lamb in the oven and cook for 15 minutes. Cover with aluminum foil, return to the oven, and reduce the oven temperature to 350°F. Cook until the lamb is tender; the cooking time is usually 30 minutes per pound, or 10 hours for a 20-lb lamb.

When ready to serve, place the lamb on a large platter and set the platter in the middle of the table in the manner of a buffet. The lamb should be served piping hot; Lawrence himself described it as "scalding."

Coriander in Yogurt
Kuzbara bi-Laban
Palestine and Jordan

Serves 6 to 8

In Palestine and Jordan, when a roast lamb is served, a dish of *kuzbara bi laban* is always served as a side-dish. This simple, delightful dish adds a delicate touch to the famous roast lamb.

4 cloves garlic, crushed	1 bunch fresh coriander leaves
salt	(cilantro), thoroughly washed and
1 quart yogurt	finely chopped

Thoroughly mix the garlic, salt, and yogurt and stir until smooth; then add the coriander and stir. Chill and serve.

Stuffed Crown Roast of Lamb
Kharoof Mihshee
Kuwait

Serves 8

1 lb lean lamb, cut into small cubes	1/4 teaspoon powdered ginger
1 medium onion, diced	2 cups cooked rice
1 cup water	1/4 cup raisins
salt and pepper to taste	1/4 cup toasted almonds
1/4 teaspoon cinnamon	5 lb crown roast of lamb
1/4 teaspoon powdered cardamom	3 hard-boiled eggs
1/4 teaspoon powdered cloves	

Simmer the cubes of lamb and the onion in the water for 20 minutes or until liquid is reduced to about 1/4 cup.

Mix together the salt, all the spices, the rice, raisins, and half of the almonds. Stir into the meat mixture and toss lightly to form a stuffing.

Place the crown roast on a rack in a shallow roasting pan. Fill the center cavity with the stuffing. Cut 2 of the eggs in quarters lengthwise and arrange on top of stuffing.

Cover the top of roast and stuffing with aluminum foil; then bake in a 325°F oven for 2 1/2 hours. Remove foil during the last 15 minutes of roasting in order to brown the roast. Garnish with the remaining sliced eggs and almonds. Serve with rice.

Stuffed Breast of Lamb
Kaboorga
Saudi Arabia

Serves 8 to 10

1/4 cup olive oil	2 breasts of lamb, approx. 2 lbs each
1 cup rice	1 can tomatoes (19 oz or 540 ml)
4 cloves garlic, crushed	1/4 cup finely chopped fresh coriander
3 medium onions, finely chopped	leaves (cilantro)
2 small green peppers, chopped	1 teaspoon oregano
1/2 cup finely chopped parsley	2 tablespoons Worcester sauce
salt and pepper to taste	pinch of cayenne
1/2 cup pine nuts	

In a frying pan, heat the oil; then add the rice, half of the garlic, the onions, and the green peppers, and stir-fry for 5 minutes. Add the parsley, salt, pepper, the pine nuts, and 2 cups water. Bring to a boil, then lower the heat, cover and let simmer for about 15 minutes over medium heat.

In the meantime, sew the two breasts of lamb together, forming a pocket—see illustration below. Stuff with the rice mixture, close by sewing, and place in a baking pan. Rub the breasts of lamb with salt and pepper, and the remainder of the garlic.

Mix the tomatoes, 4 cups of water, the coriander leaves, the oregano, the Worcester sauce, and the cayenne, and pour the mixture over the meat. Bake for about 1¹/₂ hours at 350°F, or until the meat is done, basting occasionally with the sauce. Cover with foil, and bake for another 30 minutes. Serve hot.

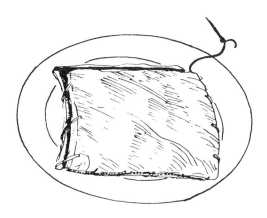

Stuffed Breast of Veal
Dul'a
Palestine and Jordan

Serves 8 to 10

5 lbs breast of veal	1 teaspoon allspice
¹/₂ cup vinegar	1 teaspoon garlic powder
2 teaspoons pepper	1 quantity rice stuffing (see recipe, p. 15)

Place the veal, salt and vinegar in a bowl and cover with water; let soak for about 1¹/₂ hours. Drain and dry.

Using a sharp, pointed knife cut a pocket between the ribs and the meat. Mix the pepper, allspice and garlic powder; then rub the mixture all over the meat, including the inside of the pocket.

Stuff the pocket with rice stuffing, then sew the pocket closed. Bake in a 350°F preheated oven, allowing 35 minutes per pound.

FROM THE LANDS OF FIGS AND OLIVES

Grilled Meat Cubes
Qudban
Morocco

Serves 4 to 6

2½ lbs beef or lamb, cut into 1 inch cubes

2 medium onions, finely chopped

1 tablespoon finely chopped parsley

2 cloves garlic, crushed

2 tablespoons finely chopped fresh coriander leaves (cilantro)

salt and pepper to taste

¼ cup olive oil

Combine all ingredients in a large bowl; leave to marinate for about 2 to 3 hours.

Place the meat on skewers; reserve marinade. Grill over glowing coals or under the broiler, turning often. Baste two or three times with the marinade.

Note: In Morocco, *qudban* are always served with small dishes of a sauce made from ground cumin and red pepper mixed with a little oil.

Grilled Meat Kababs
Laham Mishwee
Syria and Lebanon

Serves 6

2 lbs lean beef or lamb, cut into 1 inch cubes

pinch of cinnamon

8 small onions, peeled and halved

2 sprigs mint, chopped

salt and pepper to taste

Sprinkle the meat with the cinnamon, salt, and pepper. Place on skewers, alternating the meat and the onions. Grill over charcoal or under the broiler. Remove the meat from the skewers and place on a serving plate. Garnish with the mint. Serve with salad and/or rice.

Grilled Meat Yemeni Style

Serves 4

2 tablespoons olive oil

juice of 1 lemon

1½ lbs beef or lamb, cut into 1 inch cubes

2 medium onions, cut in thick slices

3 tomatoes, cut into wedges

8–12 bay leaves

1 small green pepper, cut into 1 inch squares

1 small eggplant, cut into 1 inch cubes

salt and pepper to taste

Mix the oil, lemon juice, salt, and pepper; then add the meat and stir until the meat is coated. Cover with the onions, tomatoes, and bay leaves; let stand for 2 hours.

On skewers, place a piece of onion, tomato, pepper, eggplant, and a bay leaf between each piece of meat. Grill over charcoal or under the broiler, turning skewers until the meat is done.

Raw Kibbeh
Kibbeh Nayyeh
Syria and Lebanon

Serves 6 to 8

Anyone who has a taste for steak tartare will enjoy this dish, which can be served as a main dish or as an appetizer. Kibbeh is one of the most popular dishes among the Arabs of the eastern Mediterranean, who think that it is the best of all foods. There are many types of kibbeh, but the ones made with meat are the most liked. In the West, kibbeh is eaten with a fork, but the Arabs prefer to eat it with their flat bread made into tiny scoops.

1½ cups of fine or medium burghul	¼ teaspoon cinnamon
2 lbs leanest lamb or beef	pinch of cayenne
2 medium onions, finely chopped	1 teaspoon dried mint leaves, crushed
salt	a few sprigs fresh parsley
1 teaspoon pepper	5 tablespoons olive oil
1 teaspoon allspice	

Soak the burghul in cold water for 10 minutes. Drain by squeezing out the water in a strainer, and set aside.

In a food processor, process the meat until it is finely ground. Transfer to a mixing bowl and add the burghul and the remaining ingredients except the parsley and olive oil. Mix thoroughly; then process a portion at a time until all is well ground and mixed. Place on a flat serving plate and chill well. Remove and decorate with the parsley; then sprinkle with the olive oil just before serving.

Kibbeh Stuffing

Syria and Lebanon

This stuffing is used for many types of kibbeh dishes.

3 tablespoons butter
$^1/_4$ cup pine nuts or chopped walnuts
1 lb ground lamb or beef
1 medium onion, finely chopped

$^3/_4$ teaspoon nutmeg
$^3/_4$ teaspoon allspice
salt and pepper to taste

In a frying pan, melt the butter; then add the nuts and sauté until they turn light brown. Stir in the meat and sauté for 10 minutes. Add the remaining ingredients and sauté until the onion is limp; then set aside for use as stuffing.

Baked Kibbeh

Kibbeh bis-Sayniyyeh
Syria and Lebanon

Serves 6 to 8

To the Syrians and the Lebanese emigrants, spread throughout the world, kibbeh evokes memories of a never-to-be forgotten dish eaten in their lands of origin. Traditions, language, and the Arab way of life may be forgotten or neglected, but the preparation and eating of all the various types of kibbeh will always be remembered.

1 quantity raw kibbeh (see p. 82)
1 quantity kibbeh stuffing (above)
$^1/_2$ cup olive oil

Divide the raw kibbeh in half. Spread 1 portion on the bottom of a buttered or oiled baking pan. Cover evenly with the kibbeh stuffing; then top the stuffing with the remaining portion of the raw kibbeh.

Cut into 2-inch squares and spread $^1/_2$ cup of oil evenly over the top. Bake for 50 minutes in a 350°F preheated oven. Can be served warm or cold.

Fried Kibbeh

Syria and Lebanon

Serves 6 to 8

The word "kibbeh" derives from the Arabic verb meaning to "form into a ball," and now this name is applied to this dish no matter what form it takes. The name is also pronounced by many as "kubbeh."

1 quantity raw kibbeh (see p. 82)
1 quantity kibbeh stuffing (see p. 83)
oil for frying

Take a small handful of raw kibbeh and, using your forefinger, make a hole in the middle. Shape by turning and pressing until you have an elongated, oval shell about ¼ inch thick and 3 inches long (see illustration below).

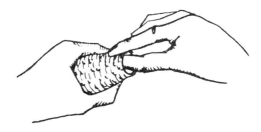

Place 1 tablespoon of stuffing into the hollow shell; then close the opening, making an egg-like shape. (Use cold water on your hands to help shape and close the shells.)

Fry in oil in a frying pan until golden brown or put into an oiled pan and bake at 350°F until browned. If baked, the shells should be turned over once during baking.

FROM THE LANDS OF FIGS AND OLIVES

Kibbeh Iraqi Style

Serves 6

1 cup fine burghul	3 tablespoons pine nuts or slivered
¼ cup flour	almonds
4 tablespoons butter	¼ teaspoon allspice
1 large onion, finely chopped	oil for frying
½ lb ground beef, lean	salt and pepper

Soak the burghul in warm water for 15 minutes; then place in a strainer and press to remove all the water. Place the burghul in a mixing bowl and mix in a little of the flour at a time. Squeeze a little of the mixture to see if it holds together; if not, add more flour. Form into balls the size of golf balls and set aside.

Melt the butter in a frying pan; then add the onions and sauté for 10 minutes over medium heat. Add the meat and continue sautéeing until the meat begins to brown; then add the pine nuts or slivered almonds, allspice, salt, and pepper and mix well to make a stuffing. Set aside. Take one ball of burghul at a time and form shells as for fried kibbeh (see illustration, p. 84). Fill each shell with 1 heaping tablespoon of the stuffing; then close the opening by pinching together, using a little water. Flatten the filled shells slightly; then fry in hot oil, turning until golden brown.

Kibbeh with Lemon
Kibbeh ma' Laymoon Hamid
Syria and Lebanon

Serves 6 to 8

During the cold winter days in southern Saskatchewan, some of us remember as youngsters how eagerly we looked forward to our evening meal when our mothers were preparing this delicious dish.

½ quantity raw kibbeh (p. 82)	salt and pepper to taste
½ quantity kibbeh stuffing (p. 83)	1 large onion, finely chopped
½ lb boned lamb or beef, cut into	1 can chickpeas (19 oz or 540 ml),
1 inch cubes	drained
1 teaspoon nutmeg	1 cup lemon juice
1 teaspoon allspice	3 cloves garlic, crushed

Form raw kibbeh into round shells as shown in the recipe for fried kibbeh (see illustration, p. 84). Fill shells with kibbeh stuffing, seal, and set aside.

Place the cubed meat, pepper, nutmeg, allspice, and salt in a pot and add water to cover by one inch. Cover and cook over medium heat for 45 minutes. Add the onion and chickpeas; cook for a further 10 minutes.

Add the lemon juice and the garlic and bring to a boil, stirring occasionally. Gently add the stuffed Kibbeh so as not to break the shells. (If more liquid is needed, add water). Return to a boil; then cook for approximately 30 minutes and serve hot.

Potato Kibbeh with Meat

Kibbet Batata

Syria and Lebanon

Serves 6 to 8

1 cup fine burghul	¹/₄ teaspoon cinnamon
3 cups mashed potatoes (about 4 large potatoes, boiled, peeled, and mashed)	pinch cayenne
	3 large cups onions, finely chopped
1¹/₂ tablespoons flour	6 tablespoons olive or vegetable oil
salt and pepper to taste	1 lb beef or lamb, cut into very small pieces
1 teaspoon oregano	
¹/₄ teaspoon allspice	

Soak burghul for 10 minutes, then place in a strainer and drain well, squeezing out the water. In a mixing bowl, place the burghul, potatoes, flour, salt, oregano, pepper, allspice, cinnamon, cayenne, and 1 cup of the onions. Combine and knead until dough-like, then set aside.

In a frying pan, heat 4 tablespoons of the oil; then stir-fry the meat over medium heat until it begins to brown. Stir in the remaining salt, pepper, and onions; then cook further until the onions begin to brown and the meat is cooked. Set aside.

Divide the kibbeh mixture in half. Spread one portion on the bottom of a greased 8 inch by 12 inch pan. Spread the meat mixture evenly over the top; then cover with the remaining portion of the kibbeh and pat down. Using a wet knife, cut into 2 inch by 2 inch squares; then sprinkle with the remaining oil and bake in a 400°F preheated oven for 30 minutes.

Kufta Barbecue
Kufta Mishwiya
Syria and Lebanon

Serves 4

The traditional way to serve kufta in Aleppo, Syria, is with a side dish of tomatoes that have been grilled separately, then peeled, mashed, and seasoned.

1 lb finely ground lean beef steak
1 small onion, finely chopped
¹/₂ cup finely chopped parsley
1 teaspoon dried mint
salt and pepper to taste

¹/₄ teaspoon cinnamon
pinch of allspice
pinch of cayenne
4 tablespoons butter, if frying.

Mix all the ingredients thoroughly until the mixture reaches a dough-like consistency. Form into long, cylinder shapes around skewers (see illustration below).

Broil in oven or over charcoal or sauté in a frying pan in heated butter, turning frequently to brown evenly. Serve with Arabic (pita) bread, yogurt, and salad.

Note: Vary the seasoning, using ground cumin and coriander in place of the mint, to make a Moroccan version.

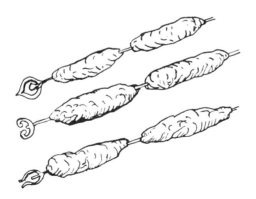

Kufta in the Pan
Kufta bis-Sayniya
Syria and Lebanon

Serves 4

1 lb finely ground lamb or beef
2 small onions, minced
1 egg
$^1\!/_2$ cup cracker or bread crumbs
salt and pepper to taste
$^1\!/_4$ teaspoon cinnamon
2 cloves garlic, crushed

$^1\!/_4$ teaspoon allspice
2 tablespoons parsley, chopped
4 medium potatoes, peeled and sliced
   $^1\!/_2$-inch thick
1 can tomato sauce (8 oz or 230 ml)
3 cups water

Thoroughly mix all the ingredients except the potatoes, tomato sauce, and water. Spread in a lightly oiled 9 inch by 13 inch baking pan. Layer the potato slices over the meat.

Mix the tomato sauce with the 3 cups water and pour over the potatoes. Bake in a 400°F preheated oven for 40 minutes.

Kufta in Sesame Sauce
Kufta bi-Taheena
Palestine and Jordan

Serves 6

2 lbs finely ground lamb or beef
2 onions, finely chopped
1 cup finely chopped fresh parsley
1 egg
salt and pepper to taste

$^1\!/_2$ teaspoon cinnamon
$^1\!/_2$ teaspoon allspice
4 tablespoons *taheena* (see p. 18)
$^1\!/_4$ cup lemon juice
2 cloves garlic, crushed

Mix meat, onions, parsley, egg, salt, pepper, cinnamon, and allspice well. Form into 24 oval patties. Bake in a greased pan for 30 to 45 minutes at 350°F in a preheated oven until well browned.

In the meantime mix the *taheena* with the lemon juice and crushed garlic. Pour this mixture over the baked kufta, then return the pan to the oven for about 10 minutes, or until the *taheena* thickens. Serve with rice.

Kufta in Yogurt Sauce
Kufta ma' Laban
Palestine and Jordan

Serves 6

2 lbs lamb or beef, coarsely ground
1 large onion, finely chopped
¹/₂ cup minced fresh parsley
1 teaspoon hot pepper
1 teaspoon allspice
1 teaspoon nutmeg
3 tablespoons butter

1 teaspoon cornstarch
1 quart yogurt
2 cloves garlic, crushed
4 sprigs mint, finely chopped
1 beaten egg
salt
pieces of Arabic (pita) bread, toasted
³/₄ cup of pine nuts

Combine the meat with the onion, parsley, pepper, allspice, and nutmeg, and form into walnut-sized balls. Sauté the balls in the butter until browned. Keep warm in a low oven while you make the sauce.

In a large pot, mix the cornstarch in a little water until smooth. Stir in the yogurt, garlic, mint (keep some aside for garnishing), egg, and salt. Cook the sauce over medium heat and stir clockwise until it bubbles; then let stand for a few minutes.

Arrange the meatballs on individual plates ringed with toast pieces. Pour the sauce over meatballs and garnish with pine nuts and chopped mint. Serve with rice if desired.

Kufta Stuffed with Eggs
Kufta Mihshee bil-Bayd
Syria and Lebanon

Serves 6 to 8

2 lbs finely ground lamb or beef
1 large onion, finely chopped
¹/₄ teaspoon cinnamon
¹/₄ teaspoon allspice
salt and pepper to taste

¹/₂ cup cracker or bread crumbs
1 egg, lightly beaten
1 cup parsley, finely chopped
6 hard-boiled eggs

Thoroughly mix all the ingredients except the parsley and the hard-boiled eggs. Divide into 3 portions. Flatten the portions into rectangles about 1 inch thick. Sprinkle generously with the parsley. Place 2 eggs on each rectangle, then roll as for a jelly roll. Place in a buttered baking pan and bake in a 375°F preheated oven for 40 minutes or until the meat is done.

Kufta with Pine Nuts
Kufta Mabrooma
Syria and Lebanon

Serves 6

This is a specialty of Aleppo, where it is traditionally baked in a round tray and served on a round dish, with the rolls arranged in diminishing circles.

2 medium sized onions, finely chopped	1/2 teaspoon allspice
3 cloves garlic, crushed	1/4 cup pine nuts
1 egg, beaten	3 tablespoons butter, melted
2 lbs lean lamb or beef, finely ground	chopped parsley and slices of lemon to
salt and pepper to taste	garnish

In a bowl, mix the onions, garlic, egg, beef, salt, pepper and allspice. Knead vigorously by hand or in a food processor until the mixture is soft and pasty. Flatten the mixture on a board, and cut into 6 rectangular pieces; then press a row of pine nuts into one of the longer sides of each rectangle and roll up into a sausage shape. Place in a small pan close together; then brush the rolls with the butter. Sprinkle the rolls with 1/4 cup of water, then bake in a 375°F preheated oven for 1 hour or until the rolls are well cooked. Place on a hot serving dish and garnish with chopped parsley and slices of lemon. Serve hot with rice or French fries.

Veal and Egg Pie
Malsooka
Tunisia

Serves 4 to 6

1/2 lb boneless veal, cut into 1/2 inch cubes	pinch of saffron
1 large onion, finely chopped	1 cup cooked white beans
3/4 cup water	1/2 cup grated cheese
2 tablespoons olive oil	1/4 cup finely chopped fresh coriander leaves
1/4 cup tomato paste	(cilantro)
salt and pepper to taste	2 hard-boiled eggs, coarsely chopped
pinch of cayenne	1/2 package filo dough sheets
5 eggs, beaten	3/4 cup butter, melted

Place the meat, onion, water, olive oil, tomato paste, salt, pepper, and cayenne in a saucepan. Bring to a boil over medium heat and cook for 15 minutes, stirring occasionally. Remove and allow to cool; then stir in the eggs, saffron, beans, cheese, coriander leaves and the hard-boiled eggs to make a filling.

Layer half of the filo dough sheets in a small pan (8 by 11 inches), buttering each sheet well. Let the edges hang over the sides of the dish. Pour in the filling mixture, spreading it evenly.

Cut the remaining filo dough sheets to the size of the pan; then brush each sheet with butter and arrange them over the filling. Fold the overhanging sheets over the filling and brush the top with the remaining butter. Bake in a preheated 325°F oven for 45 minutes, or until the pastry is golden brown. Remove and allow to cool for 30 minutes; then cut into wedges and serve.

To steam the couscous more efficiently, the bottom and top parts of the couscousière are traditionally sealed with a piece of cloth soaked in a solution of flour and water.

Iraqi Meat Pies
Booraq

Makes about 20 small pies

2 cups flour	¹/₂ teaspoon allspice
3 eggs	3 medium onions, finely chopped
6 tablespoons butter	3 cups beef broth
1¹/₄ oz package dried yeast, dissolved in	2 cups yogurt
¹/₄ cup lukewarm water	1¹/₂ teaspoons paprika
¹/₂ cup lukewarm water	salt and pepper to taste
1¹/₂ cups ground beef	

Thoroughly mix the flour with 2 of the eggs, 2 tablespoons of the butter, the yeast, water, and salt. Knead to a smooth dough, cover and let stand for 1 hour.

In the meantime, make a filling by mixing the beef with the remaining salt, pepper, allspice, and onions. Set aside.

Roll out the dough as thin as possible; then cut into 2 inch to 3 inch squares using a sharp knife. Place a heaping teaspoon of the filling on each square. Fold each square in half diagonally to form triangles; seal firmly by pinching the edges together.

Beat the remaining egg with a little water. Brush each pie with a little of the beaten egg and place in a shallow, greased baking dish. Bake in a 350°F preheated oven for about 20 minutes or until the pies turn golden brown.

Pour the beef broth over the pies; then lower the heat to 300°F, cover the baking pan, and return to the oven. Continue to bake for about 45 minutes to an hour until most of the liquid has been absorbed.

Make a sauce by mixing the remaining 4 tablespoons of the butter with the yogurt and paprika; then serve with the hot pies.

Meat and Yogurt Pies

Fatayar Laban ma' Laham

Syria and Lebanon

Makes 12 large pies

In the Middle East, the types of delicious meat, dairy and vegetable pies are countless. This *laban* (yogurt) pie can match in taste the best meat pies in the world.

1 lb frozen pizza dough or equivalent amount of homemade dough

2 tablespoons butter

¹/₂ cup beef or lamb cut into very small pieces

1¹/₂ cups *labana* (see p. 17); cream cheese may be substituted for the *labana*

1 medium onion, finely chopped

salt and pepper to taste

Thaw out the dough; then roll into 12 balls (golf ball size), and allow to rest in a warm place for 1 hour.

Melt the butter in a frying pan; then add the meat and fry until it is well done. Make the filling by mixing the meat thoroughly with the rest of the ingredients.

Roll out each ball into a 4 inch or 5 inch round. Place a heaping tablespoon of the filling on each round; then shape into a triangle and close firmly by pinching the edges (see illustration below).

Place the pies on a well greased baking pan. Bake in a 400°F preheated oven for 10 to 15 minutes or until the pies turn golden brown. If a darker color is desired, brown lightly under the broiler. Brush the tops of the pies with butter; serve hot.

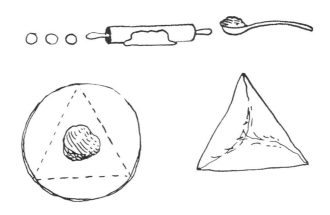

Meat and Egg Pie
Brik
Tunisia

Briks are as popular in Tunisia as hamburgers are in North America. They are sold in small restaurants and are often to be found on the housewife's daily menu.

9 small eggs
4 tablespoons butter
$^1/_2$ lb ground lean beef or lamb
2 medium onions, finely chopped
2 cloves garlic, crushed
$^1/_4$ cup finely chopped fresh coriander leaves (cilantro)

1 small hot pepper, finely chopped
salt and pepper to taste
1 teaspoon sumac (see p. 6)
$^1/_2$ cup crumbled feta cheese
8 sheets filo dough
oil for frying

Beat one of the eggs and set aside.

In a frying pan, melt the butter; then sauté the meat over medium heat for 6 minutes. Stir in the onions, garlic, coriander leaves, hot pepper, salt, sumac, and pepper and stir-fry for a further 10 minutes; then remove from the heat and stir in the cheese. Set aside.

Take a sheet of filo dough and fold it twice to make a square; then place $^1/_8$ of the filling in the center and make a well in the filling. Brush the edges of the square with some of the beaten egg; then break an egg into the well and fold the edges over to form a triangle (see illustration below). Press the edges together to seal, turning them a little to make certain they are well sealed.

In a frying pan, heat cooking oil about $^1/_2$ inch deep. Gently slide the *brik* in and fry over medium heat, turning over once so that both sides are golden brown. Set aside, but keep warm. Continue the same filling, sealing, and frying process until all the *briks* are done; then serve immediately.

Meat Stuffed Pancakes
Marik
Algeria

Makes about 12 pancakes

The Pancake

1¹/₂ cups flour
1 teaspoon baking powder
¹/₂ teaspoon salt

1 egg, beaten
1¹/₂ cups milk
1 tablespoon vegetable oil

The Filling

¹/₂ lb ground beef or lamb
1 medium onion, chopped
3 tablespoon olive oil
¹/₂ teaspoon cumin
pinch nutmeg

salt and pepper to taste
1 tablespoon chopped fresh coriander
   leaves (cilantro)
4 tablespoons yogurt

Sift together the dry ingredients. Make a well in the middle, then add the egg, milk, and oil to make a very thin batter. If the batter thickens, add milk to keep it thin.

Lightly grease an 8 inch frying pan and pour ¹/₄ cup batter into the pan, tilting it so that the batter covers the bottom of the pan. Cook on one side only over medium heat until firm; then remove and set aside. Cover each pancake with waxed paper and continue until all the batter has been used.

Make the filling by sautéeing the meat and onion in the oil until light brown; then stir in the cumin, salt, pepper, coriander leaves and yogurt. Place a tablespoon of filling in each pancake and fold it in half; then fold open edges back toward the middle of the pancake, tucking in the ends (see illustration below). Brush generously with oil or melted butter on all sides and bake in a preheated oven (325°F) for 30 minutes until crisply browned. Serve hot, with the sauce below.

The Sauce

2 large onions, diced
2 tablespoons olive oil
1 head of garlic, peeled and minced
2 tablespoons freshly chopped coriander
   leaves (cilantro)

salt and pepper to taste
2 bay leaves
5 large tomatoes, peeled and chopped

Sauté the onions in the oil until they turn golden brown; then add the remaining ingredients and cook over high heat for 5 minutes. Add ¹/₂ cup water; then turn the heat to low and cook for 15 minutes. Pour over pancakes to serve.

FROM THE LANDS OF FIGS AND OLIVES

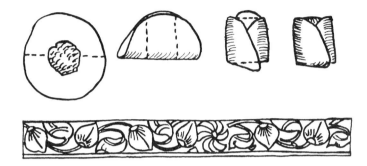

Meat Pies

Fatayar bi-Laham

Syria and Lebanon

Makes 15 to 20 pies

¹/₄ cup olive oil

1 lb lamb or beef, ground or cut into
  very small pieces

6 medium onions, chopped

2 cloves garlic, crushed

salt and pepper to taste

2 tablespoons allspice

pinch cayenne

2 medium tomatoes, chopped

¹/₄ cup lemon juice

2 tablespoons butter

1 quantity basic dough for pies
  (see p. 11)

Heat the oil in a saucepan over medium heat. Add the meat, onions, garlic, salt, pepper, allspice, and cayenne; then stir and sauté until the meat is well cooked with all signs of pink gone. Do not brown.

Add the tomatoes, lemon juice, and butter, and mix thoroughly, then taste and add more seasoning or lemon juice if required.

Form and fill pies as for *kishk* pies (see p. 98). Bake at 400°F for 15–20 minutes until well browned.

Beef, Spinach, and Bean Pie
Tajin
Tunisia

Serves 6 to 8

1/4 cup olive oil	1 teaspoon oregano
1/2 lb beef, cut into small pieces	1/2 teaspoon cumin
2 medium onions, chopped	2 cups water
4 cloves garlic, crushed	4 tablespoons butter
1 small hot pepper, finely chopped	1 bunch fresh spinach, thoroughly washed
1/4 cup tomato paste	and chopped
1 can white kidney beans (19 oz or 540 ml),	1/2 cup grated white cheese
undrained	1/2 cup breadcrumbs
salt and pepper to taste	6 eggs, beaten

In a casserole, heat the oil; then sauté the meat over medium heat until it begins to brown. Add the onions, garlic, and hot pepper; then stir-fry until the onions begin to brown. Stir in the tomato paste, beans, salt, oregano, pepper, cumin, and water and bring to a boil; then cover and cook over medium heat for 1 hour.

In the meantime, in a frying pan, melt the butter; then stir-fry the spinach until it wilts. Stir the frying pan contents and the remaining ingredients into the casserole and place in a 350°F preheated oven; then cover and bake for 40 minutes.

Note: Excellent for snacks, as a side dish or as an entrée.

Pomegranate Pizza Arabic Style
Safeehat Rumman
Syria and Lebanon

Makes 15 to 18 pies

Pomegranates are bright colored and range in hue from pinkish to purple-red. The choicest are a bright reddish color with thin leathery skin. Inside they are filled with a myriad of large red seeds which appear like masses of scarlet berries embedded in a translucent, slightly pinkish pulp.

An excellent autumn-winter fruit, pomegranates are picked before they are fully mature. However, they continue to ripen in cold storage, where they will keep in excellent condition for as long as six months. Compared to other fruit, they are exceptionally free of disease.

This pizza is an exotic version of an international favorite.

2 lbs frozen pizza dough or	1 small can tomato paste (5 1/2 oz or 156 ml)
equivalent amount of homemade dough	1 teaspoon paprika

1 lb beef or lamb with some fat, cut into very small pieces

1 cup pomegranate seeds (from 2 medium-size fruits)

2 medium onions, finely chopped

2 cloves garlic, crushed

salt and pepper to taste

$\frac{1}{2}$ teaspoon ground coriander

$\frac{1}{2}$ cup finely chopped chives

$\frac{1}{4}$ teaspoon cayenne

3 tablespoons olive oil

Form the dough into 18 balls (golf ball size); then cover with a damp cloth and allow to rest for 2 hours.

In the meantime, make a filling by thoroughly mixing the remaining ingredients. Set aside.

Roll the dough balls into rounds about 5 inches in diameter; then pinch the edges to make a raised rim (see illustration below). Spread approximately 2 tablespoons of the filling inside of the rim and pat down evenly with the fingers. Continue until all the rounds are finished.

Bake on a well greased cookie tray in a 350°F preheated oven for 20 minutes or until the rims of the pizza turn light brown. Serve hot.

Kishk Pies

Fatayar bi-Kishk

Syria and Lebanon

Makes 12 pies

Kishk can be found in most Middle Eastern grocery stores.

1 lb frozen pizza dough or equivalent
   amount of homemade bread dough
1 cup of coarse or fine *kishk*
   (see p. 12)
1 cup water

1 cup *qawarma* (see p. 12) with a
   little of its fat ($^1/_2$ lb lamb or beef,
   diced and fried, may be substituted)
1 bunch scallions, finely chopped
$^1/_2$ cup olive oil
salt and pepper to taste

Thaw out the dough; then cut into 12 balls the size of golf balls, and allow to rest for 2 hours.

In the meantime, make the filling by mixing the *kishk* with the water. Mix thoroughly with the rest of the ingredients.

Roll each ball into a round 4 or 5 inches across. Place 1 heaping table-spoon of the filling on each round; then shape into a triangle and close firmly by pinching the edges together (see illustration below). Bake on a greased baking sheet in a 400°F preheated oven for 10 or 15 minutes or until pies turn medium brown. If a darker color is desired, brown lightly under broiler. Brush the tops with butter and serve hot.

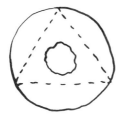

Ground Beef and Potato "Sandwich"

Imbattna

Libya

Serves 10

8 eggs

1 lb ground lamb or beef

2 bunches fresh parsley, chopped

1 medium onion, chopped

salt and pepper to taste

3 cloves garlic, crushed

5 large potatoes cut lengthwise into ¼ inch slices

1 cup flour seasoned with ½ teaspoon salt and ½ teaspoon pepper

oil for frying

Beat two of the eggs; combine with the beef, parsley, onions, salt, pepper and garlic.

With the potato slices, make sandwiches using the potato slices as "bread" and the meat mixture as the filling. Dip each of the sandwiches into the flour, coating well. Beat the remaining eggs with a pinch of salt; then dip each sandwich into the beaten eggs. Coat again with the flour. In a heavy frying pan, heat the oil (about 2 inches deep) over medium heat. Fry the sandwiches, turning until both sides are well browned.

Lower the temperature and continue frying for about 20 minutes, until a fork can pierce all layers. Drain and serve immediately or let cool to serve at a later time.

Note: These sandwiches may be frozen after cooking; thaw and place in a 350°F oven for 10–15 minutes to heat through.

Dumplings in Yogurt

Sheesh Barak

Syria and Lebanon

Serves 6

1 lb frozen pizza dough, thawed, or the equivalent amount of homemade dough

1 lb ground lean lamb or beef

2 tablespoons butter

¼ cup pine nuts

¼ teaspoon ground coriander

¼ teaspoon cinnamon

salt and pepper to taste

2 medium onions, finely chopped

2 cloves garlic, crushed

yogurt sauce (see p. 17)

Form the dough into ¾ inch balls and allow to rest for 1 hour. In the meantime, make a filling by browning the meat in the butter. Add the pine nuts and seasoning and sauté until the pine nuts are light brown. Stir in the onions and garlic and stir-fry for a further 5 minutes.

Roll out the dough balls with a rolling pin to make circles ¼ inch thick.

Place ½ teaspoon of filling in the center of each circle and fold in half. Pinch the edges of the semicircles together to seal. Fold in half again to shape dumplings like a thimble and pinch to close.

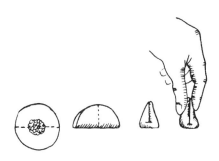

Place the dumplings on a buttered tray and broil for a few minutes, turning each one over to brown evenly.

Bring the yogurt sauce to a simmer in a large pot. Lower the dumplings into the simmering sauce, a few at a time; simmer for about 15 minutes. Serve hot.

Garlic Meatballs

Muththawin

Algeria

Serves 8 to 10

In North Africa, as well as the Middle East and in the countries of eastern and southern Europe, garlic forms an essential part of the daily menu. This Algerian dish is a fine example of how garlic is used to enhance the flavor of an ordinary dish like meatballs.

4 tablespoons butter
1 large onion, finely chopped
1 lb beef, cut into $^1/_2$ inch cubes
1 head garlic, peeled and crushed
salt and pepper to taste
1 teaspoon cinnamon
pinch cayenne

1 lb ground beef
$^1/_4$ cup rice, rinsed
1 bunch parsley, finely chopped
1 egg beaten
4 tablespoons tomato paste
1 can chickpeas (19 oz or 540 ml), undrained

In a saucepan, melt the butter and sauté the onions until they begin to brown. Add the cubed meat, half the garlic, salt and pepper, $^1/_2$ teaspoon of the cinnamon, and the cayenne. Sauté for a few minutes. Add water to a depth of one inch and bring to a boil; then cover and simmer over medium heat for 45 minutes.

In the meantime, thoroughly mix the ground beef, rice, parsley, egg, and the remaining garlic, salt, pepper, and cinnamon. Form into small meatballs; then gently place the meatballs in the simmering saucepan. Bring to a boil, and simmer for about 15 minutes. Add the tomato paste and the chickpeas; then simmer over a medium heat until the meatballs are done.

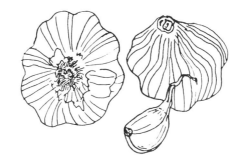

Meatball Parcels

Bariwat

Morocco

Serves 6

2 medium onions, diced
4 tablespoons butter
salt and pepper to taste
1 lb finely ground lamb or beef
1 teaspoon paprika
pinch cinnamon

$^1/_2$ cup finely chopped fresh coriander
    leaves (cilantro)
$^1/_2$ cup finely chopped parsley
5 eggs
1 package filo dough
2 cups cooking oil

Sauté the onions in the butter, with pepper and salt. Cook on low to medium heat until the onions are light brown. Set aside.

In a separate bowl, mix the ground meat, pepper and salt, paprika, cinnamon, and 1 tablespoon of mixed coriander leaves and parsley. Add the meat to the onions and fry until the meat is cooked, breaking the meat up with a fork. Add the rest of the parsley and coriander and cook for a further 5 minutes.

Beat 4 of the eggs. Stir into the meat and cook for a further 3 minutes or until the eggs are done.

Beat the remaining egg in a bowl and set aside. Cut the filo dough into 3 inch strips. Place 1 teaspoon of the meat on the bottom of each strip. Roll the strips into rolls with the edges tucked in. Seal the rolls with the beaten egg spread over the edges and ends. Fry the rolls or *bariwats* in hot oil until they become golden brown.

Note: The *bariwats* should be eaten hot. For an added exquisite and typically Moroccan taste, they may be dipped into a mixture of $^1/_2$ teaspoon of cinnamon and 1 tablespoon of sugar.

Meatballs with Yogurt

Kufta ma' Laban

Iraq

Serves 4 to 6

2 cups ground beef or lamb
¼ cup breadcrumbs
1 medium onion, finely chopped
½ cup finely chopped fresh coriander
   leaves (cilantro)
1 small hot pepper, very finely chopped
salt and pepper to taste

pinch allspice
2 tablespoons butter
4 cups yogurt
2 cloves garlic, crushed
2 eggs, beaten
2 tablespoons finely chopped fresh mint
   or 1 tablespoon dried mint

Mix thoroughly the meat, breadcrumbs, onion, coriander leaves, hot pepper, salt, pepper, and allspice; then form into meatballs 1 inch in diameter.

In a frying pan, melt the butter; then sauté the meatballs until they are well done, and set aside.

Make the sauce: Bring the yogurt, garlic, eggs, mint, and salt to a boil over medium heat, stirring continuously clockwise; then turn off the heat and allow to stand for about 3 minutes. Remove meatballs from their fat and add to the sauce. Serve hot.

Meat Cakes

Iraq

Serves 4 to 6

1 lb ground lamb or beef
½ cup finely chopped coriander
   leaves (cilantro)
¼ cup rice, cooked

2 eggs
oil
salt and pepper to taste

In a bowl place meat, coriander, cooked rice, salt, pepper, and one of the eggs. Mix thoroughly, and set aside. Beat the other egg in a small bowl; then set aside.

Make small patties of the meat mixture; then dip each in the beaten egg and fry in oil. Serve hot.

Upside Down Casserole
Maqlooba
Palestine and Jordan

Serves 4 to 6

In many parts of Europe, it was near the end of the 16th century before eggplants were widely cultivated, and then mostly as a decorative plant. In North America, only in the last few decades have they been cultivated in appreciable quantity, mainly in the southern U.S.

Requiring long warm summers to mature, the vegetable thrives best in the tropical parts of the world. Eggplants grow from one to two feet high and produce wide gray-green leaves and fruit weighing from a few ounces to over two pounds. In the Western world it is cultivated for both culinary and ornamental purposes. However, in Eastern lands it is raised mostly for its edible fruit. In the cuisine of these countries, it has always been a gourmet delight.

1 large eggplant, unpeeled, sliced into 1/2 inch thick slices	1/4 cup pine nuts
salt	2 cloves garlic, crushed
1/2 cup olive oil	3 1/2 cups boiling water
4 tablespoons butter	1 cup rice, rinsed
1 lb beef or lamb, cut into 1/2 inch cubes	1/2 teaspoon pepper
2 medium sized onions, chopped	1/2 teaspoon cumin
	1/2 teaspoon allspice

Sprinkle the eggplant slices with salt; then place in a strainer, top with a weight, and allow to drain for 45 minutes.

Heat the oil in a frying pan, then add the eggplant slices and sauté over moderately high heat until they begin to brown. (Add more oil if necessary.) Remove and place in a strainer or on paper towels to drain.

In a saucepan, melt the butter; then add the meat and sauté until it begins to brown. Add the onions, pine nuts, and garlic; then sauté and stir until they turn golden brown. Add 2 cups of the boiling water; then simmer over low heat for 1 hour, until the meat is tender and the water is almost absorbed.

Place the eggplant slices over the meat. Spread the rice evenly over the top and add the remaining 1 1/2 cups of water. Sprinkle the salt, pepper, cumin, and allspice over the rice; then cover and allow to simmer over low heat until the rice is tender, about 20–25 minutes. Turn off the heat; then allow the rice to finish cooking in its own steam.

Just before serving, invert the serving platter over the top of the saucepan; then hold securely and turn over so that the rice is at the bottom and the meat on the top. Serve immediately.

Lamb with Rice

Seleq

Saudi Arabia

Serves 4 to 6

A traveler who was crossing a desert land once wrote of a typical encounter: "'*Tafaddaloo* – do us the honor!' said the Bedouin, beckoning us into his tent to share his meal. We had only halted to ask our way along a road in the desert, but such is the tradition of hospitality in the Arabian Peninsula that he was prepared to feed our large party."

In Saudi Arabia, the Bedouin family could very well have been cooking *seleq* when the travelers arrived.

2 lbs of lamb, cut into ¹/₂ inch cubes	salt and pepper to taste
3 medium onions, finely chopped	2 cups milk
2 tablespoons fresh coriander leaves (cilantro), finely chopped	2 cups rice, rinsed
	4 tablespoons butter, melted

Place the meat, onions, coriander, salt, and pepper in a saucepan; then cover with water and simmer covered over low heat for one hour. Remove the meat and set aside, but keep warm.

Add 2 cups of water and the milk to the stock in which the meat was cooked. Bring to a boil. Stir in the rice, cover, and cook very gently over low heat until the rice is nearly cooked (about 15 minutes). Turn off the heat and allow to steam 10 minutes longer.

Place the rice on a large tray. Arrange the pieces of meat on top. Pour the melted butter over the rice and meat. Serve with a vegetable salad.

Kishk Pottage

Tanaytana

Syria and Lebanon

Serves 4 to 6

¹/₂ cup fine burghul, rinsed	¹/₄ lb lean beef, finely diced
2¹/₂ cups water	1 medium onion, finely chopped
¹/₂ cup *kishk* (see p. 12) dissolved in ¹/₂ cup of water	2 cloves garlic, crushed
3 tablespoons butter	salt and pepper to taste

Bring the burghul and water to a boil and cook over medium heat for 8 minutes. Turn the heat to low; then add the *kishk* and cook for a further 8 minutes, stirring frequently.

In the meantime, melt the butter in a frying pan, add the meat and brown. Stir in the onions and garlic; sauté further until they turn golden brown.

Stir the contents of the frying pan into the burghul, add the salt and pepper, and cook over low heat for 5 minutes, stirring occasionally.

Rice with Meat and Fava Beans

Fool ma' Rizz

Syria and Lebanon

Fava beans are popular as an hors d'oeuvre in Italy and southern France, but it is the Arabic cook who makes best use of this legume. Also known as the broad bean, vicia bean, Windsor bean, English dwarf bean, and horse bean, the fava bean has been domesticated for perhaps 4,000 years. A wild form can still be found in Algeria.

¹/₂ cup butter	2 cups frozen green fava beans or
1 lb lamb or beef, cut into small pieces	1 can of drained green fava beans
¹/₂ cup onions, chopped	(19 oz or 540 ml)
¹/₄ teaspoon allspice	1 cup rice, rinsed and drained
salt and pepper to taste	3 cups boiling water
	2 tablespoons finely chopped fresh coriander leaves (cilantro)

In a frying pan, sauté the meat in the butter over a medium heat until it begins to brown. Add the onions, allspice, salt, and pepper; then stir and continue sautéeing until the onions turn golden brown. Add the fava beans, rice, and water, and mix thoroughly; then cover and cook for half an hour or until the rice is tender but not mushy and the water has evaporated. Place in a serving dish; then sprinkle with the coriander.

Date and Meat Pottage

Saudi Arabia

Serves 6 to 8

In Islam, the Prophet Muhammad enjoined his followers to honor the date palm as "one blessed among all plants as Muslims are blessed among men," and the Holy Qur'an states that Mary gave birth to Jesus under a palm tree whose fruit she ate to ease the pain of childbirth.

5 tablespoons butter	¹/₂ teaspoon cinnamon
2 lbs beef or lamb, cut into	pinch pepper
¹/₂ inch cubes	pinch allspice
2 medium onions, chopped	1 cup dates, pitted and cut into quarters
4 cloves garlic, crushed	1 cup rice, rinsed
¹/₄ cup finely chopped fresh coriander leaves (cilantro)	salt

In a saucepan, melt the butter and sauté the meat until it begins to brown. Stir in the onions, garlic, and coriander; then sauté further until the onions begin to brown.

Add all the remaining ingredients except the dates and rice; then cover with water to a depth of one inch and cook covered over medium heat for about 40 minutes or until the meat is nearly cooked. Stir in the dates and rice and add more water if necessary; then lower the heat, cover and cook for about 20 minutes or until the rice is tender but not mushy.

Burghul Pottage
Burghul Mufalfal
Syria and Lebanon

Serves 4 to 6

Burghul (also bulgur) is prepared by cooking, drying and breaking up wheat kernels. It may be served as a boiled morning cereal, or eaten like potatoes with other foods. Boiled with sugar and raisins, it makes a filling dessert. In this recipe, it is used to bulk out a simple meat stew.

4 tablespoons cooking oil	1 cup coarse burghul, rinsed
1/2 lb beef, cut into 1/2 inch cubes	2 cups water
4 medium onions, finely chopped	salt and pepper to taste

In a frying pan, heat the oil and sauté the meat for 5 minutes; then add the onions and continue cooking, stirring from time to time until the onions turn light brown.

Stir in the burghul, and stir-fry for about 3 minutes; then add salt, pepper, and water. Bring to a boil; then turn heat down to low and simmer for about 30 minutes, until all the water is absorbed. Put a close-fitting lid on the frying pan and turn off the heat. Let stand for about 15 minutes before serving.

Stuffed Zucchini
Mihshee Koosa
Algeria

Serves 4 to 6

The Stock

4 tablespoons butter	1 cup boiling water
2 lbs stewing meat, cubed	salt and pepper to taste
1 onion, chopped	

In a saucepan, melt the butter; then fry the meat with the onion until they begin to turn brown. Add the remaining ingredients, bring to a boil, then let simmer over low heat for 40 minutes. Set aside.

The Zucchini and its Stuffing

1 lb ground beef or lamb
$^1/_3$ cup chopped parsley
1 onion, diced
$^1/_2$ cup rice
1 egg, beaten

salt and pepper to taste
$^1/_2$ teaspoon cinnamon
2 lbs green zucchini, preferably slender
   and 6–8 inches long

Make the stuffing by combining all ingredients except the zucchini. Cut stem ends off zucchini; then cut into halves crosswise. Core each piece, leaving one end solid (see illustration below); then fill with stuffing mixture and set aside.

Place the zucchini in a pot of stock vertically with the open ends upward. Bring to a boil; then let simmer over medium heat for about 10 minutes. Lower the heat and allow to simmer for about 30 minutes or until cooked. Do not let the pot boil dry; add more water if needed.

The Sauce

To be prepared while the zucchini is cooking.

$^1/_4$ cup parsley, chopped
1 egg, raw

juice of 1 lemon

Mix all the ingredients into a sauce; then pour over the cooked zucchini. Let simmer about 10 minutes over a very low heat; then serve piping hot.

Stuffed Eggplant

Ablama

Syria and Lebanon

Serves 6 to 8

Some historians have suggested that the eggplant originated in China about 4,000 years ago, and was introduced into the Middle East by the Arabs in the 8th century. Others say that since 1500 BC, eggplants have been grown and eaten as a vegetable in Iran and India. However much the origin is disputed, its history of increasing popularity since the Arab-Islamic expansion is well documented.

In the 7th century AD, the Arab armies entered Iran and India, and returned home, bringing with them the vegetable, which they called *bathinjan*, an Arabized form of the Persian *badnjan*. In the next century, after the Islamic conquest of the Iberian Peninsula, the Arabs introduced this vegetable to Europe. In the villas and palaces of Muslim Spain, the eggplant, which had been unknown to the Europe of that age, often graced the tables of the Moors.

Soon the eggplant's cultivation spread through the Iberian Peninsula, and in later centuries to the rest of Europe. The Arabic name for the eggplant is still carried by many European languages, attesting to its introduction by the Arabs. The Spanish *berenjena*, Portuguese *berinjela* and the French *aubergine*, all derive from the Arabic *bathinjan*.

12 eggplants, from 3 to 4 inches long, stemmed	salt
$^{3}/_{4}$ cup olive oil	$^{1}/_{2}$ teaspoon pepper
1 medium onion, finely chopped	$^{1}/_{2}$ teaspoon allspice
3 cloves garlic, crushed	$^{1}/_{4}$ teaspoon cinnamon
$^{3}/_{4}$ lb ground beef	$^{1}/_{4}$ teaspoon oregano
$^{1}/_{2}$ cup rice, rinsed	$^{1}/_{2}$ cup pine nuts
	yogurt sauce (see p. 17)

Core the eggplants with a sharp knife or, better yet, with an eggplant corer (found in Middle Eastern stores), making sure not to break the skins.

In a frying pan, heat $^{1}/_{2}$ cup of the oil and sauté the eggplants over a medium heat, turning often until they cook on all sides; then remove and place in a strainer to drain and cool.

To the same oil, add the onion and garlic; then sauté over a medium heat for a few moments. Add more oil if the onions begin to stick. Stir in the meat, rice, salt, pepper, allspice, cinnamon, and oregano and stir-fry until the meat is browned. Remove and allow to cool.

In the meantime, heat the remaining $^{1}/_{4}$ cup of oil in another frying pan and add the pine nuts; then stir-fry over a medium heat until they turn golden brown. Remove and drain.

Make a filling by mixing the pine nuts with the meat mixture. Stuff the eggplants; then set aside.

Prepare the yogurt sauce. Place the stuffed eggplants in the yogurt; then simmer uncovered over very low heat, for 30 minutes. Serve hot.

Cabbage Rolls
Mihshee Malfoof
Syria and Lebanon

Serves 6 to 8

"*Mihshee*" means "stuffed," from the verb "*hasha*" to stuff. This category includes many dishes whose simple, versatile filling comprises ground or diced meat, rice, and spices.

1 cabbage, medium size	$^1/_2$ teaspoon allspice
1 lb beef or lamb, cut into very small cubes	$^1/_4$ teaspoon cumin
a few bones, if available, cut into 2 to 3 inch lengths	2 tablespoons butter, melted
1 cup rice, rinsed	1 can tomatoes (19 oz or 540 ml)
salt and pepper to taste	4 cloves garlic
	$^1/_4$ cup lemon juice

Place the cabbage head in a pot half filled with boiling water, and simmer for 10–15 minutes until the outer leaves become soft. Remove the softened outer leaves, and repeat the process until you reach the center leaves, which are too small to stuff.

Cut the big outer leaves in half and remove the stem; cut out the stem of the smaller inner leaves. Use the stems and bones to line the bottom of the pot.

Make the stuffing by mixing well the meat, rice, salt, pepper, allspice, cumin, butter, and half of the can of tomatoes.

Place 1 tablespoon of the stuffing on each cabbage leaf half and roll, making sure to tuck in the ends. Arrange the rolls on top of the stems in the pot, tucking the garlic cloves in between. Spread the rest of the can of tomatoes over the rolls; then sprinkle with salt and the lemon juice.

Insert an inverted flat dish large enough to cover the top of the rolls to prevent them from opening during cooking; then add enough boiling water to barely cover the dish. Cover the pot and bring to a boil; then reduce the heat and simmer for about one hour or until the cabbage is tender and the rice inside the rolls is cooked.

Note: Burghul can be used instead of rice, and kohlrabi, grape, or Swiss chard leaves may be substituted for the cabbage.

Algerian Couscous

Algeria

Serves 12 or more

The Stew

2 large onions, diced
3 lbs stewing beef, in large pieces
1/2 cup oil
1 roasting chicken, cut into quarters
2 cans chickpeas (19 oz or 540 ml),
  drained and rinsed

6 large zucchinis, unpeeled
6 parsnips, peeled
1/2 teaspoon cinnamon
1 tablespoon *mazahar* (orange blossom
  water)
salt and pepper to taste

In a large saucepan, sauté the onions and beef in oil until browned. Add water to cover and boil, covered, for 20 minutes. Lower the heat and simmer for about 20 minutes, until the meat is almost cooked.

Cut the zucchini and parsnips in half lengthwise and crosswise, to make quarters. Add the chicken, chickpeas, all the vegetables, seasoning, and the *mazahar*. Cook for 1 hour. Check occasionally and add water if necessary; the stew should be fairly wet. Season to taste; keep warm while preparing the couscous.

The Couscous

1 tablespoon salt
2 lbs couscous
1 cup butter

5 tablespoons *mazahar (orange blossom*
  water)
2 tablespoons cinnamon

Dissolve the salt in 5 cups of lukewarm water; stir in the couscous and allow to stand for 5 minutes. Drain and squeeze to remove excess water if necessary. Using your hands, mix in 3 tablespoons of the butter to coat the couscous.

Half fill the lower pot of the couscousière or double boiler with boiling water; place the couscous in the steamer section. If necessary, wrap a dampened folded cloth around the division of the two sections to prevent steam from escaping. Steam the couscous for 20 minutes. Place the couscous in a large deep dish. Taste for moistness. If not moist enough, sprinkle with hot water and mix gently. Add the *mazahar*, the rest of the butter, and 1 teaspoon of cinnamon. Mix well.

To Serve

Mound the couscous on a large platter. Sprinkle the top of the mound with the rest of the cinnamon. Serve the stew separately; spoon onto the couscous on individual plates as desired.

Couscous

Morocco

Serves 10 to 12

Couscous, the national dish of Morocco, is fast becoming world renowned. At one time, it was the national dish of Arab Spain, but when the Arabs were expelled, the eating of couscous was made a crime by the Inquisition, and this culinary delight was lost to Europe for centuries. It has been in recent years rediscovered by the West, and now many Europeans talk with great relish about this fine dish that was once referred to as the food of the infidel.

To prepare this dish, a couscousière is needed. However, if one is not available, a double boiler with a perforated top or a pot with a fine strainer to hold the couscous may be substituted.

$\frac{1}{4}$ cup olive oil

$\frac{1}{2}$ lb lamb or beef, cut into $\frac{1}{2}$ inch cubes

1 large onion, chopped

4 cloves garlic, crushed

$\frac{1}{4}$ cup finely chopped fresh coriander leaves (cilantro)

1 small hot pepper, finely chopped

1 small can tomato paste (5.5 oz or 156ml)

1 can chickpeas (19 oz or 540 ml), undrained

$1\frac{1}{2}$ teaspoons ginger

1 teaspoon cumin

$\frac{1}{2}$ teaspoon cinnamon

pinch of saffron

2 medium potatoes, peeled and quartered

2 medium carrots, scraped and cut into quarters, lengthwise, then chopped into 2 inch pieces

1 turnip, about 3 inches in diameter, peeled and cut into 1 inch cubes

2 cups couscous

5 tablespoons butter, melted

1 zucchini, chopped into large pieces, unpeeled

1 large sweet pepper, seeded and chopped into large pieces

$\frac{1}{4}$ cup raisins

$\frac{1}{2}$ cup toasted pine nuts

$\frac{1}{2}$ teaspoon paprika

In the bottom part of the couscousière, heat the oil, then sauté the meat over medium heat for 10 minutes. Add the onion, garlic, coriander leaves, and hot pepper; then stir-fry for a further 10 minutes. Stir in the tomato paste, chickpeas, salt, ginger, cumin, pepper, cinnamon, saffron, potatoes, carrots, and turnip. Cover with water to a depth of 1 inch, and bring to a boil. Cover and cook over medium heat for 20 minutes.

In the meantime, mix the dry couscous with the butter until all the kernels are coated; then place in the top part of the couscousière and set aside.

Add the zucchini, sweet pepper, and raisins to the stew and bring to a boil; then set the top part of the couscousière firmly on top and seal tightly. To steam the couscous more efficiently, the bottom and top parts of the couscousière are traditionally sealed with a piece of cloth soaked in a solution of flour and water. Cook for 15 minutes, stirring the couscous a few times; then sprinkle the remaining 1 cup of water over the couscous while stirring all the time to make sure no lumps are formed.

Cook for another 20 minutes, stirring the couscous every few minutes; then place the couscous on a flat serving plate in a pyramid shape with a large well on top. Place the vegetables and meat with some of the sauce in the well; then decorate the couscous with the pine nuts and paprika.

Serve hot with the remainder of the sauce in a gravy boat.

Couscous of Marrakesh
Morocco

Serves 8 to 12

In Morocco, saffron is used extensively in all types of dishes, appreciated for its faint, delicate aroma, and for the magnificent yellow color it gives the food.

The Couscous

1 lb couscous	salt to taste
1 cup cold water	4 tablespoons butter

Stir the water, salt, and butter into the couscous. Set aside.

The Stew

4 tablespoons cooking oil	3 medium carrots, scraped clean and cut into $1/4$ inch slices
2 lbs chicken pieces	2 medium potatoes, peeled and cut into quarters
1 lb lamb or beef, cut into 1 inch cubes	1 can tomatoes (19 oz or 540 ml)
2 medium onions, chopped	2 medium zucchini, cut into large pieces
1 teaspoon ground coriander	1 cup fresh or frozen peas
salt to taste	1 can chickpeas (19 oz or 540 ml)
$1/8$ teaspoon saffron	1 cup raisins
1 teaspoon ground cumin	

In the bottom section of the couscousière, heat the oil; then add the chicken, lamb or beef, and onions. Simmer for about 10 minutes. Add the seasonings and water to cover to a depth of one inch; then bring to a boil, and cook for 30 minutes.

Add all the vegetables and return to a boil. Place the couscous in the top part of the couscousière and cook for 45 minutes, stirring the couscous once in a while to see that the grains do not stick together.

Mound the couscous on a platter and place the stew in a serving bowl.

Note: This dish is enhanced by either a tossed salad, an eggplant salad, or romaine salad with pimentoes.

Couscous of Tunisia

Although believed to be Moroccan in origin, couscous is so popular throughout Tunisia that it is often called "Land of the Couscous."

¹/₄ cup olive oil
1 lb beef or lamb, cut into 1 inch cubes
¹/₂ cup chickpeas, washed and soaked
    overnight in 4 cups water
2 medium onions, diced
4 cloves garlic, crushed
4 medium potatoes, peeled and quartered
3 medium carrots, scraped and halved
    lengthwise; then each half cut into
    4 pieces
1 small turnip, chopped into large pieces
1 hot pepper, finely chopped

4 tablespoons tomato paste
¹/₂ cup finely chopped fresh coriander
    leaves (cilantro)
1 teaspoon thyme
1 teaspoon tarragon
¹/₂ teaspoon cinnamon
pinch saffron
5 cups water
6 tablespoons butter
2 cups couscous
salt and pepper to taste

In the bottom part of a couscousière, sauté the meat in the oil until it begins to brown. Add the chickpeas with their water and bring to a boil; then cover and cook over a medium heat for 45 minutes.

Add the remaining ingredients except the butter and couscous and bring to a boil; cover and cook over medium heat for a further 30 minutes.

In the meantime, mix the butter and couscous with the fingers until the couscous kernels are all coated with butter; then place in the top part of the couscousière. Place the top part of the couscousière over the bottom part and seal with a wet piece of cloth impregnated with flour, pulled tightly and fastened around where the two parts of the couscousière join. Allow the coucous to steam for 20 minutes over medium heat; then sprinkle with about 1 cup of water, stirring the couscous all the time to make sure it does not become lumpy.

Cook for a further 40 minutes, stirring the couscous once in a while; then remove the couscous and place on a serving plate. Remove the vegetables and meat with a slotted spoon and arrange over the top of the couscous; then spoon a portion of the gravy over the top just before serving. Serve the remaining gravy in a separate bowl.

Almond Stew
Al-Qidra bi-Lawz
Morocco

Serves 4 to 6

Every dish cooked in North Africa entices with its subtle aroma. In Morocco and Algeria, the dishes are generally mild, but the stews of Tunisia and Libya are fiery with ginger and hot peppers. In all these countries, the spices used add a dimension to the work-a-day salt and pepper.

3 tablespoons butter
1 lb onions, coarsely chopped
4 cloves garlic, crushed
1/2 teaspoon ginger
pinch cinnamon
pinch saffron

2 lbs beef or lamb, cut into 1 inch cubes
1/2 cup slivered almonds
1/2 cup finely chopped fresh coriander leaves (cilantro)
1/2 cup finely chopped parsley
salt and pepper to taste

In a saucepan, melt the butter and add 1 cup of the onions, the garlic, salt, pepper, ginger, cinnamon, and saffron. Stir fry until the onions turn golden brown.

Add the meat and continue to stir fry until the meat begins to brown.

Stir in the almonds and water to cover, then cover the saucepan and cook for 1 1/2 hours, or until the meat is tender.

Stir in the remaining onions, coriander, and parsley. Simmer over low heat for 30 minutes more.

Baked Beef (or Lamb) and Cheese with Peppers
Tajin Shakshooka
Tunisia

Serves 8 to 10

6 tablespoons olive oil
2 lbs beef or lamb, cut into 1/2 inch cubes
1/2 teaspoon cinnamon
2 medium onions, diced
2 medium sweet green peppers, coarsely chopped

3 medium tomatoes, diced
1/2 cup finely chopped fresh coriander leaves (cilantro)
1/2 teaspoon chilli powder
3/4 cup grated cheese
6 eggs, beaten
salt and pepper to taste

In a large frying pan, heat 3 tablespoons of the oil over a high heat. Stir in the meat, cinnamon, pepper, and salt. Brown the meat cubes, stirring frequently; then pour in 2 cups of water and bring to a boil. Lower the heat, cover and simmer for about 45 minutes. Remove the meat with a slotted spoon and place in a casserole. Reserve the meat juices in the frying pan.

In another frying pan, sauté the onions in the remaining 3 tablespoons of oil over medium heat until they become limp. Stir in the peppers, tomatoes, coriander, chilli powder, 1 cup of water, and salt. Bring to a boil over a high heat. Reduce the heat to low and, stirring often, simmer for about 15 minutes or until most of the liquid in the pan has evaporated. Add the onion mixture and the eggs to the meat in the casserole, and stir in the cheese. Mix thoroughly.

Bake covered in a 350°F preheated oven for 45 minutes or until the meat is tender. Serve directly from the casserole with rice and salad. Heat the reserved meat juices and serve separately as desired.

Beef and Bean Stew
Yakhnat Fassoolya
Syria and Lebanon

Serves 6 to 8

In Arab *yakhnas* and *tajins*, all types of cheap cuts of meat and fresh or dried vegetables can be utilized interchangeably. For centuries, the Arab peasants have dined on these simple dishes, and in the process have learned the art of blending and balancing textures and aromas. To appreciate these foods, one must eat at a villager's home where there is always a pot of stew simmering on the fire. With large families and limited incomes, goulashes are the mainstay of the housewife's menu. Renowned for their hospitality, the Arab peasants always make plans for unexpected guests. When one arrives, the housewife exercises her inventiveness by adding a little more water, and, perhaps a few vegetables to her simmering pot of *yakhna* or *tajin*.

1 cup white navy beans, soaked overnight in 6 cups water	1 medium potato, peeled and cubed
4 tablespoons olive oil	1 can tomatoes (19 oz or 540 ml)
1 lb beef, cut into $^1/_2$ inch cubes	$^1/_4$ cup finely chopped fresh coriander leaves (cilantro)
a few bones, if available, broken in 1 to 3 inch pieces	3 cloves garlic, crushed
2 medium onions, diced	$^1/_4$ teaspoon tarragon
1 medium carrot, peeled and sliced into thin rounds	$^1/_4$ teaspoon cumin
	salt and pepper to taste

Cook the beans in their soaking water for $1^1/_2$–2 hours, until they are tender. Set aside, do not drain.

Heat the oil in a saucepan; add the meat and bones and sauté on a medium heat until the meat begins to brown. Add the onions, carrots, potatoes, and the cooked beans with their water; then simmer on a medium heat until the meat and the vegetables are tender, adding more water if necessary.

Stir in the tomatoes, coriander, garlic, salt, pepper, tarragon, and cumin and bring to a boil; then reduce the heat and simmer for another 30 minutes, stirring once in a while. Serve with rice.

Fava Beans and Meat Stew
Tajin
Morocco

Serves 6

Garlic and onions are regarded as essential ingredients in every one of the enormous repertoire of Arab stews. To maximize their function, they are always sautéed to a golden brown. They are then combined with some of the numerous exotic herbs and spices, many of which the Arabs first introduced into Europe. Some of these condiments still carry their Arabic names. Caraway is the Arabic *karawaya*, cumin *kammoon*, ginger *zanjabeel*, saffron *za'faran*, and tarragon *tarkhoon*.

1 lb beef or lamb, cut into medium
   size pieces
salt and pepper to taste
1 teaspoon ginger
$^1/_2$ teaspoon turmeric
4 cloves garlic, crushed
1 large onion, finely chopped
$^1/_2$ cup finely chopped fresh coriander
   leaves (cilantro)

$1^1/_2$ cups water
4 tablespoons olive oil
2 cups frozen or fresh shelled fava
   beans, or 1 can fava beans
   (19 oz or 540 ml), drained
5 tablespoons lemon juice
$^1/_2$ cup pitted black olives

In a pot, place the meat, salt, pepper, ginger, turmeric, garlic, onion, coriander, water, and oil; then cover and cook over a medium heat until the meat is tender.

Add the fava beans and continue cooking until the beans are tender. Stir in the lemon juice. Place in a serving bowl and decorate with the olives.

Chickpea Stew
Markit Ommala
Tunisia

Serves 6 to 8

¹/₄ cup olive oil
1 lb beef, cut into ¹/₂ inch cubes
2 medium onions, chopped
4 cloves garlic, crushed
¹/₂ cup finely chopped fresh coriander
  leaves (cilantro)
1 hot pepper, finely chopped
2 cans chickpeas (19 oz or 540 ml each),
  undrained

4 medium tomatoes, diced
salt and pepper to taste
¹/₂ teaspoon cumin
¹/₂ teaspoon thyme
2 cups water
¹/₄ cup green olives, pitted and chopped
2 tablespoons lemon juice

In a saucepan, heat the oil, then sauté the meat over medium heat until it begins to brown. Add the onions, garlic, coriander leaves, and hot pepper; stir-fry for a further 5 minutes.

Stir in the undrained chickpeas, tomatoes, salt, pepper, cumin, thyme, and water, and bring to a boil; then cover and simmer over medium heat for 1 hour or until the meat is done. Stir in the olives and lemon juice and simmer over low heat for 5 minutes.

Dervish's Casserole
Masbahat Darweesh
Syria and Lebanon

Serves 6 to 8

1 large eggplant, peeled and cut into
  ¹/₂ inch slices
¹/₂ cup olive oil
4 tablespoons butter
1 lb beef, cut into ¹/₂ inch cubes
4 cloves garlic, crushed
2 large potatoes, peeled and cut into
  ¹/₂ inch slices
2 medium zucchini, cut into ¹/₂ inch slices

2 large tomatoes, cut into ¹/₂ inch slices
2 large onions, peeled and cut into
  ¹/₂ inch slices
2 tablespoons finely chopped fresh
  coriander leaves (cilantro)
¹/₂ teaspoon cinnamon
¹/₂ teaspoon allspice
1 cup tomato juice
salt and pepper to taste

Sprinkle the eggplant slices with salt; then place in a strainer, top with a weight, and allow to drain for 45 minutes.

Sauté the eggplant slices in the oil over moderately high heat until they begin to brown. (Add more oil if necessary.) Remove and place in a strainer or on paper towels to drain the oil.

In another frying pan, heat the butter; then add the meat and garlic and sauté until the meat begins to brown. Set aside.

Layer the potatoes, zucchini, meat, eggplant, tomatoes, and onions in a casserole. Sprinkle with salt, coriander, pepper, cinnamon, and allspice. Pour in the tomato juice, adding water if necessary to barely cover the vegetables.

Cover the casserole and bake in a 350°F preheated oven for about 1 hour or until the meat and vegetables are tender. Cook uncovered for the last 10 minutes to brown the top.

Eggplant Beef Stew
Yakhnat Bathinjan
Syria and Lebanon

Serves 6 to 8

2 medium eggplants, peeled and cut into 1 inch cubes	2 large potatoes, peeled and cut into 1 inch cubes
4 tablespoons butter	1 can tomatoes (19 oz or 540 ml)
1 lb beef, cut into $^1/_2$ inch cubes	$^1/_4$ teaspoon nutmeg
2 medium onions, chopped	$^1/_4$ teaspoon cumin
4 cloves garlic, crushed	salt and pepper to taste

Sprinkle the eggplant cubes with salt; then place in a strainer, top with a weight, and allow to drain for 45 minutes.

In a saucepan, melt the butter; then add the meat cubes and sauté over medium heat until they begin to brown. Stir in the onions and garlic and sauté further until they turn golden brown. Cover with water and bring to a boil; then lower the heat and simmer for 30 minutes.

Add the eggplant cubes, potatoes, tomatoes, pepper, nutmeg, cumin, and salt. Simmer for a further 45 minutes or until the meat and vegetables are cooked. Serve with cooked rice.

Lamb and Okra Stew
Bani Bamya
Sudan

Serves 4

4 tablespoons butter	$^1/_2$ cup tomato paste, diluted in $1^1/_2$ cups of water
$^1/_2$ lb lean lamb, cut into $^1/_2$ inch cubes	
2 medium onions, chopped	$^3/_4$ lb fresh okra, or 1 10 oz package frozen okra
3 cloves garlic, crushed	
3 tablespoons finely chopped fresh coriander leaves (cilantro)	salt and pepper to taste

In a frying pan, melt the butter; then sauté the meat over medium heat until it begins to brown. Add the onions, garlic, and coriander; sauté further until the onions begin to brown.

Stir in the diluted tomato paste, salt, and pepper. Bring to a boil, then lower the heat, cover, and simmer for 1 hour.

Add the okra and cook, covered, over medium heat for 10 minutes or until the okra is tender. Serve hot with cooked rice.

Note: Beef may be substituted for the lamb.

Lamb and Potato Stew
Tajin
Tunisia

Serves 4 to 6

The *tajins* of North Africa differ somewhat from the *yakhnas* of the Middle East. In North Africa, more use is made of the herbs and spices which Arab traders carried through their countries on their way to Europe. Also the stews are often sweetened with honey and fruit and decorated with nuts.

4 tablespoons butter	$^1/_2$ teaspoon allspice
1$^1/_2$ lbs lamb, cut into 1 inch cubes	$^1/_4$ teaspoon cayenne
3 medium onions, chopped	1 teaspoon sage
4 cloves garlic, crushed	3 medium tomatoes, halved
3 medium potatoes, cubed	$^1/_2$ cup finely chopped fresh parsley
salt and pepper to taste	$^1/_2$ cup slivered almonds, toasted
$^1/_2$ teaspoon caraway, ground	

Melt the butter in a frying pan; then add the meat, onions, and garlic and sauté until the meat begins to brown. Transfer the contents of the frying pan to a casserole. Stir in the potatoes, salt, pepper, caraway, allspice, cayenne, sage, and water to cover, and bring to a boil.

Arrange the tomato pieces, cut-side down, on top of the stew; then cover the casserole and bake in a 350°F preheated oven for 90 minutes, or until the meat is tender. Garnish with the parsley and slivered almonds, and serve hot with cooked rice.

Iraqi Meat Stew
Muraq

Serves 6 to 8

4 tablespoons butter
2 lbs beef or lamb, cut into
$^{1}/_{2}$ inch cubes
$^{1}/_{2}$ cup finely chopped fresh coriander
leaves (cilantro)
3 cloves garlic, crushed

1 can tomatoes (19 oz or 540 ml)
2 cups water
$^{1}/_{4}$ teaspoon cumin
$^{1}/_{4}$ teaspoon allspice
salt and pepper to taste

In a saucepan, melt the butter and add the meat. Sauté over medium heat until the meat begins to brown, stirring often. Add the coriander leaves, onions, and garlic; sauté further until the onions begin to brown. Stir in the tomatoes, water, salt, pepper, cumin, and allspice. Bring to a boil, then lower the heat, cover and simmer for 40 minutes. Add the peas and cook for 15–20 minutes longer, until the meat is tender and the peas are cooked. Serve hot with cooked rice.

Lamb Tajin with Plums and Honey
Tajin Fass
Morocco

Serves 4 to 6

$^{1}/_{4}$ cup olive oil
2 lbs lamb, cut into 1 inch cubes
1 medium onion, finely chopped
$^{1}/_{2}$ cup fresh coriander leaves (cilantro),
finely chopped
2 cloves garlic, crushed
salt and pepper to taste
$^{1}/_{2}$ teaspoon ginger

$^{1}/_{2}$ teaspoon tarragon
$^{1}/_{2}$ teaspoon cinnamon
2 cups water
1 lb small plums, pitted
3 tablespoons honey
1 teaspoon *mazahar* (orange blossom
water)
2 tablespoons toasted sesame seeds

Heat the oil in a saucepan; then add the lamb cubes, onions, coriander, garlic, salt, ginger, pepper, tarragon, cinnamon, and water. Cover the saucepan and bring to a boil; then lower the heat and simmer for about an hour, until the lamb is tender. Check occasionally, and add more water if necessary.

Stir in the plums and honey; continue cooking for 15 minutes, stirring frequently.

Add the *mazahar* and bring to a boil. Place in a serving dish and sprinkle with the toasted sesame seeds. Serve immediately with cooked rice.

Lentil and Eggplant Stew with Meat
Yakhnat 'Adas ma' Bathinjan
Yemen

Serves 6 to 8

3 tablespoons olive oil
1 lb beef or lamb, cubed
a few bones (optional)
2 cups chopped onions
2 cloves garlic, crushed
1 cup lentils, soaked overnight in
   6 cups of water

salt and pepper
1 teaspoon powdered ginger
1 teaspoon allspice
$^1/_4$ cup rice, washed and drained
4 medium tomatoes, chopped
1 medium eggplant, cut into
   medium cubes

Stir-fry the meat in the oil until the meat begins to brown. Add the onions and garlic; then continue frying until the onions and garlic are golden brown. Transfer all to a casserole; then add the lentils with their water, the salt, pepper, ginger, and allspice. Mix well. Cover and bake in a 350°F oven for 40 minutes or the lentils are nearly cooked.

Remove the cover and stir in the rice, tomatoes, and eggplant. Cover again, return to the oven and cook for 40 minutes, until the rice is tender but still intact. This dish can be served hot or cold.

Lentil and Meat Stew with Potatoes
Yakhnat 'Adas ma' Laham wa Batata
Syria and Lebanon

Serves 6

1 cup lentils, washed
6 cups water
3 tablespoons butter
$^1/_2$ lb beef or lamb, cut into 1 inch cubes
2 medium onions, chopped
2 cloves garlic, crushed

3 medium tomatoes, chopped
5 medium potatoes, cubed
salt and pepper to taste
1 teaspoon cumin
1 teaspoon dried crushed thyme

Bring the lentils and water to a boil, then cook over medium heat for 15 minutes. Set aside.

In a frying pan, melt the butter and sauté the meat over low heat until it begins to brown. Add the onions and garlic and continue sautéeing until the onions turn golden brown.

Put the lentils with their water in a casserole. Add the fried meat mixture and the remaining ingredients; stir and cover. Place the casserole in a 350°F preheated oven and bake for approximately 1 hour.

> *In the foreground: chicken with sumac (p. 147). Top left: eggplant casserole with tomato and chicken (p. 148). Top right: Moroccan pie (p. 149).*

Meat and Carrot Stew
Shtatha Zrudiya
Algeria

Serves 4 to 6

Intoxicating in their flavor and fragrant with tantalizing aromas, Arab stews will pacify a restless soul searching for culinary perfection. Known to the eastern Arabs as *yakhna*, and to the North Africans as *tajin*, these zesty dishes are, perhaps, the most tasty stews in the world. Although their savor points to gastronomic magic, they are simple to prepare.

1 lb beef or lamb, cut into ¹/₂ inch cubes
3 tablespoons olive oil
1 head garlic, finely chopped
1 teaspoon paprika
1 teaspoon ground caraway

salt and pepper to taste
¹/₂ cup finely chopped fresh coriander leaves (cilantro)
¹/₂ lb carrots, peeled and sliced into thin rounds
5 tablespoons tomato paste

Sauté the meat in the olive oil until it begins to turn light brown; then add the garlic and sauté further until the garlic turns golden brown. Add the rest of the ingredients except the tomato paste, with about 3 cups of boiling water (to cover). Bring to a boil; then lower the heat and simmer for one hour until the meat and the carrots begin to get tender. Stir in the tomato paste; then simmer further for 30 minutes, or until the meat and carrots are well cooked.

Meat and Noodle Stew
Saudi Arabia

Serves 4 to 6

3 tablespoons butter
2 large onions, chopped
1¹/₂ lbs beef or lamb, cut into ¹/₂ inch cubes
2 large tomatoes, chopped

¹/₄ cup finely chopped fresh mint
4 cloves garlic, crushed
salt and pepper to taste
¹/₂ teaspoon tarragon
2 oz wide noodles

In a saucepan, sauté the onions and the meat in the butter until they turn golden brown. Add the rest of the ingredients, except the noodles, with water to cover by one inch and bring to a boil. Lower the heat and simmer for 1¹/₂ hours or until the meat is tender.

Stir in the noodles and simmer for a further 20 minutes, or until the noodles are cooked. Served hot with cooked rice.

Stuffed crown roast of lamb (p. 79)

Meat and Tomato Stew
Yakhnat Banadoora

Syria and Lebanon

Serves 6 to 8

In the cities, the wealthy look down upon appetizing *yakhnas* as peasant foods; in the fine restaurants or on the tables of the rich, they are rarely found. However, to the toiling masses, it is another story. A working house-wife makes a stew which lasts the family for two to three days. There is no question of these dishes becoming tasteless or stale: Arab stews, in many cases, improve when they are reheated. Thus, the woman of the house need only cook once or twice a week for her family and guests to dine like gourmets.

¹/₄ cup olive oil	¹/₂ teaspoon basil
1 lb beef, cut into 1 inch cubes	¹/₄ teaspoon nutmeg
3 medium onions, chopped	1 can tomatoes (19 oz or 540 ml)
4 cloves garlic, crushed	5 medium potatoes, peeled and cubed
salt and pepper to taste	

In a saucepan, heat the oil; then add the meat, onions, and garlic and sauté until the meat turns slightly brown. Add the salt, pepper, basil, nutmeg, tomatoes, and enough water to cover by one inch; then bring to a boil, lower the heat, and simmer for 30 minutes. Add the potatoes and bring to a boil again, then lower the heat and simmer for 1 hour or until the meat and potatoes are cooked, stirring occasionally. Serve hot with cooked rice.

Meat Stew with Olives and Peppers
Moarraq

Saudi Arabia

Serves 4 to 6

In the Arab world, the choice is not limited to black and green olives; olives vary in color and type of curing. Particularly favored are the ripe black olives which have been cured in brine.

¹/₄ cup olive oil	pinch cayenne
2 medium onions, finely chopped	2 cups boiling water
2 cloves garlic, crushed	1 cup rice, rinsed
1 lb lamb or beef, cut into 1 inch cubes	6 large or 12 small black olives
1 red pepper, finely chopped	3 tablespoons fresh chopped parsley or
salt	2 tablespoons dried parsley

Cook the onions in the oil for a few minutes; then add the garlic, meat, red pepper, salt, and cayenne and cook for a further 5 minutes, stirring frequently to prevent sticking. Add the boiling water, cover, and cook for 1 hour over medium heat, stirring occasionally. Stir in the rice and olives and cover; then cook over low heat for another 15 to 20 minutes, until liquid is absorbed and the rice is tender but not mushy. Stir in the parsley at the last minute and serve hot.

Note: Vary this dish by using fresh coriander instead of parsley, as the Bahrainis do.

Meat with Zucchini and Chickpeas

Egypt

Serves 4 to 6

2 medium onions, chopped
4 cloves garlic
3 tablespoons butter
½ lb lean beef, cubed
3 tablespoons tomato paste
salt and pepper to taste

1 teaspoon ground allspice
3 medium potatoes, peeled and quartered
5 medium zucchinis, washed and cut
   into 2 inch lengths
1 can chickpeas (19 oz or 540ml)

Fry the onions and the whole garlic cloves in the butter until golden. Add the meat cubes and fry for about 20 minutes or until brown.

Stir in the tomato paste and cover with water; then add the salt, pepper, and allspice. Bring to a boil, stir well, and cover; then reduce the heat to low and simmer for about 1 hour.

Add the potatoes, zucchinis, and chickpeas, then simmer for a further 40 minutes or until the meat and vegetables are tender and the liquid has been mostly absorbed. Adjust seasoning to taste before serving.

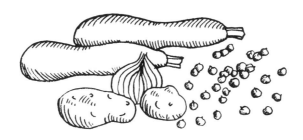

Okra with Meat
Bamya bil-Laham
Syria and Lebanon

Serves 4 to 6

Okra, which in the Arab world is known as *bamya*, was introduced to North America from Africa. In the Southern states of the U.S. it is also known as "gumbo."

1 lb tender okra, stemmed and washed
6 tablespoons oil
3/4 lb lamb or beef, cut into 1/4 inch
   cubes
1 medium onion, chopped
2 cloves garlic, chopped

1/4 cup finely chopped fresh coriander
   leaves (cilantro)
salt and pepper to taste
1/2 cup tomato sauce, diluted in 1 cup
   of water
1/4 cup lemon juice

    In a frying pan, sauté the okra in 2 tablespoons of the oil for 5 minutes over a medium heat, until they turn light brown; then remove the okra with a slotted spoon, and set aside. Add the remaining 4 tablespoons of oil; then sauté meat for 5 minutes, stirring constantly. Add the onions, garlic, coriander leaves, salt, and pepper, stirring and sautéing until onions are limp. Add the diluted tomato sauce and lemon juice; then cook about an hour, until the meat is almost done.

    Add the okra and gently stir once.

Note: Do not stir again; then cook for 10–15 minutes or until the okra is tender.

Peas with Meat
Bazilla ma' Laham
Syria and Lebanon

Serves 4 to 6

1/4 cup olive oil
1 lb lamb or beef, cut into 1/2 inch cubes
salt and pepper to taste
1/4 teaspoon oregano
1 large onion, chopped

3 cloves garlic, crushed
1 cup tomato sauce
1 lb shelled fresh peas (frozen peas
   may be substituted)

    Heat the oil in a saucepan. Add the meat and sprinkle on the salt, pepper, and oregano. Sauté until the meat turns light brown; then add onions and garlic and sauté further until the onions turn golden brown.

    Add water to cover and simmer over low heat for 30 minutes; then add the tomato sauce and simmer for another 30 minutes. Stir in the peas and simmer for another 15 minutes; then serve hot with cooked rice.

Somali Meat Stew

Serves 4 to 6

1/4 cup lemon juice

1/4 cup grapefruit juice

1 tablespoon orange blossom water (*mazahar*)

1/2 teaspoon nutmeg

1/2 teaspoon ginger

2 lbs beef, cut into steaks

salt and pepper to taste

1/4 teaspoon cayenne

1 cup finely chopped fresh parsley

1 teaspoon flour or cornstarch, mixed with 1 tablespoon water until smooth

2 cups water

1/2 cup raisins

In a bowl, mix the lemon juice, grapefruit juice, orange blossom water, nutmeg, and ginger. Place the steaks in a roasting pan and pour the mixture over the meat. Let stand for 1 hour, turning a few times; then remove the steaks. Add the salt, pepper, cayenne, and parsley to the juice in the roasting pan and mix well.

Return the steaks to the mixture and place in a 350°F preheated oven. Bake for 45 minutes or until meat is cooked. Remove the steaks and place on a heated serving platter.

Transfer the sauce to a saucepan, scraping the pan well. Stir in the flour or cornstarch, then add the water and mix well. Simmer for a few minutes, then pour into a serving bowl.

Spread the raisins evenly over the steaks on the platter. Serve with the sauce and cooked rice.

Yemeni Kidney Stew

Serves 4 to 6

When coriander leaves are harvested for use, the plant is about 6 inches high. Their racy-mild flavor differs from that of the seed, and their pronounced pungency always adds an exotic and delectable touch to the taste of food.

4 tablespoons butter

2 calf kidneys (1 to 1 1/2 lbs), cut into 1/2 inch cubes

2 medium onions, finely chopped

4 cloves garlic, crushed

1 can tomatoes (19 oz or 540 ml)

1/2 teaspoon cumin

1/2 teaspoon cayenne

1/4 cup very finely chopped fresh coriander leaves (cilantro)

salt and pepper to taste

Melt the butter in a saucepan over medium heat; then add the kidney cubes and sauté for a few minutes. Stir in the onions and garlic; then sauté further until the onions begin to brown, stirring constantly. Turn the heat to low; then stir in the remaining ingredients except the coriander, and cover. Simmer until the kidney cubes are cooked (about 1 hour); then stir in the coriander leaves and serve hot with cooked rice.

Yogurt Meat Stew

Laban Ummoo
Syria and Lebanon

Serves 4 to 6

1 lb beef or lamb, cut into ¹/₂ inch cubes	2 tablespoons butter
2 medium onions, finely chopped	3 cloves garlic, crushed
2 eggs, beaten	¹/₄ cups finely chopped fresh coriander
4 cups yogurt	leaves (cilantro)
2 cups water	salt and pepper to taste

Place the meat and onions in a saucepan, then cover with water and cook over medium heat for about 1 hour or until the meat is tender.

In another saucepan, place the eggs, yogurt, and the two cups of water, and stirring constantly clockwise, bring to a boil over medium heat. Turn the heat to low, and simmer for about 5 minutes, stirring occasionally.

While the yogurt is simmering, melt the butter in a frying pan. Add the garlic, coriander leaves, salt, and pepper, and sauté over medium heat for a few minutes.

Add the yogurt sauce and the contents of the frying pan to the meat; then simmer over low heat for about 15 minutes or until the yogurt begins to thicken. Serve hot with cooked rice.

Liver Brochettes

Morocco

Serves 6

In Moroccan cities, your nose will draw you to the outdoor stalls where brochettes are being barbecued over glowing charcoal. No other aroma can arouse your hunger more.

2 lbs lamb or calf liver	pinch cumin or allspice
salt and pepper to taste	pinch cayenne

Cube liver into 1 inch pieces. Sprinkle with the seasonings, then place on skewers and grill over an outdoor barbecue fire, preferrably of glowing charcoal.

Note: For added flavor, the liver may be marinated for a couple hours in olive oil, lemon juice, and garlic. You may also alternate the pieces of liver with vegetable pieces, such as sweet green or red pepper, onion, mushrooms, and tomato chunks.

Eggplant and Meat on Skewers
Laham Qasma Mishwee
Iraq

Serves 6

1 large eggplant, cubed
1½ lbs lamb or beef, cubed
16 small onions, peeled
2 green peppers, cut into large chunks
½ teaspoon allspice

3 tablespoons lemon juice
¼ cup vegetable oil
1 can tomato juice (19 oz or 540 ml)
salt and pepper to taste

Marinate the eggplant, meat, onions, and green peppers in the salt, pepper, allspice, and lemon juice for 2 hours in the refrigerator in a non-metallic bowl. Alternate the vegetables and meat on 8 inch skewers. Heat the vegetable oil over medium heat in a frying pan. Brown the skewered vegetables and meat very quickly, turning the skewers a few times. Add the tomato juice; then cover the frying pan and simmer over low heat for 15 minutes. Add 1 cup of water and bring to a boil; then reduce the heat and cook for about a hour or until the sauce is just below the level of the meat and vegetables. Serve with rice.

Fried Liver
Mi'laq Maqlee
Palestine and Jordan

Serves 4

4 cloves garlic
1 small hot pepper, very finely chopped
¼ cup chopped fresh parsley
1 lb beef liver

¼ cup oil
½ teaspoon allspice
salt and pepper to taste

In a mortar and pestle, crush the garlic with salt. Combine thoroughly with the finely chopped pepper and the parsley. Set aside.

Cut the beef liver into ½ inch cubes. Fry in the oil over medium heat until it starts to brown. Add the garlic mixture, pepper, and allspice. Stir-fry for a few more minutes until done to taste.

Note: This is one of the best ways of preparing fried liver. The delicious taste of the liver is unequaled by any other method of cooking.

Meat and Walnuts
Nadi
Saudi Arabia

Serves 4

3 tablespoons butter
1 lb ground lamb or beef
3 tablespoons finely chopped coriander
   leaves (cilantro)
$^1/_2$ cup orange juice

zest of 1 orange, finely chopped
$^1/_4$ cup finely chopped walnuts
salt and pepper to taste
$^1/_2$ teaspoon allspice

Heat the butter in a saucepan; then add the meat and coriander leaves, and sauté for 10 minutes over medium heat. Add the orange juice and cook a further 5 minutes; then stir in the orange peel, walnuts, salt, pepper, and allspice. Place in the center of a large serving plate and surround with plain rice.

Savory Lamb
Syria and Lebanon

Serves 6

2 lbs lean lamb, cut into 1 inch cubes
1 medium onion, finely chopped
4 cloves garlic, crushed
salt and pepper to taste
$^1/_2$ teaspoon oregano
$^1/_2$ teaspoon ground cinnamon
$^1/_2$ teaspoon ground cloves

1 bay leaf
3 tablespoons shredded coconut,
   unsweetened
$^1/_4$ cup cooking oil
2 medium tomatoes, chopped
$^1/_2$ cup lemon juice

Combine the meat, onion, garlic, salt, pepper, oregano, cinnamon, cloves, bay leaf, and coconut; mix thoroughly and leave in a cool place for 3 hours.

In a saucepan, heat the oil; then add the meat mixture and sauté for 10 minutes. Add the tomatoes and the lemon juice; then cover and cook over low heat for 1 hour. Add water if necessary, to make a moist stew. Serve with rice.

Tunisian Spaghetti

Serves 6 to 8

1/4 cup olive oil	4 bay leaves
1 1/2 lbs beef or lamb, cut into large pieces	4 cloves garlic, crushed
1/4 cup finely chopped fresh coriander leaves (cilantro)	1 can tomato paste (5 1/2 oz or 156 ml), diluted in 1 cup water
salt and pepper to taste	3/4 cup tomato sauce
1/4 teaspoon cayenne	2 cups water
	1 lb package of spaghetti

Heat the oil in a saucepan; then add the meat and sauté over medium heat until it begins to brown.

Stir in the coriander leaves and sauté for a further few minutes, then add salt, pepper, cayenne, bay leaves, garlic, the diluted tomato paste, tomato sauce, and water. Cover the saucepan and cook over medium heat for about 1 1/2 hours; then remove the bay leaves and turn off the heat, but keep warm.

In another saucepan, place the spaghetti with 8 cups of water and salt; then bring to a boil and cook over medium heat for 10 minutes. Drain the spaghetti and mix with the sauce. Serve immediately.

Hummus Dip with Meat
Hummus bi-Taheena ma' Laban
Palestine and Jordan

Serves 8–10

This tasty dish is a popular breakfast dish throughout the Arab world.

1 quantity chickpea dip (hummus; see p. 23)	salt and pepper to taste
3 tablespoons butter	1 teaspoon cinnamon
3 cloves garlic, crushed	1 teaspoon allspice
1 lb ground beef	1/2 cup pine nuts

Prepare the hummus dip according to the recipe, but omit the final garnish of oil, pomegranate seeds, and parsley. Spread the dip on a plate; set aside.

Melt the butter in a large skillet. Add the crushed garlic and stir until slightly browned. Add the meat and sauté until the meat is slightly browned. Stir in the spices and pine nuts and cook over a medium heat, stirring occasionally, until the meat is cooked.

Spread the meat mixture over the prepared hummus dip. Serve immediately with pita bread.

Steak with Pepper and Coconut

Mauritania

Serves 4

¹/₄ cup vegetable oil	¹/₂ coconut, water reserved
pinch cayenne	1 tablespoon soy sauce
salt and pepper to taste	1 beef bouillon cube
4 cloves garlic, crushed	2 tablespoons cornstarch
2 large green peppers, cut into ¹/₂ inch strips	¹/₄ cup grape juice
1¹/₂ lbs beefsteak, cut into thin strips	

Heat the oil in a heavy frying pan over medium heat; then add cayenne, salt, pepper, garlic, and green pepper. Sauté for about 2 minutes; then add beef strips and sauté for a further 5 minutes.

Remove the coconut meat from the shell and cut into ¹/₂ inch strips. Add to the pan and sauté for another 10 minutes. Transfer to a platter.

Add water to the coconut milk to make 2 cups. Bring to a boil in a separate saucepan, then lower the heat. Stir in the soy sauce and beef bouillon cube.

In a bowl, mix the cornstarch and grape juice; stir till smooth. Slowly add the cornstarch mixture to the hot liquid while stirring constantly till smooth and thickened to sauce consistency. Pour over the beef mixture. Serve with cooked rice.

Poultry

Like most other peoples, the Arabs are great consumers of chicken. In many parts of the Arab world, chicken is used in cooking more than red meat since it is cheaper in price. The poor, on feast days, often substitute chicken and, at times, turkey. When served on these festive occasions, they are stuffed with rice or with burghul or couscous, just as the more affluent would stuff lambs.

Arabs also eat chicken, fried, roasted, and in stews and soups, but perhaps the favorite method of serving chicken is barbecued. In the Arab Middle Eastern countries, the smell of barbecued chicken often permeates the alleyways of the older sections of town.

The soups and stews are usually very different from those found in the West. In parts of the Arab world, especially in North Africa, olives, fruit, nuts, spices, and herbs are added and simmered with the chicken. Every dish is a journey into the exotic world of savory foods.

Besides chicken, the other fowls utilized in cooking are turkeys and pigeons. Duck and geese are rarely used. In the Arab world, chickens reign supreme – the queen of fowl.

An Arab poet once wrote:

> To feast on chicken gives me delight;
> It tantalizes my taste and pleases my sight;
> Compared to other foods, it more than holds its own;
> Fit for a peasant or a king upon his throne.

Bukhari Chicken Stew
Dajaj Bukhari
Saudi Arabia

Serves 4 to 6

1 medium size chicken, cut into 8 pieces	1 large onion, chopped
salt to taste	2 cloves garlic, crushed
5 tablespoons butter	$^1/_2$ lb mushrooms, chopped
1 teaspoon ground ginger	1 cup cabbage, shredded
$^1/_2$ teaspoon cumin	1 cup fresh or frozen peas
$^1/_2$ teaspoon ground coriander	

Sprinkle the chicken pieces with salt; then melt the butter in a saucepan and add the chicken pieces. Sauté until they turn brown; then add water to cover by one inch, ginger, cumin, and coriander; cover and simmer over medium heat for 25 minutes.

Add the rest of the ingredients; then cover and simmer for another 20 minutes or until the peas and the cabbage are cooked. Add more water during the cooking time if necessary.

Chicken with Almonds

Dajaj bil-Lawz

Algeria

Serves 4

1 3½ lb roasting or frying chicken, cut into serving pieces	2 cloves garlic, crushed
	salt and pepper to taste
4 tablespoons butter	4 tablespoons almonds, ground
4 medium onions, diced	2 tablespoons chopped green onions

Fry the chicken in the butter in a saucepan until browned; then add the onions and garlic and fry until the onions become limp. Add water to cover by one inch, salt, and pepper; then simmer for 45 minutes to an hour, until the chicken is well cooked.

In a small bowl, mix the almonds with enough cold water to make a soft paste. Add the paste very slowly to the chicken, stirring constantly. Simmer for a few minutes; then remove from the heat and place on a platter. Sprinkle the green onions on top. Serve with fried or mashed potatoes.

Chicken with Burghul Stuffing

Dajaj Mihshee bi-Burghul

Syria and Lebanon

Serves 6 to 8

In the countries of the Middle East, chickens and turkeys are usually stuffed with a rice stuffing. The peasants and urban poor people usually substitute the less costly burghul for rice. As is often the case with peasant foods, the burghul stuffing turns out much tastier than stuffing made from rice.

½ cup pine nuts	½ teaspoon allspice
½ cup butter	1 teaspoon ground coriander
½ cup onions, chopped	1 teaspoon cinnamon
1 cup coarse burghul, soaked in water for 5 minutes and drained	1 roasting chicken (about 5 lbs), cleaned and washed
1 cup chicken stock	salt and pepper to taste
¼ cup chopped fresh parsley	

Sauté the pine nuts in the butter till golden brown; then remove with a slotted spoon and set aside.

Sauté the onions in the same butter and stir for about 10 minutes; then add the burghul, and sauté quickly for a few minutes with the onions. Add the chicken stock, the parsley, and all the seasonings, except the cinnamon, and stir over medium heat till the stock is absorbed. Leave to cool.

Add the pine nuts and mix well; then stuff the cavity of the chicken, sew or skewer closed, and place in a roaster. Any left-over stuffing can be placed in the neck opening. Brush with additional melted butter and the cinnamon; then bake covered in a 350°F preheated oven for 2 hours. Remove the cover and allow to cook another 30 minutes or until browned.

Chicken with Cashews

Saudi Arabia

Serves 4 to 6

1 3¹/₂–4 lb chicken	4 tablespoons butter
4 cups water	¹/₂ teaspoon cinnamon
2 cups of onions, finely chopped	¹/₄ teaspoon cayenne
1 carrot, peeled and finely chopped	2 bay leaves
3 tablespoons finely chopped fresh coriander leaves (cilantro)	2 cups finely chopped cashews
	1 tablespoon paprika
salt and pepper to taste	¹/₄ cup chopped parsley

Place the chicken in a pot with the water, 1 cup of the onions, the carrot, coriander leaves, salt, and pepper. Bring to a boil, then reduce the heat to low and cook for about 1 hour or until done. Remove the chicken, reserving the stock. Remove the flesh from the bones of the chicken and cut into pieces. Sprinkle with a little salt.

Melt the butter in a saucepan and add the chicken pieces; then sauté over a low heat until they turn golden brown. Add the cinnamon, cayenne, the remaining onion, bay leaves, and the reserved stock; then bring to a boil. Lower the heat and simmer covered for 30 minutes. Place on a serving platter.

Mix the cashews and the paprika in a bowl and garnish the chicken with the mixture. Sprinkle the parsley on top; then serve hot with cooked rice.

Chicken with Chickpeas

Dajaj ma' Hummus

Palestine and Jordan

Serves 6 to 8

In the Arab kitchen, chickpeas rule supreme. An Arab poet once wrote: "You can talk of your many vegetables from Morocco to Cathay, And talk of all the tasty foods the kitchen smells betray, But if you've never tasted chickpeas, you've nothing else to say, For this delicious legume rules supreme from Cairo to Bombay."

4 tablespoons butter	1 can chickpeas (19 oz or 540 ml), with
1 chicken, 3 to 5 lbs, trimmed of fat	its water
and cut into small serving pieces	1¹/₂ cups water
2 medium onions, chopped	3 tablespoons tomato paste
4 cloves garlic, crushed	¹/₂ teaspoon allspice
¹/₄ cup finely chopped fresh coriander	¹/₄ teaspoon chilli powder
leaves (cilantro)	salt and pepper to taste

In a saucepan, sauté the chicken pieces in the butter over medium heat until they turn golden brown. Turn them over several times to ensure that they brown evenly.

Remove the chicken pieces from the saucepan and set aside; then stir-fry the onions until they begin to brown. Add the garlic and coriander leaves; stir-fry for another 3 minutes. Stir in the remaining ingredients, including the chicken pieces, and bring to a boil; then cover and simmer over medium heat for 30 minutes or until the chicken pieces are well cooked. Serve hot.

Chicken with Coriander and Mint

Dajajat Maqliya

Morocco

Serves 4

In the Latin American, Chinese, Indian, and Middle Eastern cuisines, coriander leaves are used as a basic flavoring ingredient in a vast number of dishes. The sapid leaves of coriander are as important to the culinary artists in these lands as parsley is to the Western cook.

Many types of salads, sauces, curries, soups, stews, and meat loaves are made tempting by the utilization of this appetizing herb. Furthermore, in the same fashion as parsley, the strongly scented coriander leaves are used, especially in the Middle Eastern lands, to garnish the main course platters. In any event, it matters not if this historic herb is used to please the taste or please the eye. Its effect is always exciting.

2 teaspoons crushed garlic	$1/2$ teaspoon cumin
1 tablespoon paprika	2 tablespoons vegetable oil
$1/4$ teaspoon saffron	1 3 lb roasting chicken
$1/2$ cup finely chopped fresh coriander leaves (cilantro)	2 onions, chopped
	1 cup water
$1/4$ cup finely chopped fresh mint	salt and pepper to taste

In a small bowl, combine the garlic, paprika, saffron, coriander, mint, cumin, and oil. With a wooden spoon, mix and mash the ingredients into paste.

Wash the chicken and pat it completely dry with paper towels. Sprinkle it inside and out with the salt and black pepper.

Preheat the oven to 375°F. Rub the entire surface of the chicken with the herb paste, patting and spreading it as evenly as possible. Place the chicken in a casserole and surround it with the chopped onion. Pour 1 cup of water into the casserole but avoid getting any water on the chicken. Cover the casserole and bake for $1^1/2$ hours or until the chicken is done.

Transfer the chicken from the casserole to an oven-proof platter. Pour the pan juices into a gravy boat and keep warm. Turn the oven setting to broil, and broil the chicken for about 10 minutes, turning frequently until it is evenly browned on all sides. Serve the heated sauce in a gravy bowl.

Chicken with Chickpeas and Onions
Kudra bil-Dajaj wa Hummus

Morocco

Serves 6 to 8

The cuisine of Morocco is rated among the best in the world. There are few places where food is more carefully and artistically prepared, more delightfully served and more enjoyed. This dish can be counted as one of the foods which enhance the delightful Moroccan cuisine.

1 3–4 lb chicken	pinch saffron
1 lb medium onions, peeled	1 cup dried chickpeas, soaked overnight
4 tablespoons butter	$1/2$ cup finely chopped fresh parsley
salt and pepper to taste	$1/2$ cup finely chopped fresh coriander
1 teaspoon ginger	leaves (cilantro)
pinch cinnamon	

Clean the chicken and cut into small pieces. Set aside.

Dice 4 of the onions and place in a pot with the butter, salt, and pepper. Cook until the onions are golden brown. Add the ginger, cinnamon, saffron, and chicken. Cook for 10 minutes, or until the chicken begins to brown, stirring constantly.

Drain the chickpeas and add to the pot with enough water to cover by one inch. Cook over medium heat for 45 minutes or until the chicken is tender.

Chop the rest of the onions into large chunks; then add them with the parsley and coriander and cook for a further 10 minutes. Serve with rice.

Chicken with Lemon and Olives

Tajin Mseer Zaytoon

Morocco

Serves 4 to 6

In this *tajin*, the chicken is transformed in taste and texture, retaining a smoothness and buttery quality unsurpassed by most Western recipes.

¼ cup olive oil	1 teaspoon ground ginger
1 3–4 lb chicken, cleaned and cut into serving pieces	½ teaspoon black pepper
	¼ teaspoon turmeric
2 medium onions, chopped	2 tablespoons lemon juice
4 cloves garlic, crushed	1½ cups water
salt	½ cup small green olives
1 teaspoon paprika	1 lemon, peeled and sliced

In a saucepan, sauté the chicken pieces in the oil over medium heat, turning them occasionally until they become golden brown. Remove the chicken pieces and set aside. In the same pan, stir-fry the onions and garlic until they begin to brown.

Add the chicken pieces and the remaining ingredients, except the lemon slices and olives. Bring to a boil, then reduce the heat to low, cover, and simmer for about 45 minutes or until the chicken is tender.

Add the olives; then cover and simmer for a further 5 minutes. Arrange the chicken pieces on a serving platter; then place the lemon slices in a ring around them. Pour the sauce over the chicken pieces. Serve hot with cooked rice.

Chicken Milina

Morocco

Serves 4

4 eggs	3 tablespoons butter
1½ cups finely chopped cooked chicken	2 medium onions, finely chopped
salt and pepper to taste	2 cloves garlic, crushed
½ teaspoon ground coriander	2 medium tomatoes, diced

Beat the eggs well; then stir in the chicken, salt, coriander, and pepper and set aside.

In a frying pan, melt the butter; then sauté the onions and garlic over medium heat, until they turn golden brown. Stir in the egg-chicken mixture; then stir-fry over a low heat for a few minutes, until the eggs are cooked.

Remove from the heat and place in a serving dish; decorate with tomatoes and serve.

Chicken Molokhia

Egypt

Serves 4 to 6

Molokhia (also spelled *melokhia* or *milookhiyya*) is a potherb which is better known in the English-speaking world as Spanish okra or Jew's mallow. It is an annual leafy vegetable from the Linden family, and resembles both spinach and chard, but has the food properties of okra. Although its reputed land of origin is India, it is widely grown in the Middle East and parts of Africa, especially in Egypt and in the Greater Syria area.

1 3–4 lb chicken	2 tablespoons lemon juice
3 medium onions, chopped	4 tablespoons butter
1 large potato, peeled and cubed	$^{1}/_{2}$ head garlic, crushed
5 tomatoes, chopped	$^{1}/_{2}$ cup finely chopped fresh coriander
salt and pepper to taste	leaves (cilantro)
$^{1}/_{4}$ teaspoon allspice	pinch cayenne
$^{1}/_{2}$ lb fresh *molokhia* leaves, very finely chopped, or 1 cup dried and finely crushed *molokhia*	

Place the chicken, onions, potato, tomatoes, salt, pepper, and allspice in a pot with water to cover; then cook, covered, over medium heat until the water boils. Lower the heat and simmer for 1 hour, until the chicken is very tender.

Take the chicken out and remove the meat from the bones. Place the meat on a serving platter with a little of the stock and set aside.

Add the *molokhia* and lemon juice to the stock. Cover and simmer for 20 minutes, stirring occasionally.

In the meantime, melt the butter in a frying pan; then add the garlic, coriander and cayenne and fry until the garlic turns golden brown. Add the garlic-coriander mixture to the stock; then cook for a few minutes before serving. Adjust the seasoning if necessary. Serve the *molokhia* with the re-heated chicken and plain rice.

Note: Beef, lamb, rabbit, or any other meat may be substituted for the chicken.

Chicken Molokhia Palestinian Style
Palestine and Jordan

Serves 4 to 6

Besides being a food from time immemorial, *molokhia* was once thought to be a sexual stimulant, one of whose effects made women stray into the arms of strange men. Al-Hakīm bi-'Amr Allah, a Fatimid Caliph of Egypt in the 10th century, banned *molokhia* because he believed it led men and women into a life of debauchery. Even if this was only a fantasy in the mind of Al-Hakīm, his followers have, through the centuries, shied away from using *molokhia* in their cuisine.

1 medium-size chicken cut into large pieces	$^1/_2$ cup butter
salt	4 tablespoons finely chopped fresh coriander leaves (cilantro)
1 cup flour	leaves of 1 lb of fresh *molokhia*
1 teaspoon cinnamon	
2 bay leaves	$^1/_2$ teaspoon pepper
1 medium onion, chopped into large pieces	3 lemons
	1 loaf Arabic (pita) bread, toasted and broken into small pieces
$^1/_2$ head garlic, crushed	

Rub the chicken with 3 tablespoons of salt; then rinse off the salt with lukewarm water. A few moments after the salt is rinsed off, rub the chicken with the flour and rinse again with lukewarm water. Place the chicken in a pot with the cinnamon, bay leaves, and onion; then cover with water (about 10 cups) and cook for about $1^1/_2$ hours until the chicken is tender.

Take the chicken out of the stock and set aside; then strain the stock, return to the pot, and set aside.

In a frying pan, fry the garlic in the butter until it becomes golden brown; then add the coriander leaves and the chicken and fry until the chicken turns golden brown. Remove the chicken and place on a platter, ready to serve. Bring the stock to a boil; add the *molokhia*, salt, pepper, and the juice of 2 lemons and boil uncovered over medium heat for 25 minutes. Add the juice of the last lemon and cover the pot; then turn off the heat and let stand for 20 minutes. Transfer the cooked *molokhia* to a serving bowl.

To serve, place a handful of the toasted bread on a plate; then place a layer of rice on top of the bread, and over this, place the *molokhia* with its juice. Also on each plate, place one or more of the chicken pieces.

Note: For a heightened taste, make a mixture consisting of $^1/_2$ cup of table vinegar and one medium finely chopped Spanish onion; then place one to two tablespoons of this mixture (or to taste) over the *molokhia*.

Chicken Muhallabiyya

Saudi Arabia

Serves 4 to 6

1 medium size chicken (3–4 lbs)	1 teaspoon cinnamon
2 large onions, finely chopped	4 tablespoons butter
salt and pepper to taste	1½ cups rice, rinsed
1 teaspoon ginger	2 teaspoons lemon juice
3 tablespoons finely chopped fresh coriander leaves (cilantro)	

Place the chicken in a pot; then add the onions, salt, pepper, ginger, coriander, cinnamon, and water to cover. Bring to a boil; then lower the heat and simmer for an hour or till the chicken is cooked. Remove the chicken and reserve the stock; then de-bone and cut the meat into pieces. Set aside.

In a saucepan, heat the butter; then add the rice and stir-fry for 2 minutes. Add 3 cups of the reserved stock and bring to a boil on a high heat; then cover and lower the heat to very low and cook for about 15 minutes. Add the lemon juice and stir; then add the chicken pieces and adjust the seasonings if necessary; cook for a further 10 minutes on a low heat.

Chicken in Pomegranate Juice

Palestine and Jordan

Serves 4 to 6

It is believed that the pomegranate (*Punic granatum*) was first grown in Persia before the Christian era. From there it spread eastward to China and westward to the lands bordering the Mediterranean. In the countryside surrounding Carthage, the fruit became so prevalent that the Romans fell under its spell and called it the Carthaginian Apple. When the Arabs came to Europe in the 8th century C.E., they introduced the plant into the Iberian Peninsula where it was cultivated extensively. An Arab agriculturist in Moorish Spain, Ibn al-'Awwan, listed a dozen varieties thriving in all parts of Andalusia. A leftover from that age is the Portuguese name for pomegranate, *roma*, from the Arabic *rumman*.

¼ cup olive oil	¼ cup finely chopped fresh coriander leaves (cilantro)
1 3–4 lb chicken, cleaned, trimmed of fat, and cut into small pieces	1 small hot pepper, finely chopped
1 teaspoon paprika	3 tablespoons pomegranate concentrate (*dibs rumman*—see Glossary, p. 6)
salt and pepper to taste	1 can tomatoes (19 oz or 540 ml)
2 medium onions, chopped	
3 cloves garlic, crushed	

In a saucepan, heat the oil; then add the chicken pieces and sprinkle with the paprika, salt, and pepper. Stir-fry for about 5 minutes; then stir in the remaining ingredients and bring to a boil.

Cover the saucepan and cook over medium heat for 30 minutes or until the chicken is tender.

Chicken with Pomegranate Stuffing

Syria and Lebanon

Serves 6 to 8

½ cup olive oil	2 cloves garlic, crushed
1 teaspoon cumin	½ cup pine nuts or slivered almonds
1 teaspoon paprika	1 cup pomegranate seeds (from 2
salt and pepper to taste	medium pomegranates)
pinch cayenne	1 teaspoon thyme
¼ cup finely chopped fresh coriander	1 teaspoon sage
leaves (cilantro)	1 teaspoon rosemary
5–6 lb chicken	½ cup water
5 tablespoons butter	4 cups cubed toasted bread
2 medium onions, chopped	

Make a basting sauce by thoroughly mixing the olive oil, cumin, paprika, salt, pepper, cayenne, and coriander leaves. Set aside.

Clean the chicken and remove the neck; then cut the gizzard, heart, and liver into small pieces and set aside.

To make the stuffing, melt the butter over a medium heat in a saucepan. Sauté the pieces of gizzard, heart, and liver until they begin to brown. Stir in the onions, garlic, and pine nuts or almonds and sauté further until the onions begin to brown; then remove from the heat. Add the pomegranate seeds, thyme, sage, rosemary, water, and bread cubes. Combine thoroughly and set aside.

Rub the inisde of the chicken, including the neck opening, with about a third of the basting sauce. Fill both the body and neck cavity loosely with the stuffing, then sew or skewer closed. Rub sauce on the outside, then bake in a 350°F preheated oven for 2 hours until the chicken is well cooked, basting every 20 minutes with the remaining sauce.

Chicken with Prunes and Almonds

Tajin Dajaj bi-Barqooq wa Lawz

Morocco

Serves 6 to 8

1 4–5 lb chicken, cut into serving pieces	4 tablespoons butter
salt and pepper to taste	2 cups water
pinch saffron	8 oz prunes, washed and pitted
3 medium onions, finely chopped	2 tablespoons honey
4 cloves garlic, crushed	2 teaspoons cinnamon
1/2 cup finely chopped fresh coriander leaves (cilantro)	1/2 cup blanched almonds
	1 tablespoon sesame seeds, toasted

In a saucepan, place the chicken pieces, pepper, salt, saffron, onions, garlic, coriander, butter, and water; then cover and cook over medium heat for 45 minutes to an hour, until the chicken is well cooked. With a slotted spoon, remove the chicken pieces from the saucepan; then place on a serving plate and keep warm.

Add the prunes to the liquid remaining in the saucepan; then simmer over a low heat for 15 minutes. Stir in the honey and cinnamon, and continue the simmering until the sauce thickens (about 10 minutes).

Pour the sauce over the chicken pieces while it is still piping hot; then decorate with the almonds and sesame seeds. Serve with rice.

Chicken with Rice and Chickpea Stuffing

Iraq

Serves 8 to 10

There are few countries in the world where food is so well prepared and enjoyed as Iraq—a country which vies with Egypt as having the first civilization of humankind. Some scholars believe that this Mesopotamian civilization spread both east and west, and what we now know as Chinese and Western civilizations both had their beginnings in that fertile land. With this long history, it is not surprising that Iraq has a rich cuisine which covers a vast field of culinary delight. This method of cooking chicken with chickpeas in the Iraqi style is part of that rich heritage.

1 5–6 lb roasting chicken	1 cup coarse burghul, soaked for 5 minutes, then drained
6 tablespoons butter	1/2 lb dried chickpeas, soaked overnight, drained, then split
1/2 cup rice	
12 medium tomatoes	
1 teaspoon cinnamon	1 lb parsnips, peeled and cut into rounds
1 teaspoon cumin	4 cups water
salt and pepper to taste	

Wash and clean the chicken. Remove the neck, but leave the neck skin, and set aside.

Wash the rice and drain it. Stir-fry the rice in the butter over medium heat until the rice turns golden. Add to the rice 4 of the tomatoes, chopped into large chunks, ¹/₂ teaspoon of the cinnamon, ¹/₂ teaspoon of the cumin, salt, pepper, and half of the burghul. Fry and stir for a further 10 minutes.

Fill the body cavity and neck skin of the chicken with the rice and burghul mixture; then sew or skewer closed and place in a roasting pan. Mix the chickpeas, the remaining burghul, and the parsnips. Surround the chicken with this mixture and sprinkle with the remaining seasonings and spices.

Chop the remaining tomatoes into large pieces and place on top of the chickpea mixture. Pour in the water. Cover the pan with a lid or foil and place in a 300°F oven for about an hour and a half, until the chicken is done.

Remove the cover and broil for a few minutes until the chicken is golden brown.

Chicken and Rice Stew
Kabsa
Saudi Arabia

Serves 4 to 6

¹/₂ cup olive oil	1 teaspoon ground coriander
2 medium onions, chopped	salt and pepper to taste
1 3–4 lb chicken, cut into serving pieces	1 large carrot, grated
1 can tomatoes (19 oz or 540 ml)	1¹/₂ cups rice, rinsed
5 cloves garlic, crushed	3 tablespoons raisins
5 cardamom pods	3 tablespoons slivered almonds
¹/₂ teaspoon cinnamon	

In a saucepan, sauté the onions in the oil until they turn golden brown. Add the chicken, tomatoes, and garlic; then cook over medium heat for about 8 minutes, stirring a few times.

Stir in hot water to cover. Add cardamom, cinnamon, coriander, salt, pepper, and carrot. Cover and simmer over medium heat for 30 minutes or until the chicken is tender; then remove the chicken pieces and keep warm.

Measure the sauce. If less than 3 cups, add water to make up the difference; then return it to the pan, add the rice, and simmer over low heat for 15–20 minutes or until the rice is tender. Turn off the heat and allow the rice to finish cooking in its own steam.

Place the rice on a serving platter; then arrange the pieces of chicken on top and decorate with the raisins and almonds. Serve hot.

Chicken Rôti
Dajaj Muhammar
Morocco

Serves 4

2 medium onions, chopped
4 cloves of garlic, crushed
1 teaspoon paprika
salt

1 teaspoon ginger
½ cup butter
1 3–4 lb roasting chicken, cleaned

Combine the onions, garlic, paprika, salt, ginger, and butter. Put this mixture in a pot just big enough to hold the chicken and fry until the onions are light brown.

Place the chicken in the pot, turning it over a few times, for approximately 3 minutes; then add water to cover the chicken. Cover and bring to a boil, then cook over medium heat for approximately 1 hour or until done.

Uncover the pot and put the chicken with its sauce under the broiler for a few minutes until the chicken is golden brown. Serve with its sauce.

Chicken with Sauce
Dajaj Muhammar Maghrebi
Morocco

Serves 8 to 10

4 lb chicken, cut into serving pieces
½ cup butter
2 medium onions, finely chopped
salt and pepper to taste
2 tablespoons paprika
2 teaspoons cumin

¼ cup finely chopped fresh coriander
  leaves (cilantro)
4 cloves garlic, crushed
¼ cup flour, well blended with ½ cup
  of cold water

Place the chicken pieces in a pot and cover with water; then add ¼ cup of the butter, the onions, salt, pepper, paprika, cumin, coriander leaves, and garlic. Cover and cook over a moderate heat for about an hour. Remove the chicken pieces and place on a plate.

Add the flour paste to the cooking liquid, stirring often until the sauce thickens (about 10 minutes); then uncover, remove from the heat, and set aside.

Fry the chicken pieces in the remaining ½ cup of butter until the pieces are brown. Remove and place on a hot serving plate.

Add the sauce to the butter in which the chicken was fried; then heat and stir for a few moments. Pour the sauce evenly over the chicken pieces and serve at once.

Chicken with Sumac

Mussakhkhan

Palestine and Jordan

Serves 4 to 6

In Palestine and Jordan, a guest can receive no greater honor than to be served this dish.

1 3–4 lb chicken cleaned and cut into serving pieces	salt and pepper to taste
6 cardamom seeds, crushed	$1/2$ teaspoon allspice
$3/4$ cup olive or corn oil	$1/4$ cup pine nuts
4 large onions, chopped	$1/2$ cup sumac (see Glossary, p. 6)
	4 small loaves Arabic (pita) bread

In a pot, place the chicken pieces and half of the crushed cardamom seeds; then cover with water. Cook over medium heat for 45 minutes to an hour, until the chicken is tender; then remove the chicken pieces and set aside.

In the meantime, in a saucepan, place $1/2$ cup of the oil, the onions, salt, pepper, allspice, and the remaining cardamom. Cook slowly, uncovered, over a low heat for $1\frac{1}{2}$ hours.

While the onions are cooking, sauté the pine nuts in the remaining $1/4$ cup of oil until they begin to brown; then add the nuts and the sumac to the onions. Stir and allow to cool.

Divide the onion-sumac mixture in half; reserve one portion. Split open the bread loaves and layer them in a greased round or oval casserole, spreading each layer with the onion-sumac mixture. Top evenly with the chicken pieces; then spread the remaining half of the onion-sumac mixture over the chicken. Cover with foil and bake in a 350°F preheated oven for 40 minutes. Serve a portion of the bread with each chicken piece.

Note: Excellent served with yogurt or with a tomato and cucumber salad.

Chicken with Walnuts

Dajaj ma' Lawz

Saudi Arabia

Serves 6 to 8

1 4–5 lb chicken	salt and pepper to taste
4 medium onions, chopped	1 cup finely chopped walnuts
2 medium carrots, chopped into small pieces	1 tablespoon paprika
	4 tablespoons butter
³/₄ cup chopped fresh parsley	¹/₂ teaspoon cinnamon
¹/₄ cup finely chopped fresh coriander leaves (cilantro)	¹/₄ teaspoon cloves
	2 bay leaves

Place the chicken in a pot and half cover with water; then add half of the chopped onions, the carrots, ¹/₄ cup of the parsley, the coriander, salt, and pepper. Bring to a boil; then reduce the heat and allow to simmer for 45 minutes or until the chicken is cooked.

Remove the chicken and de-bone; then chop the meat into small pieces and set aside.

Strain the chicken stock and set aside. Mix the walnuts with the paprika in a small bowl and set aside.

Brown the chicken pieces in the butter. Add the remaining chopped onions, the chicken stock, the cinnamon, cloves, and bay leaves. Bring to a boil; then reduce the heat, cover and simmer for 40 minutes.

After removing the bay leaves, place on a serving platter, and garnish with the walnut and paprika mixture. Decorate with the remaining ¹/₂ cup of parsley. Serve with rice.

Eggplant Casserole with Tomato and Chicken

Tunisia

Serves 4 to 6

1 large eggplant, peeled and thinly sliced lengthwise	2 cloves garlic, crushed
	¹/₄ cup finely chopped fresh coriander leaves (cilantro)
salt	
¹/₂ cup olive oil	¹/₂ teaspoon pepper
¹/₂ lb chicken, cut into ¹/₂ inch cubes	1 cup tomato sauce
1 large onion, chopped	¹/₂ cup water
3 large tomatoes, peeled and chopped	3 eggs, hard-boiled and quartered

Sprinkle the eggplant slices with salt. Let stand for 30 minutes; then drain. Heat 6 tablespoons of the oil in a frying pan and sauté the eggplant slices until they turn limp. Remove and drain.

Add the remaining 2 tablespoons oil to the pan; then sauté the chicken until it begins to brown. Stir in the onion, tomatoes, garlic, and coriander; then sauté for a further few minutes, stirring constantly.

In a casserole, place alternate layers of the eggplant slices and meat mixture, starting with the eggplant, until all are used. Season with salt and pepper, then add the tomato sauce and water, and bring to a boil. Transfer to a 350°F preheated oven for 1 hour; then remove and garnish with the quartered eggs before serving.

A Moroccan Pie
Basteela

Serves 10

One of the most elaborate creations in Moroccan cooking is *basteela*, which no first rate Moroccan feast or *diffa* would fail to include. *Basteela* is a kind of pigeon pie which offers a subtle range of surprising tastes and textures. Although time-consuming, its preparation is not too difficult, and as anyone who has eaten *basteela* will attest, one taste is worth a thousand words—and all the effort as well. Our version is simplified but the taste is there.

5 medium onions, finely chopped	2 cups water
1¼ cups butter	1 cup finely chopped fresh parsley
salt and pepper to taste	7 eggs
pinch saffron or 1 teaspoon tumeric	½ cup oil
1 teaspoon cinnamon	1 lb blanched almonds, slivered
3 lbs boneless chicken meat, cooked and chopped into very small cubes (the chicken may be poached or baked in foil)	¼ cup sugar
	1 package filo dough

In a saucepan, cook the onions in ¼ cup of the butter, the salt, pepper, saffron or tumeric, and 1 teaspoon of the cinnamon over medium heat until the onions are light brown. Add the chicken pieces and water and stir-fry for 5 minutes; then add the parsley and cook for a further 5 minutes.

Beat 6 of the eggs and add to the chicken mixture. Stir until the eggs are almost cooked; then remove from the heat and set aside.

Heat the oil in a frying pan, and fry the almonds until they turn light brown. Remove the almonds with a slotted spoon and grind finely; place on a separate plate.

Mix 2 tablespoons of the sugar and half the ground almonds with the chicken mixture to complete the filling. Set aside.

Melt the remaining 1 cup of butter in a small pot and set aside.

Take out half of the package of filo dough and place a damp cloth over the other half to prevent drying. Place 3 sheets of filo dough on the bottom of a 10 by 15 inch baking pan, leaving approximately two inches of the dough hanging over each side of the pan. Brush with some of the butter; then repeat this procedure to make two more layers of dough.

Pour the chicken filling over the dough and spread evenly; then cover the chicken filling with 3 more sheets of dough and brush the third sheet lightly with butter. Sprinkle the remaining ground almonds over the dough; then place 1 sheet of dough over the almonds. Beat the remaining egg and brush evenly over the top and edges of the *basteela*; then fold in the overhanging edges of the dough.

Place the remaining sheets of dough over the top, trim the sides and press lightly; then brush all the remaining butter over the top.

Bake the *basteela* in a 350°F preheated oven for about 20 minutes or until the *basteela* turns golden brown. Remove from the oven and sprinkle the remaining 2 tablespoons of sugar and the $^1/_2$ teaspoon of cinammon over the top. Serve warm.

Roast Turkey
Deek Habash Mahshee
Palestine and Jordan

Serves 8 to 10

The unusual spicing and stuffing gives this old favorite an exotic twist.

1 8–10 lb turkey, cleaned and washed	$^1/_2$ teaspoon cinnamon
$^1/_2$ cup vinegar mixed with 1 tablespoon salt	$^1/_2$ teaspoon nutmeg
2 tablespoons lemon juice	rice stuffing (see p. 15)
salt and pepper to taste	$^1/_2$ cup yogurt

Rub the turkey with the vinegar and salt mixture. Let stand for about 1 hour; then drain and dry.

Rub the outside and the inside with lemon juice; then mix the salt, pepper, cinnamon, and nutmeg and rub inside and out. Stuff with rice; then sew or skewer the opening closed.

Coat the turkey with the yogurt. Place in a roasting pan and bake in a 350°F preheated oven, allowing 30 minutes per pound, until the turkey is done.

Roast Turkey Egyptian Style
Farkhat Mihshee

Serves 6 to 8

1 turkey (about 6 lbs)
cleaned and washed, with the liver,
gizzard, and heart reserved
1/4 cup lemon juice mixed with
1 cup of water
4 medium carrots, quartered
4 cloves garlic, crushed
1/2 cup butter

1 1/2 cups onions, finely chopped
2 tablespoons pine nuts
1 cup uncooked rice, rinsed
2 medium tomatoes, chopped
1/2 teaspoon dried basil
salt and pepper to taste
1/2 teaspoon savory
1/2 teaspoon ginger

Place the turkey in a roasting pan with the lemon juice and water, carrots, garlic, 1/4 cup of the butter, and 1 cup of the onions. Place in a 350°F preheated oven, basting from time to time with pan juices, for about 2 hours or until the bird is tender. Uncover and broil until the turkey turns to golden brown; then set aside and keep warm.

Strain the pan juices and measure; add water if necessary to make 2 cups. Set aside.

Cut the liver, gizzard, and heart into small pieces; then place in a frying pan and sauté in 2 tablespoons of the butter for 6 minutes. Remove with a slotted spoon and set aside; then add the remaining butter, the remaining onions, and the pine nuts and sauté over medium heat for 10 minutes.

Add the rice and stir-fry for a further 5 minutes; then add the reserved liquid, tomatoes, basil, salt, pepper, savory, and ginger. Cover and cook over reduced heat until all the liquid has been absorbed; then add the sautéed liver, gizzard, and heart, and combine thoroughly to make a stuffing. Stuff the turkey; then place in a 300°F preheated oven for 40 minutes and serve hot.

Fish and Shellfish

edieval Arab cookbooks give very few recipes for fish, and modern cooks in the inland parts of the Arab world rarely use it. Because fish spoils so easily, its consumption as one travels inland diminishes drastically.

But for the people of the Arabian Gulf countries, and those who inhabit the shores of North Africa, fish is often on the daily menu. Stuffed with herbs, curried, cooked with *taheena* (but rarely breaded and fried as is common in the West), fish dishes regularly grace the tables of the workers and the affluent alike.

Perhaps the most appetizing way the Arabs prepare fish is to barbecue it. When used for kababs, fish must always be fresh, just out of the sea if possible. Seasoned with herbs and spices, then cooked over glowing coals, its taste of sea and smoke has no equal.

Fish Salad

Sudan

Serves 6 to 8

4 tablespoons butter	6 tablespoons lemon juice
2 lbs fish fillets (a firm-fleshed fish such as cod, haddock, salmon, or bass works best)	$^1\!/_2$ cup olive oil
	1 cup finely chopped fresh coriander leaves (cilantro)
1 cup shredded cabbage	pinch cayenne
5 medium tomatoes	2 hard-boiled eggs, sliced
$^1\!/_2$ teaspoon cumin	$^1\!/_2$ cup black olives
salt and pepper to taste	$^1\!/_2$ cup coarsely chopped fresh parsley

In a frying pan, melt the butter, then sauté the fish fillet for about 10 minutes or until it turns light brown, turning it over once. Remove and flake with a fork.

Dice 3 of the tomatoes. Mix the fish, cabbage, cumin, salt, pepper, 2 tablespoons of the lemon juice, and 4 tablespoons of the olive oil, and place on a serving plate.

Make a sauce by mixing the coriander leaves, cayenne, salt, pepper, lemon juice, and olive oil. Pour evenly over the fish mixture.

Garnish with the eggs, the remaining 2 tomatoes (sliced), the olives, and the parsley.

Clockwise from bottom left: fish rolls (p. 161) with sesame sauce (p. 18), fish kabab (p. 156), Somali crabmeat stew (p. 166), baked herb-stuffed fish (p. 155).

Baked Fish

Samak fil-Furn

Egypt

Serves 6

2 lbs filleted white fish (such as cod,
    flounder, sole, etc.), cut into 6 pieces
salt and pepper to taste

¹/₄ cup lemon juice
3 tablespoons vegetable oil
2 oranges, peeled and sliced

    Season the fish with the salt and pepper and place in a baking dish. Mix the lemon juice with the oil and pour evenly over the fish. Arrange the slices of orange over the top and cover; then bake in a 400°F preheated oven for approximately 30 minutes or until done. Serve on a bed of rice.

Baked Herb-Stuffed Fish

Kuwait

Serves 6 to 8

A cook can always tell if a fish is fresh by the brightness of the eyes and the firmness of the flesh. All types of fish spoil quickly; hence, if not utilized immediately, they should be frozen. The modern method of blast freezing preserves the flesh so well that decomposition is barely detectable.

    If frozen, to preserve its fresh taste, fish should be thawed slowly in cold water and cooked soon thereafter.

4 tablespoons butter
2 medium onions, chopped
¹/₂ cup finely chopped fresh parsley
¹/₄ cup finely chopped fresh coriander
    leaves (cilantro)
1 lemon, with peel, very finely chopped
6 cloves garlic, crushed

1 teaspoon finely chopped hot pepper
1 teaspoon paprika
salt
¹/₂ teaspoon cumin
1 4–5 lb fresh salmon or similar fish,
    scaled, cleaned, and washed
garlic sauce (see p. 19)

    In a frying pan, melt the butter; then sauté the onions over a medium heat for 8 minutes. Stir in the parsley, coriander leaves, lemon, garlic, and hot pepper; then stir-fry for 4 minutes.

    Remove from the heat and stir in the paprika, salt, pepper, and cumin to make a filling; then stuff the fish and sew closed. Rub the fish with cooking oil; then wrap in aluminum foil and bake in a 400°F preheated oven for 30 minutes.

    Remove the foil and place under the broiler for a few minutes to lightly brown; then serve immediately with garlic sauce.

Clockwise from bottom right: sesame cookies (p. 223), Arabian shortbread (p. 209), stuffed pancakes (p. 225), shredded dough cheesecake (p. 224), baklawa (p. 210).

Fish Fillets Baked in Taheena

Palestine and Jordan

Serves 6 to 8

In the past, in the parts of the world where the oceans teem with fish, cities and states rose and fell with the rise and fall in the richness of their nearby fishing fields. In the future, there is little doubt that fish could be the deciding factor between starvation and plenty. A truly versatile fare which at times decided the destiny of empires, this ancient food has a bright future.

$^1\!/_2$ cup cooking oil

2 lbs fish fillet (any kind), cut into
   2 inch cubes

4 medium potatoes, peeled and sliced

5 tablespoons *taheena* (see p. 18)

$^1\!/_4$ cup lemon juice

$^1\!/_2$ small hot pepper, chopped

3 tablespoons fresh coriander leaves
   (cilantro), finely chopped

2 cloves garlic, crushed

$^3\!/_4$ cup water

1 teaspoon sage

salt and pepper to taste

In a frying pan, heat the oil; then fry the fish pieces over medium heat for 10 minutes, turning them over once. Remove the fish pieces with a slotted spoon and place in a casserole. Set aside.

In the same oil, fry the potato slices until they begin to brown, turning them over once. Add more oil if they begin to stick. Remove and place over the fish in the casserole.

Place all the remaining ingredients in a blender and blend for a few moments; then pour over the potatoes and fish. Cover and bake in a 400°F preheated oven for 15 minutes; then serve immediately.

Fish Kabab

Morocco

Serves 4 to 6

Fish can be eaten raw, baked, boiled, broiled, pickled, or steamed. However, the epitome of flavor is reached if served grilled. This method requires very careful cooking because the fish tends to fall apart if turned on the grill too frequently. Halibut and salmon have a fairly solid flesh and are the best type of fish to barbecue.

1 small onion, finely chopped

$^1\!/_4$ cup finely chopped fresh coriander
   leaves (cilantro)

4 cloves garlic, crushed

$^1\!/_4$ cup vegetable oil

$^1\!/_2$ teaspoon cumin

pinch cayenne

2 lbs halibut fillet, cut into 1$^1\!/_2$ inch cubes

2 medium green peppers, cut into
   1 inch squares

¼ cup lemon Juice	2 medium firm tomatoes, quartered
1 teaspoon oregano	garlic sauce (see p. 19)
salt and pepper to taste	

In a large bowl, thoroughly mix all the ingredients except the fish, green peppers, and tomatoes; then add these three ingredients and gently toss. Allow to marinate for 4 hours, tossing every 30 minutes.

Thread the fish, green peppers, and tomatoes intermingled onto skewers. Grill over charcoal for about 15 minutes or until the fish is cooked, basting with the marinade juice every few minutes. Serve immediately with garlic sauce.

Fish Kibbeh

Kibbet Samak

Syria and Lebanon

Makes about 48 small patties

1 cup burghul, soaked for 10 minutes in warm water and thoroughly drained by pressing out the water through a strainer	2 tablespoons flour
	salt and pepper to taste
	¼ teaspoon allspice
	¼ teaspoon cinnamon
1 lb cod or similar fish fillet, cut into 2 inch pieces	¼ teaspoon nutmeg
	pinch cayenne
1 medium onion, chopped	oil for frying
2 cloves garlic, crushed	
¼ cup finely chopped fresh coriander leaves (cilantro)	

Place all the ingredients except the oil in a food processor and process to a firm paste. Form into small patties about 1½ inches in diameter.

Heat oil ½ inch deep in a frying pan. Fry the patties over medium heat, turning them over once until they turn golden brown. Serve warm with garlic sauce (see p. 19).

Fish and Rice

Sayadia

Syria and Lebanon

Serves 4 to 6

A number of the beliefs of the early cultures and religions passed into the Greek, Roman, and later the Christian traditions. The early Christians employed the fish as a symbol for Christ. Later the Christians' abstinence from meat on Fridays and in Lent, and the Church's enjoining its members for hundreds of years to eat fish, has given fish consumption a great impetus.

4 tablespoons butter	¹/₂ cup pine nuts
1 lb fish fillets (any kind),	1 cup rice, rinsed
cut into large pieces	salt
¹/₂ teaspoon cumin	2 cups water
1 large onion, chopped	

In a frying pan, melt the butter. Sprinkle the fish with the cumin, then sauté over medium heat until it turns brown. Remove the fish with a slotted spoon or spatula.

In the same butter, sauté the chopped onion and pine nuts over medium heat until the onions turn a golden brown.

Grease a 2-quart casserole; then place a layer of onion and pine nuts, a layer of fish and a layer of rice. Repeat the layers until all the ingredients are used. Mix the salt and water and pour over all the ingredients; then cover and bake at 350°F in a preheated oven for 1 hour or until the rice is cooked. Remove cover for the last 15 minutes of baking.

Fish with Rice

Samak bil-Rizz

Morocco

Serves 4 to 6

Hunted for food by stone age man about 40,000 years ago, fish is believed to be the first of the world's creatures consumed by humans. From the lordly caviar to the lowly smelt, these animals of the sea have for centuries been a major contributor to the human diet. Today, more so than in the past, they are becoming important as a nourishing food. With the increase in the world's population and the shortage of fertile land, humankind is looking more and more to the three quarters of the earth's surface covered with water as a source of human subsistence.

3 to 4 lb whole fish

$^1/_2$ small head of garlic, peeled

$^1/_2$ cup finely chopped fresh coriander leaves (cilantro)

salt and pepper to taste

1 tablespoon paprika

1 teaspoon cumin

$^1/_2$ cup lemon juice

4 tablespoons butter

$^1/_2$ cup rice, washed, and drained

$1^1/_2$ cups water

5 medium tomatoes, sliced

$^1/_2$ cup cooking oil

Clean the fish; then wash and set aside.

Crush the garlic with the coriander and salt. Put this mixture in a dish, and add the paprika, cumin, and lemon juice. Mix well.

Rub the fish inside and out with half of this mixture; then set aside both the fish and the remaining half of the mixture.

In a frying pan, sauté the rice in the butter until crisp. Add $^1/_2$ cup of the water and cook covered for about 5 minutes over low heat.

Mix the rice with the rest of the coriander-garlic mixture; then stuff the fish with this filling and close the cavity with toothpicks.

Place the fish in a baking pan. Cover with the tomato slices and pour the oil and the rest of the water over the tomatoes and fish. Cover the pan with foil; then place in the oven and cook for 1 hour at 350°F.

Curried Fish

Samak Karee

Kuwait

Serves 4 to 6

$^1/_2$ cup oil

1 large onion, sliced

$^1/_2$ small head of garlic, chopped

$^1/_2$ fresh hot pepper, seeded and thinly sliced

$^1/_2$ teaspoon fresh grated ginger root

$^1/_4$ cup tomato paste

2 medium tomatoes, diced

salt and pepper to taste

$^1/_2$ teaspoon turmeric

$^1/_4$ teaspoon cardamom

$^1/_4$ teaspoon cumin

$^1/_4$ teaspoon cinnamon

$^1/_4$ teaspoon nutmeg

pinch cayenne

1 cup water

2 lbs fish fillets, cut into pieces

Heat the oil in a large frying pan; then add the onions, garlic, hot pepper, and ginger root, and fry until golden brown. Add tomato paste and the fresh tomatoes; simmer for a few minutes. Stir in the salt, all the spices, and the water; cook for 25 minutes over low heat.

Add the fish pieces and simmer in this sauce for about 30 minutes or until the fish is cooked. Serve with rice.

Curried Shrimp with Tomato Sauce and Rice Pilaf

Bahrain

Serves 6 to 8

2 medium onions, chopped
1 clove garlic, crushed
2 tablespoons butter
2 tablespoons curry powder
salt

1 can (8 oz or 227 ml) tomato sauce
1 cup chicken stock
3 tablespoons lemon juice
$\frac{1}{2}$ cup light cream
2 lbs shrimp, cooked, shelled, and
deveined

The Curried Shrimp

Fry the onions and garlic in butter in a saucepan until tender; then add the curry powder, salt, tomato sauce, and chicken stock, and stir. Cover and simmer for 20 minutes. Remove from the heat and stir in the lemon juice. Slowly add the cream, stirring all the while; then add the shrimp and place over low heat until the shrimp is heated through. Keep hot until ready to serve.

The Rice Pilaf

$\frac{1}{4}$ cup oil
$1\frac{1}{2}$ cups rice, soaked for 15 minutes
    and drained
salt

3 cups boiling water
2 cups frozen peas
2 tablespoons butter
$\frac{1}{2}$ cup split toasted almonds

Place oil in a frying pan and heat; then add the rice and sauté over medium heat for 10–15 minutes, stirring all the while, until the rice is crispy.

Add the salt and boiling water to the rice; then stir for a few minutes and cover. Turn the heat to low and cook for 15 minutes; then add the frozen peas and butter to the rice and stir. Allow to cook a further 5 minutes; then place on a platter and garnish with almonds. Serve with the shrimp.

Fish Rolls
Samak Miqlee
Syria and Lebanon

Serves 6 to 8

2 lbs white fish
1 carrot, sliced
2 onions, chopped
10 black peppercorns
3 slices white bread with crusts
    removed, or ¾ cup breadcrumbs
milk for moistening
1 egg

1 teaspoon ground coriander
2 cloves garlic, crushed
1 teaspoon thyme
salt
pinch cayenne
5 tablespoons flour
oil for frying

    In a large pot, put the cleaned fish, carrot, half the onions, and the peppercorns in water to cover; then bring to boil and simmer until tender. Remove the fish from the liquid; then flake the flesh from the bones and put into a mixing bowl.

    Soak the bread in milk for a few minutes; then squeeze dry and mix with the flaked fish. Mix in the egg, the remaining onion, coriander, garlic, thyme, salt, and cayenne, and knead together.

    Form the mixture into finger-like cylinders; then roll in the flour and fry in hot oil until they are golden brown. Serve hot or cold with garlic sauce (see p. 19) or sesame sauce (p. 18), for dipping.

Fish Stew
Yakhnat Samak
Kuwait

Serves 4 to 6

salt
6 tablespoons lemon juice
2 lbs filleted fish, cut into large pieces
5 tablespoons olive oil
1 medium onion, chopped
3 tablespoons finely chopped fresh
    coriander leaves (cilantro)
3 cloves garlic, crushed

1 teaspoon pepper
½ teaspoon thyme
¼ cup tomato paste
1 cup water
1½ cups cooked rice
½ lemon, sliced
1 small tomato, sliced
a few sprigs of parsley

    Sprinkle salt and 3 tablespoons of the lemon juice on the fish fillets and allow to stand for 4 to 6 hours.

    In a frying pan, heat the oil; then add the onion, coriander, garlic, pepper, thyme, and salt. Sauté and stir until the onion turns golden brown. Stir in the tomato paste, water, and the remaining 3 tablespoons of lemon juice;

then simmer on a low heat for 5 minutes, stirring occasionally.

Place the fish in another frying pan and pour the onion mixture over the fish. Bring to a boil, then lower the heat and allow to simmer for 25 minutes or until the fish is done.

Place the cooked rice on a serving dish; then carefully arrange the fillet pieces over the top of the rice.

Pour the sauce on the pieces of fish and rice; then decorate with the lemon and tomato slices and sprigs of parsley.

Fish Stew Tunisian Style

Serves 8 to 10

Besides being an important food, fish has been associated with religion since the dawn of civilization. In a good number of the early cultures, sea animals were held sacred and holy, only fit for the gods. The Babylonians, Assyrians, Aramaeans, Phoenicians, and ancient Egyptians worshiped a fish, god called Nun. In India, the Buddhists have for centuries venerated the "Lord of the Fishes," Matsyendranatha. And in Christianity, a fish is used to symbolize Christ.

$^1/_2$ cup cooking oil	3 medium potatoes, peeled and cut into
2 lbs fish fillets, cut into 1 inch cubes	$^1/_2$ inch cubes
2 medium onions, chopped	$1^1/_2$ cups water
4 cloves garlic, crushed	salt and pepper to taste
$^1/_4$ cup finely chopped fresh coriander	$^1/_2$ teaspoon cumin
leaves (cilantro)	$^1/_4$ teaspoon allspice
1 can stewed tomatoes (19 oz or 540 ml)	pinch cayenne

In a saucepan, heat the oil; then sauté the fish cubes over a medium-high heat for 10 minutes, turning them over once. Remove the fish with a slotted spoon and set aside.

Sauté the onions, garlic, and coriander leaves in the same oil over a medium heat for 10 minutes. Add the remaining ingredients except the fish and bring to a boil; then cover and cook over medium heat for 20 minutes. Add the fish cubes and heat through; then serve hot.

Fish Stuffed with Dates

Morocco

Serves 6 to 8

$^1/_2$ lb dates, chopped into small pieces	4 to 5 lb whole fish, cleaned, scaled,
$^1/_2$ cup blanched ground almonds	and washed, sprinkled with salt on
3 tablespoons butter, melted	the inside
$^1/_2$ teaspoon cinnamon	2 tablespoons olive oil

¼ teaspoon ground coriander	salt
½ teaspoon pepper	1 medium onion, finely chopped
½ teaspoon ginger	¼ cup chopped parsley
6 tablespoons lemon juice	1 lemon, thinly sliced

Make a stuffing by mixing the dates, almonds, butter, cinnamon, coriander, ½ teaspoon of the pepper, ¼ teaspoon of the ginger and 2 tablespoons of lemon juice; then stuff the fish and sew closed.

Mix the olive oil, salt, and the remaining pepper with the ginger, and 2 tablespoons of the lemon juice. Rub the outside of the fish with this mixture.

On a large piece of aluminum foil, sprinkle half the onions to make a bed roughly the size and shape of the fish; then place the fish on top of the onions and sprinkle the remaining onions on top. Wrap the foil tightly around the fish and place in a pan; then bake for about 1 hour in a 350°F preheated oven. Remove the tin foil about 5 minutes before the end of the cooking time to brown the fish, turning over once.

Place on a serving plate; then sprinkle with the remaining lemon juice and decorate with the parsley and lemon slices.

Fish Stuffed with Coriander
Tajin Samak
Morocco

Serves 6 to 8

Olive oil is favored by a fair number of health-conscious people, since it is practically free of fatty acids and, in contrast with other oils, it is utilized in its original form, unhydrogenated.

Besides its use in cooking, the oil of the initial pressing is also employed as a hair dressing and as a massage ingredient to soften the skin. Many Mediterranean beauties through the ages have utilized this oil to enrich their flowing black tresses, inspiring romantic poets for many centuries. Perhaps the most renowned women who prepared their hair and anointed their bodies with olive oil were the legendary eastern queens, Cleopatra and Zenobia. It is believed that Cleopatra would have an olive oil massage before her rendezvous with Caesar or Anthony.

1 cup finely chopped fresh coriander leaves (cilantro)	4 to 5 lbs whole fish, cleaned, scaled, and thoroughly washed
1 cup finely chopped scallions	5 medium tomatoes, sliced
1 medium head of garlic, peeled and crushed	4 medium potatoes, peeled and cut into thin slices
salt	2 medium carrots, scraped and thinly sliced
2 teaspoons paprika	

pinch cayenne
½ cup lemon juice

½ cup olive oil
½ cup water
½ cup pimento stuffed green olives

In a small bowl, thoroughly mix the coriander, green onions, garlic, salt, paprika, cayenne, and lemon juice. Stuff the fish with half the mixture and sew; then place in a deep pan and spread the remaining mixture over the top of the fish.

Arrange the tomatoes, potatoes, and carrots in alternate layers over and around the fish; then pour the olive oil and water over the vegetables.

Cover with foil and place in a 350°F preheated oven; bake for 1 hour or until the fish and vegetables are tender. Remove from the oven and spread the olives evenly over the vegetables and fish; then return to the oven and bake uncovered for a further 10 minutes.

Garlic Fried Fish Steaks

Algeria

Serves 4 to 6

Fish have excellent nutritive properties. Equal to lean meat in their food composition, fish contain about 20% protein and small amounts of calcium, iodine, iron, magnesium, phosphorous, potassium, and sodium. In addition, most fish contain vitamins A, B, D, and E. Almost free of carbohydrate and fat, fish are gaining in popularity as a low-fat fare.

6 cloves garlic, crushed
¼ cup olive oil
2 tablespoons lemon juice
1 teaspoon tarragon
salt and pepper to taste
½ teaspoon ground coriander

pinch cayenne
2 lbs fish steaks (any kind)
flour
oil for frying
garlic sauce (see p. 19)

Make a paste by thoroughly mixing all the ingredients, except the fish steaks, flour ,and cooking oil; then rub the steaks with the paste. Refrigerate for 2 hours.

Dredge the steaks in flour. Heat oil ½ inch deep in a frying pan and fry the steaks until they turn golden brown; then serve hot with the garlic sauce.

Shrimp with Rice

Bahrain

Serves 4

½ cup oil
1 cup rice
1 cup sliced onions
1 clove garlic, crushed

1 can stewed tomatoes (19 oz or 540 ml)
2 cups water
1½ lbs raw shrimp, shelled and deveined
salt and pepper to taste

Place oil in a frying pan and heat; then add the rice, onions, and garlic and cook over low heat, stirring until the rice is lightly browned. Add tomatoes, water, salt, and pepper and mix; then add the shrimp and cover. Simmer over low heat for 30 minutes or until the rice is cooked.

Sole with Grape Juice
Samak Musa
Egypt

Serves 4

2 lbs sole fillets
½ cup flour seasoned with salt and
  pepper
½ cup butter
1 large onion, finely chopped

1 cup mushrooms, sliced
salt and pepper to taste
½ cup white grape juice
½ cup light cream or half and half

Moisten the fillets with a little sprinkling of water; then dip in the seasoned flour and set aside.

Heat the butter in a frying pan; then add fillets and sauté over a medium heat for approximately 10 minutes, browning both sides. Remove the fish and place in a casserole.

In the same butter, sauté the onion over medium heat for 5 minutes. Add the mushrooms, salt, and pepper and stir-fry until the onion turns golden brown; then add the grape juice, and simmer for a few minutes. Remove from the heat and stir in the cream. Pour the sauce over the fish. Cover and bake at 350°F for half an hour; then serve hot from the casserole.

Somali Crabmeat Stew

Serves 4

3 tablespoons butter
1 large onion, finely chopped
2 cloves garlic, crushed
2 tablespoons finely chopped fresh
   coriander leaves (cilantro)
salt

$1/_2$ teaspoon ginger
$1/_2$ teaspoon chilli pepper
$1/_2$ teaspoon cumin
5 medium tomatoes, chopped
1 lb lump crabmeat, canned, fresh, or
   frozen

   Melt the butter in a frying pan and sauté the onion, garlic, coriander, salt, ginger, pepper, and cumin, stirring occasionally, until the onion begins to brown. Add the tomatoes and simmer until they become soft. Add the crabmeat and sauté over low heat for 20 minutes; then serve hot with plain rice.

Stuffed Salmon Tunisian Style

Serves 6 to 8

In Tunisia, fish is a symbol of fertility. In parts of that land, it is customary for a bride and groom to step over a large fish after their wedding. Fish made from fabric or metal are hung in homes or pinned to clothing to bring good luck.

1 3–4 lb salmon, scaled
salt and pepper to taste
2 tablespoons lemon juice
4 tablespoons butter
1 medium onion, finely chopped
2 cloves garlic, crushed
1 small hot pepper, finely chopped
$1/_4$ cup finely chopped fresh coriander
   leaves (cilantro)
$1/_4$ cup small pieces of feta or similar
   cheese

2 hard-boiled eggs, chopped
$1/_4$ cup breadcrumbs
$1/_4$ cup chopped green olives
$1/_2$ teaspoon thyme
1 raw egg
4 large potatoes, peeled and cut into
   $1/_2$ inch thick slices
1 tablespoon chopped parsley

   Wash the salmon thoroughly. Rub both inside and outside with salt and pepper and the lemon juice. Let stand for 1 hour.

   In a frying pan, sauté the onion in the butter until golden-brown. Stir in the garlic, hot pepper, and coriander leaves and sauté for a further few minutes; then transfer the frying pan contents into a mixing bowl. Add the salt and pepper, cheese, boiled eggs, breadcrumbs, olives, thyme, and the raw egg and mix thoroughly. Stuff the fish with this mixture and sew up the opening.

Place in a baking pan and brush liberally with oil; then arrange the potato slices around the fish and add $\frac{1}{2}$ cup of water. Cover and bake in a 375°F preheated oven for 20 minutes; then remove the cover and bake for a further 25 minutes, basting a few times with extra oil.

Place on a serving platter and arrange the potato slices around the sides; then decorate with the parsley and serve hot.

Egg Dishes

As in parts of the Western world, Arabs today get their eggs from modern chicken factories. Gone are the days when they gathered their eggs from the chickens scratching for their food in the fields or in the barnyard. However, as in the past, eggs are still very popular throughout the Arab world.

The Arab omelette is made with numerous vegetables and meats and is almost always very tasty. It is believed that the Spanish *tortilla* was introduced, like many other foods, into the Iberian Peninsula by the Arabs. Arab omelettes are flat, like the tortilla or the Italian frittata, as opposed to the folded or souffléed types more commonly known in the West.

Besides omelettes, the dozens of other ways in which Arabs eat their eggs all have their special appeal. Yet no matter how eggs are consumed, they are always eagerly anticipated as a treat.

An Arab poet wrote:

> My wife always brings me
> For breakfast a covered tray
> Containing the best of treats,
> But for only one I pray.
>
> When I find eggs offered,
> Like a penetrating sun ray,
> It revives my spirits,
> And nourishes me for the day.

Casserole of Eggs and Peas

Tunisia

Serves 4

3 tablespoons olive oil	³/₄ cup water
2 medium onions, finely chopped	salt and pepper to taste
2 cloves garlic, crushed	¹/₄ teaspoon cumin
5 tablespoons finely chopped fresh coriander leaves (cilantro)	4 eggs
2 cups fresh or frozen peas	1 teaspoon paprika

In a frying pan, heat the oil; then add the onions, garlic, and coriander, and sauté over medium heat until the onions begin to brown. Transfer to a casserole and add the peas, water, salt, pepper, and cumin; then cover and bake in a 350°F preheated oven for 20 minutes until the peas are done.

Break the eggs, side by side, over the peas; then cover the casserole and bake for a further 10 minutes or until the eggs are set but still soft. Garnish with the paprika and serve from the casserole.

Egg and Almond Stew
Tajin Tufaya
Morocco

Serves 4 to 6

People who come to know Moroccan cooking usually find it among the most sensual in the world.

3 tablespoons butter
2 medium onions, finely chopped
salt and pepper to taste
$\frac{1}{2}$ teaspoon paprika
pinch cayenne
pinch saffron
$1\frac{1}{2}$ lbs beef, cut into 1 inch cubes

1 cup water
$\frac{1}{4}$ cup finely chopped fresh coriander leaves (cilantro)
$\frac{1}{4}$ cup olive oil
$\frac{1}{2}$ cup slivered almonds
3 large eggs

Melt the butter in a saucepan and sauté the onions, salt, pepper, paprika, cayenne, saffron, and meat. Stir and sauté over medium heat until the meat begins to brown. Add the water and coriander, then cover the saucepan and cook until the meat is tender. Remove from the heat and set aside.

In a frying pan, heat the olive oil; then add the almonds and sauté until they turn golden brown. Remove from the oil and set aside.

Hard-boil the eggs; then shell and divide into quarters.

Place the meat with its sauce in a serving platter; then garnish with the almonds and arrange the egg quarters in a pattern on top.

Eggs in Mint Yogurt Sauce
Bayd bil-Laban
Syria and Lebanon

Serves 4

2 cloves garlic
2 tablespoons dried mint, or 3 or 4 sprigs fresh mint
salt to taste
2 tablespoons butter

1 tablespoon cornstarch, dissolved in 2 cups water
1 quart plain yogurt
6 eggs

Mash the garlic, mint, and salt together; then sauté the mixture in the butter and set aside.

Mix the dissolved cornstarch with the yogurt in a heavy saucepan. Bring to a boil over medium heat, stirring constantly to prevent curdling.

Break the eggs, dropping quickly into the boiling yogurt; then allow to cook for a few minutes over medium heat. Add the sautéed garlic mixture, and continue cooking for 15 minutes. Serve with plain rice.

Eggs and Potato Omelette
Bayd ma' Batata
Morocco

Serves 4 to 6

½ cup cooking oil
5 medium potatoes (a waxy type, such as new potatoes, is more suitable than baking potatoes), peeled and diced into very small pieces

salt and pepper to taste
½ teaspoon paprika
1 cup water
5 eggs, beaten

In a frying pan, heat the oil over a medium heat; then add the potatoes, salt, pepper, paprika, and water, and cook until the water has been absorbed by the potatoes, which should be tender, but still intact.

Pour the eggs over the potatoes, and turn the heat down very low; then cook without stirring for about 5 minutes, or until the eggs are done.

Egg and Tomato Casserole
Shakshooka
Tunisia

Serves 4 to 6

According to culinary historians, the Arab cuisine includes perhaps 40,000 dishes. Yet most public eating places in the Arab world, especially those catering to the upper and middle classes, offer only a dozen or so meat dishes on their daily menus. The vegetarianism of the masses, with the exception of falafel and hummus, is rarely known within the portals of the restaurants.

¼ cup olive oil
1 small green pepper, finely chopped
1 medium onion, finely chopped
5 medium tomatoes, chopped
2 cloves garlic, crushed

salt and pepper to taste
¼ teaspoon cumin
pinch allspice
pinch chilli powder
6 eggs

Sauté the green pepper and onion in the olive oil for 3 to 5 minutes over medium heat. Stir in the tomatoes and garlic; then sauté further until the tomatoes are tender. Turn the heat to low; then mash the tomatoes with a fork and add the salt, pepper, cumin, allspice, and chilli powder and sauté for a further 5 minutes. Break in the eggs; then cover and cook until the eggs are done.

Eggs with Tomatoes
Bayd ma' Banadoora
Syria and Lebanon

Serves 4

The attractive coriander plant, which can be grown from seeds retailed as a spice, is an annual of the parsley family. It grows from one to two feet high with slender, hollow stems, parsley-like leaves, and tiny pinkish-white flowers. The plant can be easily grown in all types of gardens, but to thrive, it needs a dry sunny climate and a well-drained light soil. When mature, it produces a very small oval fruit containing a pungent oil. The smell of this oil repels insects from both the plant and nearby growth. When dried, the fruit gives out a pleasant aromatic odor and makes a tasty spice.

2 tablespoons butter	2 tomatoes, finely chopped
1 medium potato, cut into 1 inch cubes	5 eggs, beaten
2 tablespoons finely chopped fresh coriander leaves (cilantro)	salt and pepper to taste
	$^1/_4$ teaspoon cumin

In a frying pan, melt the butter; then add the potato cubes and sauté over medium heat until they begin to brown. Stir in the coriander leaves and sauté for a few minutes longer; then add the tomatoes and sauté for a further 3 to 5 minutes, stirring often.

In the meantime, combine the remaining ingredients; then add to the potato-tomato mixture and mix well. Cover and turn the heat to low; then cook until the eggs are done.

Fried Bread with Eggs
Fattoot
Syria and Lebanon

Serves 4

4 tablespoons butter	5 eggs
1 8 inch loaf pita bread, cut into small pieces	salt and pepper to taste
1 tablespoon finely chopped fresh coriander leaves (cilantro)	

In a frying pan, melt the butter over medium heat; then add the bread pieces and coriander leaves. Stir-fry until the bread pieces turn light brown; then stir in the eggs, salt, and pepper and continue to stir-fry until the eggs are cooked.

Garlic Omelette
Bayd ma' Thoom
Syria and Lebanon

Serves 4

In the Arab East, *Bayd ma' Thoom*, a tasty garlic omelette, is served to a mother who has just given birth. It is believed that the garlic purifies the blood and speeds the recovery of the new mother. No one has proved that this omelette purifies the blood, but it makes a delicious breakfast dish.

1 large head of garlic	6 eggs
¼ cup olive or vegetable oil	salt and pepper to taste

Peel the garlic cloves and dice into small pieces. Heat the oil in a frying pan over medium heat; then add the diced garlic and stir-fry until golden brown. Remove from the heat and take the garlic out with a slotted spoon, but reserve the oil in the frying pan.

In a bowl, beat the eggs with a fork; then add the salt, pepper, and the fried garlic and mix thoroughly. Pour the egg and garlic mixture back into the frying pan and fry over low heat until the eggs are cooked.

Hard-boiled Eggs with Cumin
Bayd Maslooq ma' Kammoon
Morocco

In Morocco, vendors in the streets sell eggs which are sprinkled with a seasoning similar to the following:

1 teaspoon salt	12 eggs, hard-boiled and peeled
2 teaspoons cumin	

Mix the salt and cumin; then place in a small bowl. Serve the eggs whole, accompanied by the bowl of salt and cumin, with each person dipping the eggs into the mixture.

Kishk with Eggs
Kishk ma' Bayd

Syria and Lebanon

Serves 4

2 tablespoons butter
2 cloves garlic, crushed
1 small onion, finely chopped
3 cups water

¹/₄ cup *kishk* (powdered cheese—see p. 12),
   dissolved in ¹/₂ cup milk
4 eggs
salt and pepper to taste

Melt the butter in a saucepan and add the garlic and onions; then sauté until they turn golden brown. Stir in the remaining ingredients except the eggs and bring to a boil; then turn the heat to low and cook for 10 minutes, stirring once in a while.

Break the eggs into the *kishk*, and poach for a further 5 minutes; then serve 1 egg in a bowl of *kishk* to each person.

Potato with Eggs
Batatis ma' Bayd
Iraq

Serves 4

It is believed that the Iraqis acquired this dish from the British troops after the First World War.

2 cups mashed potatoes
1 tablespoon flour
salt and pepper to taste
4 eggs, hard-boiled and shelled

1 raw egg
4 tablespoons breadcrumbs
oil for frying

Mix the potatoes with the flour, salt, and pepper; then divide into 4 portions. Place 1 hard-boiled egg on each part of the potato mixture; then round into an oval shape.

Beat the raw egg in a small bowl. Dip each oval in the beaten egg, then coat with breadcrumbs.

Heat the oil and fry the ovals until they turn golden brown. Serve whole, or cut each oval into 4 parts.

Scrambled Eggs with Hot Sausages and Peppers

Tunisia

Serves 4

The Tunisian cuisine is neither Western nor Oriental but a mixture of the two. It has borrowed much from the neighboring Mediterranean countries and the previous civilizations which once thrived in that land. Phoenicians, Romans, Arabs, Andalusian Muslims, Turks, French, and the native Berbers all contributed to the creation of the modern Tunisian kitchen. From this blend of numerous cultures, cooking from the land of Hannibal has evolved into a world of exciting and unique culinary pleasure.

1/4 cup olive oil	1/4 cup water
1/2 lb seasoned Polish, Italian, or similar sausage, cut into chunks	salt and pepper to taste
2 cloves garlic, crushed	2 sweet peppers (green, yellow, or red) with seeds removed, cut into 1/2 inch strips
1/4 teaspoon caraway	
2 large tomatoes, cut into eighths	3 eggs

Heat the oil in a heavy frying pan over high heat until sizzling; then add the sausage, garlic, and caraway. Stir frequently and cook till the sausage is lightly browned. Add the tomatoes, water, pepper, and salt; then lower the heat to medium and cook until most of the liquid in the frying pan is absorbed.

Add the sweet peppers and simmer, partially covered, for about 10 minutes.

Break the eggs into a bowl and stir briskly with a fork; then pour them into the sausage mixture and stir the mixture gently. Cook over low heat until the eggs are done.

Scrambled Eggs with Yogurt

'Ujja ma' Laban

Palestine and Jordan

Serves 4

5 eggs, beaten	5 tablespoons *labana* (curd cheese or yogurt spread—see p. 16)
salt and pepper to taste	2 tablespoons butter

Thoroughly mix the eggs, salt, pepper, and cheese. Set aside.

Melt the butter over low heat; then pour in the egg-yogurt cheese-mixture, and stir for a few minutes until the eggs are cooked.

Eggplant Omelette
Bathinjan ma' Bayd
Syria and Lebanon

Serves 4 to 6

1 medium eggplant, peeled and diced
  into small pieces
salt
6 tablespoons olive oil

1 medium onion, finely chopped
2 cloves garlic, crushed
$\frac{1}{2}$ teaspoon pepper
5 eggs, beaten

Sprinkle the eggplant pieces with salt; then place in a strainer, top with a weight, and allow to drain for 45 minutes.

In a frying pan, heat the oil over medium heat; then add the eggplant pieces, onions, and garlic and sprinkle all with salt and pepper. Sauté and stir gently until the eggplant is cooked. (Add more oil if necessary.)

Stir in the eggs and lower the heat; then continue to sauté and stir for a few minutes until the eggs are cooked.

Vegetarian Dishes

In the historical Biblical lands, vegetarian dishes have been the food of the masses since time immemorial. For thousands of years, the peasants in these countries have been kept nourished and healthy by the consumption of meatless foods.

On the other hand, people of wealth have through the centuries disdained vegetarian dishes as the food of the lowly poor. For them, the more meat in their kitchens, the higher their prestige. Even if they envied their servants who ate tasty vegetarian dishes in the kitchen, their status as ruling classes forced them to reject the simple food of the impecunious. The tantalizing aroma rising from the simmering pots of their servants was not for their tables.

Today, this meat status impregnates Middle Eastern society. A farmer or factory worker subsists on a daily menu consisting almost entirely of fresh and dried vegetables, and some milk products. However, when a guest arrives, meat dishes are always served, even if the host can barely afford the expense. The simply-flavored, sizzling vegetable stews and other non-meat dishes, which have kept their ancestors healthy since recorded history, are not for honored guests.

In the West, vegetarianism has until recently been subjected to the myth of engendering physical weakness if not being downright unhealthy. Author and philosopher Henry David Thoreau, a vegetarian, relates in *Walden* the story of his encounter with a farmer at his work who insisted that no one could live on vegetables alone, and that meat was necessary for the making of bones. As Thoreau accompanied the farmer behind his sturdy oxen, he points out to the reader how the vegetable-made bones of the animals jerked the farmer and his heavy plow through every obstacle in the way. The myth of vegetarianism as a cause of physical debility has been disproved by generations of peasants the world over.

Algerian Vegetarian Stew
Ijwaz

Serves 6 to 8

With vegetarian dishes, amazing meals can be produced. The never-ending storehouse of Middle Eastern and North African vegetable foods make many savory feasts possible. It matters not if one lives on a diet of garden greens or red meat, these nutritious, toothsome dishes will always seduce the diner. They are worth trying, even by the uninitiated. Anyone who experiments will find that the rich heritage of Middle Eastern and North African meatless dishes is a cuisine of exciting and delicious culinary delights.

¹/₄ cup olive oil

2 medium zucchinis, unpeeled, cut into
  ³/₄ inch cubes

1 large eggplant, peeled and cut into
  ³/₄ inch cubes

2 large green peppers, chopped into
  small pieces

1 medium carrot, peeled and chopped
  into small pieces

3 medium onions, chopped

1 head garlic, peeled and crushed

salt and pepper to taste

1 can tomatoes (19 oz or 540 ml)

1 tablespoon dried basil

In a saucepan, heat the oil over low heat; then add all the ingredients except the tomatoes and basil. Cover and cook for 45 minutes; then stir in the tomatoes and cook for a further 15 minutes. Stir in the basil; then place in a serving dish and serve with cooked rice or mashed potatoes.

Bean Pottage

Syria and Lebanon

Serves 6 to 8

¹/₂ cup dried kidney beans, soaked
  overnight

6 tablespoons butter

1 cup rice, rinsed

2 cups boiling water

2 medium onions, chopped

2 cloves garlic, crushed

¹/₄ teaspoon cumin

pinch cayenne

salt and pepper to taste

Place the beans in a saucepan and cover with water; then cook for about an hour until tender but still firm. Drain and set aside.

While the beans are cooking, melt 4 tablespoons of the butter in a frying pan, then add the rice, and stirring continually, sauté over high heat for 2 minutes. Add the water and salt, and bring to a boil; then turn the heat to low and cover. Cook for 15 minutes; then turn off the heat and allow to finish cooking in its own steam for another 20 minutes.

In another frying pan, melt the remaining butter; then add the onions and garlic and sauté until they turn golden brown. In a serving bowl, place the beans, rice, the fried onions and garlic, salt, and the rest of the ingredients; then mix thoroughly and serve hot with a salad.

Bean Salad

Fool biz-Zayt

Yemen

Serves 6 to 8

2 cups dried fava beans, soaked
  overnight

¹/₄ cup olive oil

2 tablespoons *taheena* (sesame seed
  paste—see p. 18)

6 tablespoons lemon juice

salt and pepper to taste

5 eggs, hard-boiled, shelled, and chopped

¹/₂ cup finely chopped fresh coriander
  leaves (cilantro)

In a pot, cover the fava beans with water and cook for 45 minutes to an hour, until they are tender but not soft enough to break up; then place in a shallow serving dish and allow to cool.

In the meantime, in a small bowl, thoroughly mix the olive oil, *taheena*, lemon juice, salt, and pepper; then add to the beans and mix well. Add half the chopped eggs and gently toss; then serve garnished with the remaining chopped eggs and coriander leaves.

Fava Beans of Fez

Fool Fass

Morocco

Serves 4

Since the dawn of recorded history, fava beans—also known as broad, vicia, Windsor, English, dwarf or horse beans—have been grown in western Asia and North Africa. From there, through the centuries, they have spread to every corner of the globe.

There are numerous types of fava beans. The most common plant grows from two to four feet high and produces large thick pods with flat angular seeds. The size of the seeds (or beans) vary from that of a pea to over an inch long and half an inch wide.

2 cups fresh or frozen fava beans

¹/₄ cup olive oil

1 large sweet red pepper, finely chopped

4 cloves garlic, crushed

salt

1 teaspoon cumin

¹/₂ cup finely chopped fresh coriander
  leaves (cilantro)

¹/₄ teaspoon chilli powder

Place all the ingredients in a saucepan and cover with water; then cook for 10–15 minutes until the fava beans are tender.

Fava Beans in Oil

Fooliyya

Syria and Lebanon

Serves 4 to 6

The cool climate of Europe is ideal for the growing of fava beans. From Roman times to the discovery of America, fava beans were the only edible beans known to the inhabitants of that continent. In pre-Columbian Europe, this legume, which some have labeled "the bean of history," nourished all strata of society. It was only after the discovery of the New World that it was replaced by newly introduced beans from the Americas.

Why fava beans lost favor is still a mystery, as they are among the most delicious of legumes. Perhaps the long period required for growth had something to do with their replacement. Other types need a much shorter time period from seeding to harvest. To produce a good crop, fava beans must be planted very early in spring.

¹/₄ cup olive oil

3 cloves garlic, crushed

1 large onion, chopped

salt and pepper to taste

¹/₄ teaspoon allspice

¹/₄ cup finely chopped fresh coriander leaves (cilantro)

3 cups shelled fresh fava beans

3 tablespoons lemon juice

Heat the olive oil in a saucepan, then add the garlic, onion, salt, pepper, allspice and coriander and sauté over a medium heat until the onions begin to brown. Stir in the fava beans; then cover with water and cook over medium heat for approximately 30 minutes or until the beans are tender. Stir in the lemon juice and cook for a few more minutes. Serve either hot or cold.

Fava Bean Pottage

Fool Mudammas

Egypt

Serves 4

In Egypt, *fool mudammas* is the common breakfast for 90% of the Egyptians. In the early morning hours, the streets of the cities in the Nile Valley are filled with people lined up in front of vendors selling tempting *fool mudammas* from earthenware pots. Although in North America there are no vendors with pots of steaming fava beans, anyone can produce delicious *fool mudammas* with hardly any effort by following this recipe.

1 cup dried fava beans, soaked overnight
   and drained
¹/₄ cup olive oil
salt and pepper to taste
¹/₂ teaspoon ground coriander
¹/₂ teaspoon cumin

¹/₄ cup lemon juice
2 cloves garlic, crushed
4 hard-boiled eggs, shelled
2 tablespoons finely chopped fresh
   coriander leaves (cilantro)

Place the fava beans in a pot and cover with water; then cover the pot and cook over medium heat for 45 minutes to an hour until they are very tender, adding more water if necessary. Drain the beans and place in a mixing bowl; then add 2 tablespoons of the olive oil, salt, pepper, ground coriander, cumin, lemon juice, and garlic and mix well until some of the beans are slightly crushed. Transfer to 4 soup plates; then place an egg in the center of each plate. Sprinkle each plate with the remaining oil; then garnish with the coriander leaves and serve.

Fava Beans and Tomatoes

Fool ma' Tomatim

Palestine and Jordan

Serves 4 to 6

¹/₄ cup olive oil
2 medium onions, finely chopped
2 cloves garlic, crushed
2 cups fresh shelled fava beans
¹/₄ cup finely chopped fresh coriander
   leaves (cilantro)

¹/₄ teaspoon chilli powder
1 can stewed tomatoes (19 oz or 540 ml)
salt and pepper to taste

In a saucepan, heat the oil and stir-fry the onions and garlic until they begin to brown. Add the fava beans and coriander leaves; then stir-fry for a few minutes. Stir in the remaining ingredients and bring to a boil; then cover, turn the heat to low, and simmer for about 1 hour. Serve hot or cold.

Burghul with Tomatoes
Burghul bi-Banadoora
Syria and Lebanon

Serves 4 to 6

¹/₂ cup butter, melted	salt and pepper to taste
2 onions, minced	¹/₄ teaspoon cinnamon
¹/₄ cup pine nuts	¹/₄ teaspoon allspice
4 medium tomatoes, chopped	¹/₄ teaspoon ground coriander
2 cups water	1 cup coarse burghul, rinsed

Melt 3 tablespoons of the butter and sauté the onions and pine nuts until they turn light brown; then add the tomatoes and cook for 5 minutes over medium heat. Add the water, salt, pepper, cinnamon, allspice, and coriander and bring to a rolling boil; then stir in the burghul and cook covered over low heat for 20–25 minutes until the liquid is absorbed. Uncover and cook until fluffy; then spoon the remaining butter over the top and stir lightly. Serve immediately.

Cabbage Rolls in Oil
Mihshee Malfoof bi-Zayt
Syria and Lebanon

Serves 6 to 8

Stuffed vegetable leaves, such as cabbage, kohlrabi, Swiss chard, and wild grape leaves, make an excellent main course for any meal or even a banquet. The herbs and spices soaking into the rice and blending with the lemon juice and vegetables enhance and perk up their flavor. For the lovers of vegetarian foods, these stuffed leaves are among the most tasty of meatless dishes.

1 large head of cabbage	¹/₂ cup finely chopped fresh mint
1 cup rice, rinsed	1 cup olive oil
¹/₂ can chickpeas (19 oz or 540 ml), drained	salt and pepper to taste
1 medium onion, finely chopped	2 large tomatoes, finely chopped
1 small bunch scallions, finely chopped	6 cloves garlic, coarsely chopped
¹/₂ cup finely chopped parsley	²/₃ cup lemon juice
¹/₂ cup finely chopped fresh coriander leaves (cilantro)	

Core the cabbage; then place in a large pot, cover with water and boil until the leaves soften. Separate the leaves and cut out the thick stem veins. Cut the large outer leaves in half; then cover the bottom of a pot with the stem trimmings.

Mix the remaining ingredients except the garlic and lemon juice to make a filling. Place a heaping tablespoon of the filling on the bottom (stem end) of the leaf; then roll, tucking in the ends. Squeeze the rolls gently and place compactly in the pot on top of the trimmings. Sprinkle the garlic pieces between the layers.

When the leaves are all rolled and placed in the pot, pour over the lemon juice. Place an inverted dish on top of the rolls to keep them from separating; then add water to cover the rolls, and bring to a boil. Cover and cook over medium heat for 30 minutes; then turn the heat to low and simmer for 15 minutes. Serve either hot or cold as a main course or as snacks.

Note: Swiss chard and other vegetable leaves or grape leaves may be substituted for the cabbage.

Carrots with Yogurt
Jazar ma' Laban
Egypt

Serves 4 to 6

2 lbs carrots, cleaned, then cut lengthwise into quarters	4 cloves garlic, crushed
salt and pepper to taste	1½ cups yogurt
boiling water	¼ cup finely chopped fresh coriander leaves (cilantro)
¼ cup butter	1 teaspoon chilli powder

In a pot, place the carrots, salt, pepper, and enough boiling water to cover the carrots; then cover the pot and cook for 20 minutes. Remove and drain.

Melt the butter in a frying pan; then add the garlic and carrots and sauté over medium heat for 10 minutes, turning over the carrots once or twice.

Arrange the carrots on a flat serving dish; then pour the yogurt evenly over the carrots. Garnish with the coriander leaves; then sprinkle with the chilli powder and serve hot.

Chickpeas with Green Beans
Hummus ma' Loobya
Syria and Lebanon

Serves 4 to 6

¹/₄ cup olive oil
4 medium onions, chopped
1 cup chickpeas, soaked for 24 hours and split
1 lb green beans, washed, trimmed, and halved

salt and pepper to taste
¹/₂ teaspoon allspice
4 large tomatoes, chopped into small pieces

In a saucepan, heat the oil and sauté the onions over medium heat until they begin to brown; then add the chickpeas and green beans and stir-fry for 10 minutes. Add the remaining ingredients and cover with water; then cover the saucepan and cook over medium heat for about an hour or until the chickpeas are tender. Serve hot or cold.

Chickpeas with Macaroni
Tunisia

Serves 4 to 6

In availability, price, food value, versatility, and taste, chickpeas are without match when compared to other legumes. There is no better way to prove this to the uninitiated than by sampling a few dishes that make use of this tasty and nourishing legume.

2 tablespoons olive oil
2 medium onions, chopped
3 cloves garlic, crushed
¹/₄ cup finely chopped fresh coriander leaves (cilantro)
1 small hot pepper, very finely chopped
1 can stewed tomatoes (19 oz or 540 ml)

1 can chickpeas (19 oz or 540 ml), undrained
1¹/₂ cups elbow macaroni
1 cup water
salt and pepper to taste
¹/₄ teaspoon allspice
¹/₄ teaspoon cumin

In a frying pan, heat the oil; then sauté the onions and garlic over medium heat until they begin to brown. Stir in the coriander leaves and hot pepper and sauté for a further few moments; then transfer the frying pan contents to a casserole. Add the remaining ingredients and stir; then bake in a 350°F preheated oven for about an hour or until the macaroni is cooked.

Chickpeas with Tomatoes and Sweet Peppers

Libya

Serves 6 to 8

In North America, chickpeas can be found in supermarkets and in Arab, Armenian, Greek, Indian, Italian, and Spanish food stores. They are also sold under the their Italian name "ceci"; Arabic "hummus"; or Spanish "garbanzo". They are to be found in bulk, packages, or cooked in cans.

2 cups chickpeas, soaked for 24 hours; then drained and split	2 cloves garlic, crushed
$^1/_2$ cup olive oil	1 lb tomatoes, chopped into small pieces
2 medium sweet red peppers, chopped into small pieces	2 tablespoons parsley, finely chopped
1 small hot pepper, finely chopped	salt
1 large onion, chopped into small pieces	$^1/_2$ teaspoon black pepper
	$^1/_2$ teaspoon basil
	$^1/_2$ teaspoon tarragon

In a pot, cover the chickpeas with about an inch of water, then cook over medium heat for about an hour or until the chickpeas are tender. (Add more water if necessary.)

In the meantime, heat the oil in a saucepan over medium heat; then add the sweet and hot peppers, onion, and garlic. Stir-fry until all the vegetables turn limp; then stir in the remaining ingredients and cover the saucepan. Turn the heat to low and simmer for 30 minutes; then stir in the chickpeas and simmer for a further ten minutes just before serving.

Note: If a thicker stew is desired, the chickpeas can be drained after being cooked.

Cucumber and Pepper Relish

Falfal bil-Labid
Tunisia

Serves 4 to 6

2 tablespoons lemon juice	2 medium sweet red peppers, seeded and cut into 1 inch squares
2 medium cucumbers peeled, sliced in half lengthwise, and cut into 1 inch long pieces	

In a serving bowl, stir the lemon juice and salt together until the salt dissolves; then add the cucumbers and peppers and stir until they are thoroughly coated. Cover the bowl and marinate at room temperature for at least 8 hours before serving.

Note: This relish is traditionally served with couscous in Tunisia.

Dates with Rice
Arabian Peninsula

1 cup rice
2¼ cups water
salt
5 tablespoons butter, melted
½ cup blanched almonds, slivered

2 tablespoons raisins, washed
¾ cup dates, chopped
½ teaspoon cinnamon
pinch ground cloves

In a pot, cook the rice in 2 cups of the water and the salt for 10 minutes; then drain, rinse with warm water, and set aside.

In the meantime, place 2½ tablespoons of the butter in a frying pan and fry the almonds until they begin to brown; then stir in the raisins, dates, cinnamon, and cloves. Sauté for 3 minutes over low heat; then add the remaining ¼ cup of water and simmer for 20 minutes, stirring often to make sure the contents do not burn.

In a saucepan, place half of the rice and dot with 1 tablespoon of the butter; then top with the frying pan contents and cover with the remainder of the rice. Dot with the remaining 1½ tablespoons of butter, then cover with an inverted plate. Simmer over very low heat for 15 minutes; then turn off the heat and allow to cook in its own steam for a further 15 minutes.

Eggplant and Cheese Casserole
Bathinjan ma' Jiben
Syria and Lebanon

Serves 4 to 6

1 large eggplant, peeled and cut into
  ½ inch thick slices
½ cup olive oil
1 can tomatoes (19 oz or 540 ml)
¼ lb feta or other white cheese, very
  thinly sliced
½ cup finely chopped parsley
¼ cup finely chopped fresh coriander
  leaves (cilantro)

3 large eggs, beaten
1 large onion, finely chopped
salt and pepper to taste
¼ teaspoon allspice
¼ teaspoon oregano
¼ teaspoon sage

Sprinkle the eggplant pieces with salt; then place in a strainer, top with a weight, and allow to drain for 45 minutes.

In a frying pan, heat the oil; then sauté the eggplant slices over a moderately high heat until they turn golden brown. (Add more oil if necessary.) Remove the slices from the oil and place in a strainer or on paper towels to drain the excess oil.

In a casserole, place the eggplant slices; then cover evenly with the tomatoes, cheese, parsley, and coriander leaves, in that order.

In a separate bowl, beat the eggs with the onion, pepper, allspice, oregano, and sage; then pour evenly over the top. Cover the casserole and place in a 300°F preheated over for 30 minutes; then remove the cover and cook for a further 10 minutes. Serve either hot or cold.

Eggplant and Chickpea Stew
Munazalit Bathinjan
Syria and Lebanon

Serves 6 to 8

Fried, puréed, made into salads or stuffed, eggplants stimulate the appetite and make the diners smack their lips. However, they reach their epitome as ingredients in stews. Browned in olive oil or butter, then simmered in herbs and spices, they enhance the other ingredients.

1 medium eggplant, peeled and cut into
  1 inch cubes
salt
6 tablespoons olive oil
1 large onion, finely chopped
3 cloves garlic, crushed
1 can chickpeas (19 oz or 540 ml),
  undrained

2 zucchinis (about 5 inches long), cut
  into 1 inch cubes
1 can tomatoes (19 oz or 540 ml)
3 tablespoons finely chopped fresh
  coriander leaves (cilantro)
¹/₄ teaspoon pepper
¹/₄ teaspoon nutmeg

Sprinkle the eggplant cubes with salt; then place in a strainer, top with a weight, and allow to drain for 45 minutes.

Heat the oil in a saucepan and sauté the eggplant cubes over moderately high heat until they begin to brown. (Add more oil if necessary.) Add the onion and garlic and sauté for a further few minutes; then stir in the chickpeas with their liquid, the zucchini cubes, tomatoes, coriander, pepper, and nutmeg, and bring to a boil. Cover the saucepan and turn the heat to low; then simmer for 30 minutes. (If not juicy enough, add more water.) Serve either hot or cold.

Eggplant in Oil
Bathinjan bi-Zayt
Palestine and Jordan

Serves 4 to 6

salt

2 medium eggplants, peeled and cut into ¹/₂ inch thick slices

³/₄ cup olive oil

4 large onions, cut into ¹/₄ inch thick slices

3 cloves garlic, crushed

¹/₄ cup finely chopped fresh coriander leaves (cilantro)

5 medium tomatoes, cut into ¹/₂ inch thick slices

¹/₂ teaspoon pepper

¹/₄ teaspoon allspice

¹/₄ teaspoon tarragon

1 cup water

Sprinkle salt on the eggplant slices; then place in a strainer and allow to drain for 45 minutes.

In a frying pan, heat the oil; then add the onions, garlic, and coriander and sauté until the onions begin to brown. Remove the onions with a slotted spoon and place at the bottom of a casserole; then sauté the eggplant slices in the oil until they turn soft. Add more oil if necessary.

Remove the eggplant slices from the oil and allow to drain; then place the eggplant and tomato slices in alternate layers on top of the onions. Sprinkle with the pepper, allspice, tarragon, and salt. Pour in the water, then place in a 350°F preheated oven and bake for 30 minutes. Serve from the casserole either hot or cold with rice or *orzo* (rice-shaped pasta).

Egyptian Falafel
Ta'amia
Egypt

Makes about 40 patties

This tasty vegetarian delight is the "hamburger" of the Middle East. The simplest way to make it is to purchase the falafel or *ta'amia* powder, ready-made, in stores selling Arabic or Middle Eastern foods.

Although ready-made falafel is simple to prepare, it is not as tasty as that made from scratch. This recipe, common in Egypt, is how true falafel or *ta'amia* is made.

4 cups dried fava beans, soaked overnight and drained	2 teaspoons cumin
	salt
3 large onions, chopped into large pieces	1 teaspoon pepper
1 head of garlic, peeled	1 teaspoon baking soda
1 large bunch of parsley, washed and stems removed	1 teaspoon baking powder
	oil for frying
2 hot green peppers, seeds removed	

Mix the fava beans, onions, garlic, parsley, and hot pepper; then put through a food processor and process until the beans are finely ground. Add the cumin, salt, pepper, baking soda, and baking powder and process for a further minute; then remove from the processor and form into patties.

In a deep fryer or saucepan, heat the oil; then fry the patties, turning them over once or twice, until they are golden brown and crisp on the outside. Serve the patties as sandwiches in $^1/_2$ rounds of Arabic (pita) bread in a bed of tossed salad, or as an entrée with a tossed salad.

Falafel

Syria and Lebanon

Makes 20 patties

1 cup fava beans, soaked overnight and drained	1 teaspoon ground coriander
	$^1/_4$ teaspoon chilli powder
1 cup chickpeas, soaked overnight and drained	2 teaspoons salt
	1 teaspoon pepper
3 medium onions, chopped	1 teaspoon baking soda
4 cloves garlic, crushed	oil for frying
1 teaspoon cumin	

Mix the fava beans, chickpeas, and onions; then put through a food processor or meat grinder, more than once if necessary. The beans and chickpeas must be finely ground. Add the remaining ingredients except the oil and mix well; then form into patties.

Heat the oil in a frying pan; then fry the patties over a medium heat, turning over, until they turn golden brown. Serve the patties warm as a main dish with fresh vegetables or as sandwiches in $^1/_2$ rounds of Arabic (pita) bread.

Fez Carrots
Jazar Fass
Morocco

Serves 4 to 6

In North Africa, fruit is sometimes included in vegetable and meat dishes to add an exotic flavor. This utilization of fruit is not common in the culinary art of the Arab East, but is unique to North Africa.

4 tablespoons butter
1 lb carrots, peeled and sliced into
    ¹/₂ inch thick rounds
2 medium onions, thinly sliced
¹/₂ teaspoon nutmeg

salt
¹/₄ cup white grape juice
¹/₄ cup seedless raisins, soaked in water
    for 30 minutes and drained
1 tablespoon sugar

Melt the butter in a frying pan; then add the carrots and sauté for 5 minutes over medium heat. Turn the heat to low and add the onions, nutmeg, salt, and grape juice; then cover the frying pan and simmer, stirring occasionally, until the carrots are tender. Stir in the raisins and sugar; then cook for a few minutes and serve.

Fried Cucumbers
Khiyar Maqlee
Syria and Lebanon

Serves 4

1 large cucumber, peeled and cut into
    ¹/₂ inch rounds
salt and pepper to taste
¹/₂ cup flour

¹/₄ teaspoon garlic salt
³/₄ cup olive or vegetable oil
¹/₂ cup scallions, finely chopped

Sprinkle both sides of the cucumber rounds with the salt, then allow to stand in a strainer for 30 minutes to drain the water.

Mix the flour, pepper, and garlic salt; then roll the cucumber rounds in the seasoned flour. Heat the oil and fry the cucumber rounds until they turn evenly brown; then place in a serving dish and sprinkle with the chopped onions.

Fried Eggplant
Bathinjan Maqlee
Syria and Lebanon

Serves 4 to 6

1 large eggplant, unpeeled, sliced into
   ³/₄ inch slices
½ teaspoon garlic powder
¼ teaspoon ground coriander

½ cup olive oil
2 tablespoons lemon juice
salt and pepper to taste

    Sprinkle the eggplant pieces with the salt and place in a strainer, top with a weight, and allow to drain for 45 minutes. Mix the garlic powder, coriander, and pepper: then sprinkle this mixture on the eggplant slices. In a frying pan, heat the oil; then over moderately high heat fry the eggplant slices on both sides until they are evenly browned. Place on a serving dish; then sprinkle with the lemon juice and serve hot or cold as a side dish.

Note: Eggplant cooked this way also makes an excellent sandwich with Arabic (pita) bread.

Fried Eggplant Palestinian style
Bathinjan Maqlee Falasteeni
Palestine and Jordan

Serves 4

1 large eggplant, peeled and cut into
   ½ inch slices
salt
1 cup cooking oil

2 cloves garlic, crushed
1 hot green pepper, very finely chopped
2 tablespoons lemon juice
6 tablespoons finely chopped parsley

    Sprinkle both sides of the eggplant slices with salt; then place in a bowl and cover with water. Leave to soak for 15 minutes; then remove the eggplant slices from the water and allow to dry on paper towels.

    Heat the oil in a frying pan and fry the eggplant slices, turning them over until they brown on both sides; then place on a serving platter and set aside.

    Make a sauce by mixing the remaining ingredients, except the parsley. Pour the sauce over the eggplant slices, making sure it is divided evenly over each piece. Garnish with the parsley and serve.

Fried Eggplant with Yogurt Sauce
Bathinjan Maqlee bi-Laban
Palestine and Jordan

Serves 4

Arab yogurt and vegetable dishes are as old as time itself. Every town and city has its own versions and the number of these recipes is endless. The vegetable and seasoning ingredients may be interchanged with others or omitted to suit the diner's taste. No matter what changes are made, the yogurt always makes them appetizing.

1 large eggplant, peeled, then quartered lengthwise, and cut into ¹/₂ inch thick slices
salt
¹/₂ cup olive oil
1¹/₂ cups yogurt

1 clove garlic, crushed
2 tablespoons very finely chopped fresh coriander leaves (cilantro)
¹/₂ teaspoon pepper
pinch cayenne

Sprinkle the eggplant slices with salt; then place in a strainer, top with a weight, and allow to drain for 45 minutes.

Heat the oil in a frying pan; then sauté the eggplant slices over medium heat, turning them over, until they brown (Add more oil if necessary.) Place the eggplant slices on paper towels and allow to drain; then arrange them on a serving dish and set aside to cool.

Make a sauce by thoroughly mixing the yogurt, garlic, coriander leaves, pepper, cayenne, and salt. Spoon the sauce over the eggplant slices, or serve separately.

Fried Tomatoes with Garlic
Banadoora Maqliya ma' Thoom
Palestine and Jordan

Serves 4

4 cloves garlic, crushed
salt and pepper to taste
¹/₂ small hot pepper, very finely chopped

2 tablespoons chopped fresh parsley
2 tablespoons oil
2 large, firm tomatoes, thickly sliced

Thoroughly mix the garlic with the pepper, salt, and hot pepper; then stir in the parsley and set aside. Heat the oil in a frying pan over medium heat. Add the tomato slices and cook for about a minute on one side; then turn and sprinkle slices with the garlic, hot pepper, and parsley mixture. Continue to cook for another minute, shaking the pan occasionally; then turn the slices again and cook until they are done, but not mushy. Slide the tomato slices onto a plate, and serve immediately.

Note: Do not try to cook more than two servings at a time or the tomatoes will end up overcooked. This type of tomato appetizer is great scooped up onto Arabic bread.

Chickpea and Burghul Patties
Kibbet Hummus
Syria and Lebanon

Makes about 60 small patties

The vegetarians of affluent North American society are always searching for a new dish to add variety to their meals. One day, they will discover kibbeh with chickpeas; and when they do, it will surely become a favorite.

1 can chickpeas (19 oz or 540 ml), drained	1 teaspoon baking powder
1 cup burghul soaked for 5 minutes in boiling water, then drained by squeezing out the water in a strainer	1 teaspoon baking soda $1/2$ teaspoon cumin $1/2$ teaspoon allspice
2 medium onions chopped	pinch cayenne
4 cloves garlic, crushed	salt and pepper to taste
$1/4$ cup finely chopped fresh coriander leaves (cilantro)	1 cup flour oil for frying

In a food processor, place all the ingredients except the flour and oil and process until all the ingredients are thoroughly ground. Transfer into a mixing bowl.

Add the flour and mix thoroughly; then form into walnut size balls. (If the batter is too sticky, add more flour.) Flatten into patties, about $1/4$ inch thick.

In a frying pan or saucepan, heat oil about $1/2$ inch deep. Fry the patties over medium high heat until they turn a golden brown, turning them over once (about 10 minutes on each side). Remove and place on paper towels to drain; then serve either hot or cold. (They reheat well on foil plates in the oven.)

Note: To make *kibbet adas*, 1 can of lentils (19 oz or 540 ml) may be substituted for the chickpeas.

Pumpkin Kibbeh
Kibbet Lakteen
Syria and Lebanon

Makes about 12 patties

When Hallowe'en is over and the North American farmers are left with thousands of unsold pumpkins, how happy they would feel if they knew that everyone was waiting to make kibbeh with pumpkin.

This recipe is best made with fresh pumpkin because canned pumpkin tends to have too much liquid. If you use fresh pumpkin, remove the seeds and rind; then cut into small pieces and bake in the oven to give you 2 cups of baked, mashed pumpkin. It may also be steamed.

2 cups of baked, mashed pumpkin	$^1/_4$ teaspoon cumin
1 cup fine burghul soaked for 10 minutes in boiling water and drained	pinch cayenne
	1 medium onion, finely chopped
salt to taste	4 cloves garlic, crushed
$^1/_2$ teaspoon black pepper	1 cup flour
$^1/_2$ teaspoon ground coriander	$^1/_2$ cup water
$^1/_4$ teaspoon ground allspice	oil for frying

Place all the ingredients, except the oil, in a food processor and process into a dough which should stick together when squeezed.

Form into small balls the size of golf balls. (If the mixture is too soft, add more flour.) Flatten these balls into patties; then set aside.

In a saucepan, heat oil to a depth of $^1/_2$ inch. Fry until the patties turn golden brown, turning them over once. Drain on paper towels, and keep warm until ready to serve.

Note: An alternate way of making this dish is to place the mixture in an oiled 9 inch square baking pan; then pat down and with a wet knife cut into 1$^1/_2$ inch to 2 inch squares. Spread a little oil over the top and bake in a 400°F preheated oven until golden brown; then put the individual pieces on a platter and serve.

Leek Pies

Fatayar Kurath
Syria and Lebanon

Makes 15 to 20 pies

1 bunch leeks (3 or 4)	¹/₂ cup lemon juice
6 medium onions, peeled and chopped	¹/₄ cup oil
3 teaspoons sumac (see p. 6)	1 quantity basic dough recipe (see
salt and pepper to taste	p. 11)

Cut off the root hairs of the leeks, and any part of the green leaf stalks that looks damaged or brown; then cut crosswise into ¹/₂ inch pieces. Wash thoroughly two or three times, ensuring the removal of all the sand and grit; then drain.

In a large bowl, place the leeks, onions, sumac, salt, pepper, lemon juice, and oil and set aside for about 30 minutes.

In the meantime, divide the dough into 15 or 20 spheres the size of golf balls. Allow to rest for 15 minutes; then roll out into 5 inch rounds.

Stir the filling well; then place spoonfuls of the mixture, including some of the juice, on the dough rounds, pinching over the circumference to make a cover. Seam along the middle line to close (see illustration below).

Place one by one on a greased baking pan; then bake in a 400°F preheated oven for 30 minutes or until the dough is cooked and slightly brown on the bottom and raised edges.

Lentils and Noodles
Rishta
Syria and Lebanon

Serves 4

1 cup lentils, rinsed

5 cups water

2 tablespoons butter

2 medium onions, chopped

2 tablespoons finely chopped coriander
   leaves (cilantro)

2 cloves garlic, crushed

4 oz fine egg noodles

salt and pepper to taste

pinch cayenne

2 tablespoons lemon juice

Place the lentils in a pot and cover with the water; bring to a boil and cook over medium heat for about 25 minutes, or until the lentils are tender, but not mushy.

In the meantime, melt the butter in a frying pan; then add the onions, coriander, and garlic and sauté until the onions are golden brown. Stir the contents of the frying pan into the lentils, then add the salt, pepper, and cayenne and bring to a boil. Lower the heat and simmer for about 10 minutes or until the noodles are tender. Add the lemon juice; then serve hot with a tossed salad.

Lentil Pottage
Mujaddara
Syria and Lebanon

Serves 4 to 6

In the Eastern Arab world, the most common dish made from lentils is "*mujaddara*," a pottage which has been popular since Biblical times. According to tradition, *mujaddara* is the mess of pottage referred to in the Biblical account of Esau's great hunger: for a dish of this pottage, he sold his birthright as the first born to his twin brother Jacob. Perhaps this Biblical story gave birth to an ancient saying, "A hungry man would be willing to sell his soul for a dish of *mujaddara*." The pottage in the Bible was probably made with red lentils, but other types of lentils can be used for this dish.

When the Arab immigrants came to North America, they not only brought with then their love for *mujaddara* but also their custom of not serving it to guests. Perhaps the few cents it costs to make this dish made the immigrants think that it could not possibly be good enough to serve to visitors. It is.

1 cup lentils, rinsed
5 cups water
6 tablespoons olive or vegetable oil
2 large onions, chopped

¼ cup rice or burghul, rinsed
salt and pepper to taste
½ teaspoon cumin

In a saucepan, bring the lentils and water to a boil; then cover and cook over medium heat for 30 minutes. In the meantime, heat the oil in a frying pan; then add the onions and sauté until they turn golden brown. Add the onions and their oil and the remaining ingredients to the lentils; then cook for a further 20 minutes or until the lentils and rice or burghul are tender but still slightly firm. Remove from the heat then serve.

Note: If this recipe is prepared as a main course, it will only serve 4. As a side dish, it will serve 4 to 6 as indicated.

Molokhia Vegetable Stew

Serves 4 to 6

Molokhia was said to have been the favorite food of the ancient Egyptians, and the taste for this vegetable has never left that historic land. Today, in Egypt, it continues to be the preferred food of the rich and the poor alike. Almost every housewife of whatever social stratum in society prepares molokhia regularly. The rich cook it with meat and the poor with vegetables. The plant is so much in demand that nearly every farmer grows a little patch for his or her own use or for sale.

1 large potato, peeled and chopped into large chunks
1 medium carrot, scraped clean and chopped into small pieces
1 small yellow turnip, peeled and chopped into small pieces
1 medium zucchini, chopped into large pieces
3 large tomatoes, chopped into large pieces
2 medium onions, chopped into small pieces

½ teaspoon cumin
pinch allspice
8 cups water
salt and pepper to taste
½ lb fresh molokhia leaves, very finely chopped or 1 cup dried and finely crushed molokhia
4 tablespoons butter
½ head garlic, crushed
½ cup finely chopped fresh coriander leaves (cilantro)
pinch cayenne

Place the potato, carrot, turnip, zucchini, tomatoes, onions, salt, pepper, cumin, allspice, and water in a pot. Cover and cook over medium heat until the water begins to boil; then lower the heat and simmer for about 30 minutes, until the vegetables are tender but still intact. Remove the vegetables with a slotted spoon, place on a serving dish, and keep warm.

Add the *molokhia* to the stock; then cover and simmer for 20 minutes; stirring occasionally. In the meantime, melt the butter in a frying pan; then add the garlic, coriander, and cayenne and fry until the garlic turns golden brown. Add the garlic mixture to the stock and simmer for a few moments, stiring occasionally.

Adjust the seasoning; then serve hot with vegetables and plain rice.

Potato Croquettes
'Ajijat
Algeria

Serves 4 to 6

With a hundred and thirty years of French occupation, French influence entered the Algerian kitchen, but this influence has not been all-pervasive. Algerian cuisine was and still is highly seasoned. If any dishes were borrowed from France, spices and herbs were added to make them fit the Algerian taste. Potato croquettes are one example of a dish borrowed from France but flavored by an Algerian touch.

6 medium potatoes	$^1/_2$ teaspoon nutmeg
6 eggs	$^1/_2$ teaspoon pepper
1 large onion, finely chopped	pinch dried sage
1 bunch fresh parsley, finely chopped	1 cup flour
6 scallions, finely chopped	oil for frying
1 tablespoon finely chopped mint leaves	salt to taste
1 teaspoon cinnamon	

Wash and boil the potatoes; then peel and mash. Add two of the eggs, the parsley, scallions, mint, cinnamon, salt, nutmeg, pepper, and sage and mix thoroughly.

In a shallow bowl, beat the remaining eggs and set aside; then place the flour on a flat plate and set aside.

Form the potato mixture into golf-ball sized spheres, dip them into the beaten eggs and roll them in the flour. Flatten them into patties. Place on a floured tray. Fry the patties in hot oil till golden, turning once. Remove with a slotted spoon onto a large platter lined with paper towel, and drain. Serve hot.

Rice with Orzo
Rizz bish-Shi'ariyya
Syria and Lebanon

Serves 4

5 tablespoons butter	2 cups boiling water
$1/_4$ cup orzo	salt
1 cup rice, rinsed	

Melt 4 tablespoons of the butter in a frying pan; then add the orzo and, stirring continually, sauté until brown. Add the rice and sauté for a further few minutes, stirring all the time. Add the water and salt and bring to a boil; then turn the heat to medium and cover. Cook for 15 minutes; then turn off the heat and allow to finish cooking in its own steam for 20 minutes. Stir in the remaining butter, then serve hot.

Spinach Pies
Fatayar bi-Sabanakh
Syria and Lebanon

Makes 24 pies

Sumac, with its lemony flavor, is a favorite spice of the Middle Eastern housewife. As a seasoning, it lends a tart taste to chicken, salads, curries, sauces, and stuffings. In the eastern Arab countries and adjoining lands, it is also employed extensively with onions and salt as a savory spice for roasts. Arab gourmet cooks say there is no substitute for this tangy condiment.

2 lbs frozen pizza dough, thawed, or equivalent amount of home-made bread dough	$1/_4$ cup pine nuts
	4 tablespoons sumac (available in Middle Eastern specialty stores)
1 bunch of spinach, thoroughly washed and finely chopped	1 tablespoon lemon juice
3 medium onions, chopped into small pieces	5 tablespoons olive oil
	salt and pepper to taste

Make the dough into 24 balls; then cover with a damp cloth and allow to stand for 2 hours in a warm place.

In the meantime, make the filling by mixing the remaining ingredients, except 3 tablespoons of the olive oil.

Flatten the dough into 5 inch circles, $1/_4$ inch thick; then place 1 heaping tablespoon of the filling on each circle. Fold the edges to form triangles (see illustration, p. 203); close by firmly pinching the edges together. Place on a well-greased baking tray and brush heavily with the remaining olive oil.

Bake in a 400°F preheated oven for about 20 minutes or until the pies turn light brown; then serve hot for lunch or snacks.

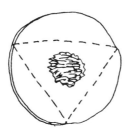

Stuffed Grape Leaves with Lentils
Mihshee Waraq 'Inab ma' 'Adas
Syria and Lebanon

Serves 6 to 8

In the eastern Arab world, grape leaves are stuffed with various combinations—rice and meat, rice and onions, rice and lentils. The latter two, of which this recipe is one, are excellent vegetarian dishes.

$^3/_4$ cup brown or green lentils	$^1/_2$ teaspoon allspice
$^1/_2$ cup oil	salt and pepper to taste
$^1/_4$ cup lemon juice	1 teaspoon cumin
$^3/_4$ cup rice, rinsed and drained	1 lb canned or bottled grape leaves,
1 cup finely chopped fresh mint, or	thoroughly washed and drained
3 tablespoons dried mint	$1^1/_2$ cups tomato juice
1 bunch scallions, finely chopped	water

Place the lentils in a pot and cover with water; then half cook (about 15 minutes) and drain. Make the stuffing by mixing the lentils, $^1/_4$ cup of the oil, half the lemon juice, the rice, mint, onions, allspice, salt, pepper, and cumin.

Place about 1 heaping tablespoon of the stuffing on each grape leaf and roll, making sure to tuck in the ends while rolling.

In the bottom of the pot, place a few of the grape leaves; then arrange the rolled grape leaves in layers. Pour the tomato juice, the remaining oil and lemon juice over the rolls, then insert an inverted plate over the top. Pour in enough water to cover the plate; then bring to a boil. Reduce the heat and simmer over low heat until the rice inside the rolls is tender but still intact.

Note: This dish may be served hot or cold.

Tomatoes Stuffed with Chickpeas

Palestine and Jordan

Serves 6

12 medium tomatoes, ripe but slightly
  firm
¹/₄ cup olive oil
2 medium onions, chopped
4 cloves garlic, crushed
¹/₄ cup pine nuts (or slivered almonds)
¹/₂ cup finely chopped fresh coriander
  leaves (cilantro)

1 can chickpeas (19 oz or 540 ml),
  drained
salt to taste
1 teaspoon pepper
¹/₂ teaspoon allspice
¹/₂ teaspoon cumin
pinch cayenne
2 tablespoons butter

Cut off the tomato tops; then scoop out the pulp with a spoon. Reserve both the cut tops and the pulp.

In a frying pan, heat the oil and sauté the onions and garlic until they begin to brown; then add the pine nuts or slivered almonds and coriander leaves and stir-fry for 5 minutes. Remove from the heat and stir in the remaining ingredients except the salt and ¹/₂ teaspoon of the pepper; then fill the tomatoes with this mixture and replace the tops.

Place the tomatoes side by side in a casserole; then mix the tomato pulp with the salt and remaining pepper and pour in between the tomatoes. Place a little of the butter on each of the tomatoes; then bake in a 350°F preheated oven for 30 minutes or until the tomatoes are cooked. Serve hot with some of the juice spooned on top.

Note: Excellent served with mashed potatoes or cooked rice.

Yogurt with Chickpeas

Laban ma' Hummus
Palestine and Jordan

Serves 4

1 can chickpeas (19 oz or 540 ml),
  undrained
1 clove garlic, crushed
salt and pepper to taste

2¹/₂ cups yogurt
2 cups croutons or pieces of well-
  toasted pita bread
2 tablespoons butter, melted

Place the chickpeas and their liquid in a pot and bring to a boil.

In the meantime, thoroughly mix the garlic, salt, pepper, and yogurt. Place in a serving bowl. Pour in the boiling chickpeas and stir; then spread the croutons or toasted bread over the top. Sprinkle with the melted butter and serve immediately.

Note: Makes an excellent breakfast dish.

Yogurt Pies
Fatayar bi-Laban
Palestine and Jordan

Makes 12 large pies

2 cups flour
³/₄ teaspoon salt
²/₃ cup lukewarm water
1¼ oz package yeast, dissolved in
   ¼ cup of lukewarm water
2 tablespoons butter, melted

1 egg, beaten
2 cups yogurt spread (*labana*—see p. 17)
2 medium onions, finely chopped
¹/₂ cup finely chopped fresh coriander
   leaves (cilantro)
¹/₄ teaspoon pepper

Make a dough by mixing the flour, ¹/₄ teaspoon of the salt, the water, yeast, butter, and egg; then knead well; cover and allow to rest for an hour.

In the meantime, make a filling by mixing thoroughly the remaining ¹/₂ teaspoon of salt, the yogurt spread, onions, coriander leaves, and pepper.

Cut the dough into 12 pieces and roll into balls, then allow to rest for 15 minutes. Roll each ball into 5 to 6 inch rounds; then divide the filling into 12 parts and place on the rounds.

Close each round firmly by pinching the edges together into triangles (see illustration for spinach pies, p. 203); then place on a well-greased baking tray.

Bake in a 400°F preheated oven for about 15 minutes or until the pies brown. Remove from the oven, brush the top of the pies with butter, and serve.

Za'tar Pies
Mana'eesh
Syria and Lebanon

1 lb frozen pizza dough, thawed, or the
   equivalent amount of home-made
   dough

6 tablespoons *za'tar* (see p. 15)
¹/₂ cup olive oil

Form the dough into 2 inch diameter balls; then cover with a damp cloth and allow to stand for one hour. In the meantime, mix the *za'tar* and oil; then set aside. Flatten the dough into ¹/₄ inch thick rounds and place on a well-greased cookie tray; then spread 1 or 2 tablespoons of the *za'tar* oil mixture evenly with the fingers over the top of each round. Bake in a 350°F preheated oven for 20 minutes or until the edges are well browned.

Zucchini Stew
Munazalit Koosa
Syria and Lebanon

Serves 4

In all the Arab countries, olive oil has been, through the centuries, the most commonly used medium of cooking. Although the cheaper vegetable oils have in our modern age made inroads into the lands of olive oil, olive oil is still the most important ingredient used to cook a daily meal. Once people are used to the taste of olive oil, rarely will another type of oil satisfy them.

2 medium onions, chopped	salt
3 cloves of garlic, crushed	$^1/_2$ teaspoon pepper
$^1/_2$ cup olive oil	pinch dried basil
2 large zucchini, finely chopped	2 eggs
3 medium tomatoes, finely chopped	

In a frying pan, sauté the onions and garlic in the oil until the onions turn golden brown; then add the zucchini and sauté for a few minutes. Stir in tomatoes and seasoning and simmer for 10 minutes over medium heat; then add the eggs and stir-fry for a few more minutes and serve.

Pastries and Sweets

I n the homes of the rich and the middle classes in the Arab world, no table of any self-respecting host would be without trays of pastries. They are served in the Middle East with tiny cups of piping-hot, strong Arab coffee, and in North Africa with refreshing mint tea. The ideal setting for serving the pastries is in attractive surroundings. A Western writer, describing a scene where Moroccan sweets were being served, wrote:

> The guests were resting on low sofas, surrounded by rich colorful cushions in a Moorish-Andalusian style room filled with the aroma of delicate perfume. Sweet mint tea with Moroccan pastries was being served. The tea was poured into silver decorated glasses while the sweets were passed around on shining, inlaid silver trays. Making the rounds, serving the guests, were beautiful maidens in fascinating Arab dress.

His picturesque description could well have been a panorama from the *Thousand and One Nights*.

Arab pastries are very different from the cakes and pies of the Western world. In the majority of cases, they are paper-thin layered pastries filled with nuts, spices, and butter, then soaked in *qater*, a syrup of sugar or honey. Their delectable, sweet taste has inspired poets and men of letters through the centuries. Poems have been composed, songs have been sung and legends born wherever these marvelously delicate pastries have been served. A poet once said: "With our exquisite and luscious sweets, can the beauty of any woman compare?"

Another wrote: "To eat the pastries of the Arabs is to make a person's life serene and happy and keep away evil."

Almond and Sesame Seed Pastry
Samsa
Tunisia

1½ cups almonds, blanched	1 package (1 lb or 454 grams)
1½ cups white sesame seeds	baklawa dough (use filo dough)
1½ cups clarified butter	1 quantity *qater* syrup (see recipe, p. 14)

Preheat the oven to 350°F; then spread the almonds and sesame seeds evenly on a large shallow pan and bake them until they are light brown, stirring them occasionally so that they brown evenly. Pulverize the browned almonds and sesame seeds in a blender; then set aside.

In a well-buttered 10 inch by 15 inch baking pan, place 1 sheet of baklawa dough; then brush with butter. Repeat the procedure until ⅓ of the dough is used.

Spread ½ of the almond and sesame seed mixture on the baklawa dough;

then add another $^1/_3$ of the dough, sheet by sheet, buttering them as before. Spread the remaining almond and sesame seed mixture on the dough; then cover with the remaining $^1/_3$ of the dough, buttering sheet by sheet as before.

Brush the top with the remaining butter; then with a sharp knife carefully cut into squares or diamond shapes. Bake in a preheated oven of 400°F for 5 minutes; then lower the heat to 300°F and bake for approximately 30 minutes, or until the sides are a light shade of brown.

While the *samsa* is baking, prepare the syrup. Before removing the *samsa* from the oven, place under the broiler for a few moments, turning the tray around until the top is evenly golden brown; then remove from the oven. Pour the syrup evenly over the top of the hot *samsa*; then allow to cool before serving.

Arabian Shortbread
Ghurayba
Syria and Lebanon

Makes 40 pieces

Arab children look forward to this delicious shortbread made by their mothers in the family kitchen.

1$^1/_2$ cups butter	1 egg yolk
1$^3/_4$ cups confectioner's sugar	3 cups flour
1 teaspoon orange blossom water (*mazahar*)	40 blanched almonds

Place the butter, 1$^1/_2$ cups of the confectioner's sugar, the orange blossom water, and egg yolk in a blender; then blend for 1 minute. Transfer to a mixing bowl; then gradually add the flour while mixing with the fingers, until a smooth dough is formed. Form the dough into balls a little smaller than a walnut; then place on an ungreased cookie sheet and flatten slightly to about $^1/_2$ inch thickness. Press an almond on each piece; then bake in a 300°F preheated oven for 20 minutes or until the bottoms turn light brown. Remove from the oven and allow to cool; then sprinkle with the remaining confectioner's sugar.

Note: The *ghurayba* may feel soft at the end of baking time, but they will harden as they cool.

Baklawa

Syria and Lebanon

Makes 35 to 40 pieces

In the banquets of the rich during past ages, Arab pastries reached their height of magnificence. At any of these feasts, baklawa, the king of Arab pastry, was always to be found. Made from a paper-thin dough, known in the West as strudel or phyllo (also spelled filo) dough, it has stood the test of centuries. Its dough, with the shredded version known as *knafa*, forms the bases of the many varieties of syrup-soaked sweets to be found on the tables of these ancient lands.

In the Arab East, it used to be said that no young lady would make a good wife unless she knew how to make baklawa dough. Fortunately today, not only in the Arab world, but also throughout the Western world, the dough is prepared commercially and young ladies are spared this ordeal of proving their suitability for marriage. With the commercially produced dough, anyone can easily make baklawa.

2 cups walnuts, chopped	1 tablespoon orange blossom
1 cup sugar	water (*mazahar*)
2 cups clarified butter, melted	1 package baklawa (filo) dough
(see note below)	(1 lb or 454 grams)
2 teaspoons cinnamon	1 quantity *qater* (syrup — see p.14)

Mix the walnuts, sugar, $^1/_4$ cup of the butter, the cinnamon, and orange blossom water; then set aside.

Butter well a 10 inch by 15 inch baking pan; then set aside.

Remove the dough from the package and spread out on a towel. Be careful to cover the unused dough with a damp towel or cling wrap to prevent it from drying out as you work. Take one sheet and place in the baking pan; then brush with butter. Keep repeating the procedure until one-half of the package is used. Place the walnut mixture over the buttered layers and spread evenly.

Take one layer of dough and spread over the walnut mixture and brush with butter; then continue this procedure until the rest of the dough is used.

Heat the remaining butter; then pour evenly over the dough. With a sharp knife, carefully cut into approximately 2 inch square or diamond shapes. Bake in a preheated oven of 400°F for 5 minutes; then lower the heat to 300°F and bake from 30–45 minutes or until the sides are a light shade of brown.

While the baklawa is baking, prepare the syrup, then set aside.

When the sides of the baklawa are lightly brown, place under the broiler and turn the pan around until the top of the baklawa is evenly golden brown. Remove from the broiler and allow to cool for 15 minutes; then spread the syrup with a spoon over each square or diamond. Allow to cool before serving.

Note: To make clarified butter, melt the butter in a pot over a low-medium heat; then raise the heat until the butter boils and becomes foamy. Skim the foam from the surface; then set aside for 15 minutes. Pour the now clarified butter into a jar, but be careful to omit the salty residue at the bottom.

Barley Pudding with Oranges and Cinnamon

Kurdistan

Serves 4

$1/2$ cup barley, washed	2 eggs, separated
4 cups milk	grated rind of 1 orange
$1/4$ teaspoon salt	1 orange, separated into segments
$1/2$ cup brown sugar	1 teaspoon cinnamon
$1/3$ cup butter	$1/4$ cup confectioner's sugar

In a saucepan, cover the barley with cold water and bring to a boil; then cook over medium heat for 20 minutes. Add the milk, salt, brown sugar, and butter; then bring to a boil, stirring until the sugar is dissolved. Lower the heat and simmer for about $1^1/4$ hours; then remove from the heat and cool slightly.

Beat the egg yolks until thick and creamy in appearance; then add the orange rind and stir into the cooled barley mixture.

Beat the egg whites until stiff and fold gently into the barley mixture. Pour into a well-buttered baking dish; then decorate with the orange segments and sprinkle the cinnamon over the top. Bake in a 350°F oven for about 30 minutes. Sprinkle with the confectioner's sugar; then serve hot.

Browned Flour Almond Dessert

Salloo

Morocco

Serves 4 to 6

2 cups flour	$1/4$ cup confectioner's sugar
$1/4$ cup cooking oil	$1/2$ teaspoon aniseed
$1/2$ cup blanched almonds	3 tablespoons butter
1 cup sesame seeds, toasted	$1/2$ tablespoon cinnamon

Place the flour in a frying pan and toast over a medium heat, continually stirring until the flour turns light golden brown. Set aside.

Heat the cooking oil in another frying pan, then add the almonds and fry until golden brown. Take out 2 tablespoons of the almonds and set aside.

Mix the sesame seeds, the rest of the almonds, 2 tablespoons of the sugar, and the aniseed; then grind to fine powder. Melt the butter; then mix with the almond-sesame seed mixture, the flour, and the cinnamon.

Place this mixture on a round plate and form into a dome; then sprinkle the remainder of the sugar evenly over the dome and decorate with the remainder of the almonds.

Candied Eggplants
Bathinjan Ma'akid
Syria and Lebanon

1 dozen tiny eggplants about 3 inches long, washed and stemmed	¹/₂ teaspoon whole cloves
2 cups sugar	2 teaspoons orange blossom water (*mazahar*)
2¹/₂ cups water	3 tablespoons lemon juice

Place the eggplants in a pot and cover with water; then bring to a boil. Cook for 3 to 5 minutes over medium heat; then remove and drain in a strainer.

In the meantime, place the sugar, water, and cloves in a pot; then, stirring all the time, boil over medium heat until the sugar melts. Add the eggplants; then cook for 20 minutes over low heat. Stir in the orange blossom water and lemon juice, and cook for a further 5 minutes; then remove and allow to cool. Serve with or without the syrup.

Coconut Squares

Morocco

A kind of coconut divinity or fudge.

2 cups grated coconut	3 tablespoons butter
³/₄ cup half and half	3 tablespoons lemon rind
1¹/₂ cups sugar	

Place the coconut, half and half, and sugar in a saucepan, and bring to a boil; then turn the heat to low and simmer until a soft ball is formed when a teaspoonful is dropped into cold water. Add the butter and lemon rind and mix; then allow to cool to room temperature. Place in an electric mixer and mix until thick and glossy. Pour into a small buttered pan and chill; then cut into squares and serve.

Croissants

Tisharaq al-Aryan

Algeria

3 egg yolks
1 cup milk
4 cups flour
1¹/₂ cup sugar
4 teaspoons baking powder
shredded peel of 2 oranges (zest)
shredded peel of 2 lemons (zest)
¹/₂ cup clarified butter

¹/₂ cup oil
1 teaspoon vanilla
1 cup pulverized almonds
1 teaspoon orange blossom water
  (*mazahar*)
1 teaspoon cinnamon
1 cup coarsely chopped or
  slivered almonds

Beat two of the egg yolks well, then mix with the milk and set aside.

In a large bowl, place the flour, 1 cup of the sugar, baking powder, the orange and lemon zests, butter, and oil; then rub well with hands to mix. Add the vanilla and the yolk and milk mixture; then combine thoroughly to make a dough and let stand for 15 minutes.

In the meantime, make a filling by mixing the remaining ¹/₂ cup of sugar, the pulverized almonds, orange blossom water, and the cinnamon; then set aside.

Roll the dough ¹/₈ inch thick with a rolling pin on a floured surface; then cut into triangles the size of pie wedges. Place the filling in the center and roll up from the bottom of the triangles; then place on a well-greased cookie sheet with the point down (see illustration below).

Brush the rolled croissants with the remaining egg yolk, well-beaten. Sprinkle the croissants with the chopped or slivered almonds; then bake in a 350°F preheated oven for 15 to 20 minutes.

Dates with Bananas

Palestine and Jordan

Serves 6 to 8

To the Arabs, the date palm has a definite personality and human qualities. Well might they have a point, for like human beings, if its head is severed, it will die. In the same fashion as a human limb, a frond cut will not grow again, and its crown is covered with a thick foliage, like the hair on a human head.

1 cup whipping cream
1 tablespoon sugar
1 cup whole dates, pitted and
   thinly sliced lengthwise

3 large bananas, sliced in half
   lengthwise, then sliced into $^1/_2$ inch
   thick pieces
1 teaspoon cinnamon

    Mix the cream and sugar and whip until stiff; then place in a bowl and add the dates and bananas. Toss gently; then place in 6 to 8 serving dishes. Sprinkle with the cinnamon; then chill for 30 minutes before serving.

Dates in Butter Sauce

Al-Rangina

Saudi Arabia

Serves 4 to 6

To thrive, the date palm needs a hot dry climate with no rain but water for the roots. It is said this majestic tree needs its head in the sun and its feet in water. The Arabs have a proverb: "The date palm must have its feet in heaven but its head in hell." Under ideal conditions, the tree usually grows from 20 to 30 feet tall. Its life span is 100 years, although it has been known, in some instances, to reach the age of 200. From the age of about five, the date tree begins to bear fruit and continues until it dies of old age. The palm has no branches, but the leaves, when the tree matures, are from 20 to 30 feet long. There are male and female species and, to bear fruit, the female must be fertilized. In the wild, this function is performed by the wind. However, when palms are commercially cultivated, they are pollinated artificially by hand. There are perhaps several thousand species bearing fruit, which range from the size of a tiny plum to that of a large orange.

$^3/_4$ lb whole dates, pitted
$^3/_4$ cup butter
$^2/_3$ cup flour

2 teaspoons cinnamon
$1^1/_2$ tablespoons confectioner's sugar

    Place the dates in 4 to 6 small serving plates in rows; then set aside.

Heat the butter over medium heat until it begins to sizzle; then add the flour and cinnamon. Sauté and stir continually for no more than 3 minutes. The butter sauce should be a soft paste. Pour the sauce over the dates and allow to cool; then sprinkle with the confectioner's sugar and serve.

Date Cookies

Iraq

Makes about 45 pieces

Dates are without doubt one of the world's most complete foods. They contain carbohydrates, fat, protein, vitamins A, B, D, and G, iron, magnesium, potassium, phosphorus, calcium, and copper. Their sugars are not acid forming and they have enough fiber to provide needed roughage. To a Bedouin of the Arabian Peninsula, dates are truly a miracle food. It is no wonder they call them the "bread of the desert."

From the days of early civilization, humankind has believed that dates have medicinal qualities. The Bedouins maintain that a diet of this rich food can cure any ailment from a simple cold to impotence. Many firmly believe that dates cure the diseases of the lung and chest, steady the blood pressure, and clear the intestines, thus helping to keep away cancer of the bowel. There could be some merit to these claims, since the Arabs who eat dates on a daily basis do not suffer from high blood pressure or many of the common digestive ailments of the West.

Beside the fruit, which is much valued as a health food, the other uses of the date palm are of great economic importance. Its fiber is utilized for ropes and mats; its wood for building materials and furniture; its leaves for roofs, baskets, and hats; and the stones of the fruit are crushed for animal food. Also, the sap, called the "drink of life" by the early inhabitants of the Middle East, is made into sugar, vinegar, or alcoholic drinks, and the tree acts as an umbrella for other fruits and vegetables growing in its shade. It is said that there are at least 800 uses for the date palm.

2 cups flour	1 cup sugar
1 teaspoon baking powder	3 eggs
¹/₂ teaspoon ground cardamom	1 cup chopped dates
¹/₂ teaspoon salt	1 cup chopped walnuts
³/₄ cup butter, melted	

Sift together the flour, baking powder, cardamom, and salt; then set aside.

Mix thoroughly the butter, sugar, and eggs; then gradually add the dry ingredients until a soft dough is formed. Stir in the dates and walnuts; then place heaping teaspoons of the dough an inch apart on an ungreased cookie tray. Place in a preheated 350°F oven and bake for 15 minutes or until the cookies turn golden brown. Remove and allow to cool before serving.

Date Crescents
Aqras Tamer
Syria and Lebanon

Makes about 36 pieces

1¼ cups butter, melted	1 cup finely chopped dates
2 eggs	¾ cup blanched almonds, ground
½ cup milk	¼ cup sugar
½ teaspoon salt	½ teaspoon cinnamon
1½ teaspoons vanilla	pinch nutmeg
3 cups flour	pinch ground cloves
2 teaspoons baking powder	½ cup confectioner's sugar

In a bowl, mix 1 cup of the butter, the eggs, milk, salt, and vanilla. Sift together the flour and baking powder, then gradually knead the flour into the butter mixture until a soft dough is formed. Form into ping-pong size balls and allow to rest, covered with a cloth, for 1 hour.

In the meantime, make the filling by thoroughly mixing the rest of the ingredients, including the remaining 4 tablespoons of the butter and excepting the confectioner's sugar. Roll out the balls to 3 to 4 inch rounds. Place 1 heaping teaspoon of filling in the center of each round, then fold over to cover the filling and form into a crescent shape. Pinch the edges together to seal.

Place on a baking tray; then bake in a 350°F preheated oven for 20 minutes or until the crescents turn golden brown. Remove from the oven and allow to cool; then place on a serving plate and sprinkle with the confectioner's sugar.

Date Fruit Cup
Khshoof al-Balah
Egypt

Perhaps at the beginning of the Pharaonic era, the cultivation of date palms spread to the Valley of the Nile. Paintings found in the tombs of the Pharaohs show that this stately tree was known in that ancient land at least since the time that hieroglyphics were invented.

In later centuries, Phoenician traders carried it from the Fertile Crescent and Egypt to North Africa and Spain. However, in Spain the date palm was not cultivated on a large scale until after the Arabs occupied the Iberian Peninsula in 711 AD. In the Alicante province of the eastern coast of Spain, palm orchards, first established by the Arabs, are still flourishing today.

4 cups water	6 whole cloves
2 cups dates, preferably pitted	2 tablespoons lemon juice
⅓ cup sugar	½ cup whipping cream
¼ cup raisins, washed	

Place the water in a pot and bring to a boil; then add the dates and cook for 5 minutes. Remove the dates with a slotted spoon and allow the dates to cool, then peel and set aside. Reserve the cooking water.

Bring the reserved water to a boil; then add the sugar and stir until the sugar dissolves. Stir in the raisins, cloves, and dates and cook for 15 minutes over medium heat. Add the lemon juice and cook for a further 5 minutes; then remove from the heat and allow to cool.

Place in fruit cups; then whip the cream and spoon over the dates before serving.

Date Jam
Maraba Tamer
Palestine and Jordan

Makes about 1 quart

The scenic palm which some people call "the Tree of Paradise" has had religions significance since the dawn of history. The ancient Mesopotamian religions regarded it as a sacred plant, and this reverence was passed on to later religions and civilizations. In the Old Testament, the story of Genesis mentions it as the "tree of life," and the Book of Psalms records that the "righteous shall flourish like a palm tree." Even today, among the Christians, its leaves are used in the celebration of Palm Sunday.

1 1/2 cups water	3 tablespoons lemon juice
2 cups sugar	1/4 cup blanched almonds, finely
10 whole cloves	chopped
2 cups finely chopped dates	1/4 cup walnuts, finely chopped

Bring the water to a boil over medium heat. Add the sugar and cloves and, stirring all the time, bring the water to a boil again.

Stir in the dates and turn the heat to low; then cook for about 10 minutes or until a paste is formed. Add the lemon juice, almonds, and walnuts; then cook for a few more minutes. Remove and allow to cool; then store in a glass jar.

Date and Nut Pie
Hilwat Tamer
Iraq

¹/₂ cup coarsely chopped
  blanched almonds
¹/₂ cup coarsely chopped walnuts
¹/₄ cup sugar
¹/₂ cup butter
1 cup half-and-half

1 lb dates, finely chopped
¹/₂ teaspoon cinnamon
1 tablespoon orange blossom water
  (*mazahar*)
2 tablespoons sesame seeds, toasted

Mix the almonds, walnuts, and sugar; then set aside.

In a heavy frying pan, melt the butter; then stir in the cream, dates, cinnamon, and *mazahar*. Sauté over a low heat until the dates become soft, stirring once in a while to make sure the dates do not stick. Add a little more cream if necessary. Stir in the nut mixture; then sauté for a further 3 minutes.

Spread evenly in a pie pan; then bake in a 300°F preheated oven for 15 minutes. Remove from the oven, sprinkle with the sesame seeds, and allow to cool; then cut into small pie-shaped wedges.

Deep-Fried Sweet Balls
'Awamee
Syria and Lebanon

Makes about 3 dozen pieces

2 cups flour
4 tablespoons cornstarch
teaspoon salt
1¹/₄ oz package dry yeast, dissolved
  in ¹/₄ cup of warm water

2 cups warm water
1 quantity syrup (qater—see p. 14)
2 cups cooking oil

In a large bowl, combine the flour, cornstarch, and salt; then pour in the yeast and mix well. Add the water and stir until the mixture resembles the texture of pancake batter; then cover and set aside for 1 hour.

In the meantime prepare the syrup and keep it warm.

Heat the oil in a saucepan over medium heat; then dip a tablespoon into cold water, spoon up 1 tablespoon of batter and drop it into the hot oil. Cook until the *'awamee* is golden brown; then remove with a slotted spoon and place the ball on a paper towel for a few minutes until the oil is absorbed. Continue until all the batter is used.

Dip the *'awamee* balls into the syrup; then remove and arrange on a serving platter.

Fig Jam

Syria and Lebanon

1 lb dried figs, ground	6 cloves
1 cup sugar	½ cup pine nuts
1 cup cold water	1 tablespoon sesame seeds
1 teaspoon fennel seeds, ground	1 tablespoon lemon juice

Place the figs, sugar, water, fennel, and cloves in a pot and bring to a boil; then cover and cook over medium heat for 20 minutes or until it reaches jam consistency, stirring every few minutes during the last 15 minutes. Remove and stir in the pine nuts, sesame seeds, and lemon juice; then allow to cool.

Note: Store in sterilized containers. Excellent when spread on buttered toast or an Arabic (pita) bread.

Gazelle's Ankles
Ka'ab Ghazal
Algeria

Makes approximately 36 pieces

In Algeria, this picturesquely named sweet is the dessert *par excellence.* No feast would be complete without this sweet, served with mint tea after the meal.

2 cups flour	½ cup finely ground blanched
½ cup clarified butter (see note, p. 211)	almonds
¼ cup vegetable oil	¼ cup sugar
½ cup water	½ teaspoon cinnamon
2 teaspoons orange blossom water	½ quantity syrup (qater—see p. 14)
(*mazahar*)	¼ cup confectioner's sugar

Place the flour, butter, and oil in a bowl and rub together until crumbly; then add the water and 1 teaspoon of the orange blossom water and knead to form a smooth dough. Cover with a cloth and set aside for 30 minutes.

In the meantime, prepare the filling by mixing the almonds, sugar, cinnamon, and the rest of the orange blossom water.

Form the dough into walnut-size balls and place on a cloth; then remove one ball at a time and roll into a very thin circle. Place 1 heaping teaspoon of the filling on the center and fold over to make a half-moon shape; then close by pinching the edges. Trim the edges with a pastry wheel; then form into a crescent shape once more.

Continue the same process until all the balls are used; then place on an ungreased baking tray. Bake on the middle rack of a 350°F oven for 15 to 20 minutes or until golden brown.

In the meantime, prepare the syrup. Place the *ka'ab ghazal* in the syrup for a few moments while they are still hot; then remove to a serving dish and sprinkle with the confectioner's sugar.

Honey Dipped Pastry
Bariwat
Morocco

Makes approximately 48 pieces

1 cup blanched almonds	1 package filo dough
¹/₂ cup sugar	2 cups cooking oil
¹/₂ teaspoon cinnamon	2 tablespoons orange blossom water
1 tablespoon butter	(*mazahar*)
1 egg	2 cups honey

Place the almonds and sugar in a blender and crush until the almonds are semi-fine; then stir in the cinnamon and butter and set aside.

In a small bowl, beat the egg; then set aside.

Cut each filo sheet into two lengthwise; then place 1 tablespoon of the almond mixture near the right hand bottom corner of each half-sheet. Fold the sheet in half lengthwise over the filling; then fold the closed sheet upward into a 3 inch by 2 inch rectangle or a triangle shape.

Using a pastry brush or your hand, paint each *bariwat* piece with the egg, especially at the openings to ensure closure.

Heat the oil in a frying pan until it becomes boiling hot; then lower the heat and place the *bariwat* in the oil, and fry until golden brown.

In the meantime, mix the orange blossom water and honey. Place in a pot and heat thoroughly; then lower the heat to very low. Take the *bariwat* out of the oil; then place in the honey for approximately 3 minutes. Remove the *bariwat* from the honey; then place in a sieve until the honey drains off.

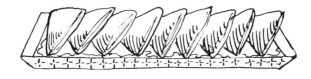

Honeyed Pastries
Griouches
Morocco

1½ cup sesame seeds, toasted
6 cups flour
1 egg
¼ cup lemon juice
3 tablespoons butter
4 cups cooking oil

4 tablespoons orange blossom water
  (*mazahar*)
1¼ oz package yeast dissolved in
  ¼ cup water
4 cups honey

Finely grind ½ cup of the sesame seeds and place in a mixing bowl; then add the flour, egg, lemon juice, butter, ½ cup of the oil, and 1 tablespoon of the orange blossom water and mix thoroughly. Add the dissolved yeast; then knead into a dough and allow to rest for 15 minutes.

Form into 2½ inch diameter balls; then roll the balls into thin sheets and trim the edges to form squares. Cut the squares into quarters to form four smaller squares and roll again into thinner sheets.

Score the sheets into ½ inch strips, starting half an inch from the edges thus leaving the ends attached. Lift each alternate strip with the fingers of one hand; then with the other hand pull lightly the other strips, and gather the strips together, forming oval-shaped "*griouches*."

Place the remaining cooking oil in a frying pan and heat; then lower the temperature and fry the *griouches* until golden brown.

In the meantime, heat the honey with the rest of the orange blossom water and leave over a very low heat. Place the hot *griouches* in the honey for a few minutes; then remove from the honey and place in a sieve or strainer. When the honey has drained, sprinkle with the remaining toasted sesame seeds and serve.

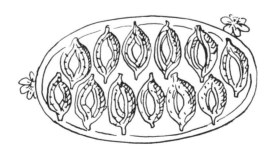

Nutty Date Delight

Ka'k Tamer

Iraq

Makes about 40 pieces

¹/₄ cup butter	1 cup flour
1 cup sugar	1¹/₂ teaspoons baking powder
3 eggs	1¹/₂ cups finely chopped dates
1¹/₂ teaspoons vanilla	1 cup coarsely chopped or
1 teaspoon cinnamon	broken walnuts
¹/₂ teaspoon salt	¹/₂ cup chopped blanched almonds

In a mixing bowl, place the butter, sugar, eggs, vanilla, cinnamon, and salt; then mix thoroughly. Sift in the flour and baking powder; then again mix thoroughly.

Add the dates, walnuts, and almonds and mix well; then place in an 8 inch by 12 inch greased baking pan and bake in a 350°F preheated oven for 30 minutes or until the cake turns golden brown. Cut into squares and allow to cool before serving.

Pomegranate and Almond Delight

Iraq

Serves 4 to 6

Wonderful to look at, appetizing in flavor, delicious in taste, and with a juice which is refreshing on a hot summer day—this is how a northern European tourist visiting the Middle East once described the pomegranate. With this description, the people of southwestern Asia, the original home of this fruit, wholly agree. There is nothing more longingly remembered by a thirsty traveler crossing the burning desert lands than a cool invigorating drink made from the fluid of the pomegranate.

This has been so since remote antiquity. In their mythology, the Greeks believed that the liquid of the pomegranate sprang from the blood of the god of wine and revelry, and thereafter became the drink of the gods. A number of historians have indicated that Eve gave Adam a pomegranate, not an apple as stated in the Bible. In later centuries, Solomon sang of an "orchard of pomegranates," and many people in the eastern lands came to believe that the juice of this historic fruit purged a person of envy and hatred.

seeds from 4 medium pomegranates	4 tablespoons soft honey
1 cup slivered almonds	2 teaspoons orange blossom water
	(*mazahar*)

Thoroughly mix all the ingredients until the honey coats all the pomegranate seeds and almonds; then place in a serving bowl and chill before serving.

Pudding
Mihallabiyya
Egypt

Serves 6

¹/₂ cup cornstarch	1 teaspoon vanilla extract
4 cups milk	1 teaspoon cinnamon
6 tablespoons raisins	2 tablespoons finely chopped walnuts

In a bowl, dissolve the cornstarch in 1 cup of the milk; then set aside.

Put the remaining 3 cups of milk into a pot with the sugar and raisins; then bring to a boil over high heat, stirring until the sugar dissolves. Reduce the heat to low; then add the dissolved cornstarch, and, stirring constantly, simmer for about 10 minutes, or until the mixture is thick enough to coat a spoon heavily. Stir in the vanilla; then pour the mixture into small individual dessert bowls. Sprinkle with cinnamon and scatter the walnuts decoratively on top; then refrigerate for at least 2 hours before serving.

Sesame Cookies
Barazek
Syria and Lebanon

Makes about 40 cookies

³/₄ cup sesame seeds	1¹/₂ cups sugar
¹/₂ cup honey	2¹/₂ cups flour
¹/₂ cup coarsely chopped pistachios	2 cups wheat hearts or semolina
2 eggs	2 teaspoons baking powder
1¹/₂ cups butter	¹/₂ teaspoon salt

Place the sesame seeds, honey, and pistachios in separate bowls; then set aside.

Place the eggs, butter, and sugar in a food processor and process into a paste; then transfer to a mixing bowl. Add the flour, wheat hearts, baking powder, and salt; then knead into a dough.

Form into golf ball-sized balls; then dip the balls, one at a time, into the pistachios and flatten with the fingers on a greased cookie tray. Continue until all the balls are finished; then brush each cookie with the honey, and sprinkle with the sesame seeds.

Bake in a 350°F preheated oven for 15 minutes or until the cookies turn golden brown; then remove and allow to cool.

Shredded Dough Cheese Cake
Knafa bil-Jiben
Syria and Lebanon

Serves 8

In the Middle East, *knafa bil-jiben* is a traditional breakfast dish. However, it is also an excellent dessert.

1 package *knafa* dough (1 lb or 454 grams), available in Middle Eastern grocery stores

1 cup clarified butter (see note, p. 211)

1 lb ricotta cheese, broken down with a fork

1 teaspoon orange blossom water (*mazahar*)

1 quantity syrup (*qater*—see p. 14)

¹/₄ cup crushed pistachios or blanched almonds

Thaw the dough if frozen; then mix it with the butter and place it in a baking pan. Place pan over *very low* heat, and gently rub the dough with your hands for about 15 minutes, ensuring that every part of the dough is moist; then divide the dough into two halves. Flatten half of the dough by hand into an 8 inch by 12 inch well-buttered baking pan that is 2 inches deep.

Mix the cheese and orange blossom water; then spread on the dough in the pan and cover with the other half of the dough. Bake in a 300°F preheated oven for 30 minutes or until the surface of the dough becomes golden brown. If the surface is not golden brown in 30 minutes, place the pan under the broiler and turn it around until the top is evenly golden brown.

In the meantime, prepare the syrup using only half the sugar listed in the syrup recipe. Remove the *knafa* from the oven and, while still hot, pour the syrup evenly over the top. Garnish with pistachios or almonds; then cut into 8 pieces and serve while hot.

Stuffed Dates

Iraq

In the date palm's native homeland, the Arabian Peninsula, the inhabitants have no doubts that it was the first grown in paradise. According to Muslim belief, the Archangel Gabriel told Adam in the Garden of Eden: "Thou art created from the same substance as this palm tree which henceforth shall nourish you."

1 lb whole dates, pitted
1/2 cup coarsely chopped walnuts
3/4 cup half-and-half
2/3 cup sugar

1 tablespoon orange blossom water (*mazahar*)
4 tablespoons cocoa
1 cup shredded coconut

Slit the dates on one side and stuff with the walnuts; then close and set aside.

Place the cream in a small pot and bring it to a boil; then add the sugar and stir over medium heat until it melts. Add the orange blossom water and cocoa and cook, stirring constantly, for about 5 minutes; then remove from the heat and allow to cool.

Dip the dates in the cocoa syrup; then roll them in the coconut and place on a serving tray.

Stuffed Pancakes
Katayif
Syria and Lebanon

The Batter

2 cups flour
1 1/2 teaspoons baking powder
1/2 teaspoon salt
2 cups milk

2 eggs
1 cup butter, melted
1 quantity syrup (*qater*—see p. 14)

Sift together dry ingredients. Place with the milk and eggs in a large mixing bowl; then beat until smooth. Add 2 tablespoons of the melted butter and beat again; then cover and let rest for a few hours.

In the meantime, prepare the syrup, and either one of the following fillings by mixing the ingredients thoroughly.

Cheese Filling	*or*	*Walnut Filling*
2 cups ricotta cheese		2 cups chopped walnuts
3/4 cup sugar		3/4 cup sugar
1 teaspoon cinnamon		1 teaspoon cinnamon
		2 teaspoons orange blossom water (*mazahar*)

Heat a griddle; then grease with shortening or butter. Pour about 2 table-spoons of the batter to make about 3 inch wide patties (on a griddle, you can make about 4 pancakes at a time). Let cook on one side only; then remove and place on a paper towel. Place about 2 teaspoons of the filling on each pancake; then fold over to make a half-moon shape and press firmly. Transfer to a buttered baking sheet or tray; then repeat the procedure until all the batter is finished.

Pour some of the remaining melted butter over each pancake; then place in a preheated oven of 375°F for 10 to 15 minutes. Remove from the oven and dip into the syrup; then drain and allow to cool before serving.

Sugared Dates
Morocco

The inhabitants of the oases in the Arabian desert and the Sahara of North Africa value the graceful palm above all other trees as a symbol of wealth and prestige. For thousands of years it has been the foundation of life for the dwellers of these arid lands. The climate in these countries is ideal for its cultivation, and its fruit is easily preserved. When ripe and dried, dates do not spoil. It is as if this valuable fruit were tailor-made for the desert lands.

1 lb dates, pitted
$^{1}/_{2}$ cup blanched almonds
$^{3}/_{4}$ cup sugar
2 tablespoons butter

1 teaspoon orange blossom water
   (*mazahar*)
pinch nutmeg

Slit each date on one side and set aside.

Place the almonds on a tray and lightly brown in the oven; then grind finely. Make a filling by thoroughly mixing the almonds, $^{1}/_{4}$ cup of the sugar, the butter, orange blossom water, and the nutmeg. Stuff each date with about 1 teaspoon of the filling; then close and roll in the remaining $^{1}/_{2}$ cup of sugar. Place on a serving dish and serve as candies or for dessert.

Tunisian Date Cookies
Makroodh

Makes about 25 pieces

In North Africa, dates with a bowl of milk are offered a visitor as a symbol of hospitality.

2¹/₂ cups semolina flour

1 cup butter, melted

1¹/₂ teaspoons vanilla

2 eggs

¹/₂ teaspoon salt

¹/₂ cup finely chopped dates

1 cup honey

¹/₂ cup water

1 tablespoon orange blossom water (*mazahar*)

2 cups oil

2 tablespoons confectioner's sugar

Mix the semolina, butter, vanilla, eggs, and salt; then knead until the dough is smooth. Add a little water if necessary. Shape the dough into about 2¹/₂ inch long cylinders, one inch in diameter; then take each one in the palm of the hand and make a small trench. Place about ¹/₂ teaspoon of the dates in each trench; then close and pat into rectangular cookies and allow to rest for one hour.

In the meantime, make a syrup by placing in a pot the honey, water, and *mazahar*; then, stirring all the time, bring to a boil. Keep warm over low heat.

Heat the oil in a saucepan; then fry the *makroodhs* until they turn golden brown. Do not overheat the oil

Dip the *makroodhs* in the honey syrup, then drain and allow to cool. Sprinkle with the confectioner's sugar and serve.

Tunisian Doughnuts
Yo-yo

Makes approximately 2 dozen small doughnuts

3 eggs

2¹/₄ cups oil

¹/₄ cup orange juice

2 tablespoons finely chopped
  fresh coconut

1¹/₄ cups sugar

2¹/₂ cups flour

1¹/₂ teaspoons baking soda

2 cups water

2 tablespoons lemon juice

1 cup honey

Place the eggs, ¹/₄ cup of the oil, orange juice, 1 tablespoon of the coconut, and ¹/₄ cup of the sugar in a blender. Blend until smooth.

Transfer to a bowl; then sift in the flour and baking soda, and knead until the mixture is soft. Cover the bowl with a towel; then set aside to rest for at least 1 hour.

In the meantime, make a syrup by placing in a pot the remaining sugar, water, and lemon juice; then boil over high heat until the sugar dissolves, stirring constantly. Reduce the heat to low and add the honey and the remaining 1 tablespoon of the coconut. Simmer for 10 minutes, then turn heat to very low to keep the syrup warm.

Place the remaining oil in a small saucepan; then heat until the oil is moderately hot. In the meantime, divide the dough into walnut-size balls; then flatten the balls slightly.

Hold the round in the palm of one hand and punch a hole through the center with the floured index finger of your other hand. Fry, a few at a time, for about 5 minutes, turning them around with a slotted spoon until they are golden brown on both sides; then transfer them to paper towels to drain. With tongs, pick up the *yo-yos*; then dip them into the warm syrup and serve at once.

Yogurt Cake

Iraq

1¹/₂ cups yogurt	2¹/₂ teaspoons baking powder
¹/₂ cup butter, melted	¹/₂ teaspoon salt
¹/₂ cup whipping cream	¹/₂ cup honey
4 eggs	¹/₂ cup water
1 cup sugar	3 tablespoons lemon juice
2 cups flour	

Thoroughly mix the yogurt, butter, cream, eggs, and sugar; then set aside.

Sift the flour, baking powder, and salt; then stir into the yogurt mixture to make a batter. Place in a well-greased 8 inch by 11 inch baking pan and let stand for an hour; then bake in a 300°F preheated oven for about 1¹/₄ hours, or until a skewer inserted into the center of the cake comes out clean.

In the meantime, make a syrup by placing the honey and water in a pot. Bring to a boil over medium heat, stirring a few times; then add the lemon juice and boil for about 5 minutes before removing from the heat.

Remove the cake from the oven and allow to cool; then turn over into a serving dish. Spoon the syrup evenly over the cake; serve warm.

Wheatheart Cakes

Syria and Lebanon

2 lbs cream of wheat
1½ cups yogurt
1½ cups whipping cream
1 cup shredded coconut
4 tablespoons baking powder
2½ cups sugar

¾ cup water
2 tablespoons lemon juice
1 tablespoon orange or
   rose blossom water
1 cup melted butter

In a mixing bowl, place the cream of wheat, yogurt, whipping cream, coconut, baking powder, and half a cup of the sugar; then mix thoroughly into a batter. Pour the batter into a 10 inch by 15 inch well-greased baking pan and place in a 350°F preheated oven; bake for 30 minutes.

In the meantime, place the remaining 2 cups of sugar and water in a pot and bring to a boil over a medium heat, stirring constantly; then add the lemon juice and simmer over low heat for a further 15 minutes. Turn the heat to very low and stir in the orange or rose blossom water; keep the syrup warm.

Before removing the cake from the oven, brown evenly for a few minutes under the broiler; then cut into 2 inch squares. Spoon the melted butter over the cake and wait for a few moments; then pour the warm syrup evenly over the top and allow to cool before serving.

Drinks

In the Arab world, during the past centuries, sherbets (from Arabic *sharba*[t] —a drink), lemonade, coffee, tea, and similar types of non-alcoholic drinks were the common beverages.

Today, even though they are still common throughout the Arab lands, Western-style drinks are slowly edging them out. Of course, this applies mostly to cold drinks, whereas coffee and tea are still very popular at all levels of society.

Perhaps the most common of the ancient kinds of drinks which are still to be found in every Arab country is liquorice root beverage, sold by street vendors everywhere. Almost every tourist is impressed by these colorfully dressed vendors clinking their cups and crying out, "'Irq as-soos, 'irq as-soos!"

Alcoholic drinks have been in the past and remain today traditional among the Christian and Jewish Arab communities, especially in Egypt, Lebanon, Syria, Tunisia, and Morocco. Muslims in every Arab land generally avoid alcohol, although lapses do occur.

Coffee and tea in all their forms are the drinks *par excellence* among the Arabs. In the Arab East, coffee rules supreme. A traditional sign of hospitality, it is the first offering to guests. A gift from the Arabian Peninsula to the world, coffee has been for centuries and still is associated with the exotic lure of Arabia. Its Arab origin is attested to by the languages of the world, most of which derive their name for coffee from the Arabic *qahwa*.

In North Africa, mint tea plays a similar role to coffee in the eastern Arab lands. A few minutes after a stranger enters a North African home, a glass of piping hot mint tea is offered. Refreshing, tasty, and diffusing an inviting aroma, it is also a great ending for a festive meal. Tourists may in time forget their adventures in the North African world, but never the lure of freshly brewed mint tea.

Arabic Coffee
Qahwa 'Arabiyya
Syria and Lebanon

Serves 4

Coffee, which derives from the Arabic word *qahwa*, was introduced into Europe via Turkey from Arabia. The drinking of coffee is a very important activity in the Eastern Arab world. Men spend hours during the long summer evenings, and whenever they can during the day, sitting in cafés, sipping cups of coffee. The women drink coffee while visiting one another in their homes.

Business and bargaining in the marketplace never take place without drinking coffee. At home, it is served as soon as visitors arrive, always freshly brewed and usually with freshly roasted and pulverized coffee beans.

4 heaping tablespoons pulverized coffee
2 tablespoons sugar

4 cups water
1 cardamom seed, crushed

Place the coffee, sugar, and water in a pot, and bring to a boil; then when the froth begins to rise, remove from the heat and stir. Heat again until the froth arises; then remove from the heat and allow to settle for a few minutes. Add the crushed cardamom and stir; then put a little froth into each cup. Pour the coffee and serve hot.

Note: The sugar may be omitted if desired, and the coffee served bitter or with an artificial sweetener.

Arabic Coffee Kuwaiti Style

2 cups water

4 heaping tablespoons very finely
  ground coffee

6 cardamom seeds, crushed

Place all the ingredients in a coffee pot; then bring to a boil. Turn the heat to low and simmer for 30 minutes; then fill about a third of each Arabic coffee cup at a time and serve. Two more servings of coffee should be offered to each guest.

Arabic Coffee Saudi Arabian Style

2¹/₂ cups water

¹/₄ cup very coarsely ground
  partially roasted coffee

1 teaspoon pulverized cardamom seeds

Place the water in a coffee pot and bring to a boil; then remove from the heat and add the coffee. Return to the heat and brew over medium heat for 10 minutes; then remove and pour slowly into a serving coffee pot (*ibreeq*), making sure the grounds remain in the first pot. Add the cardamom and boil for 3 minutes just before serving.

Cinnamon Tea

Kuwait

Serves 4

4 cups water

4 cinnamon sticks, each about
  4 inches long

2 teaspoons sugar

Place the water and cinnamon in a pot and bring to a boil; then boil over medium heat for 20 minutes. Remove the sticks; then stir in the sugar and boil for a minute before serving.

Ginger Coffee

Yemen

Serves 4

2 cups water
4 tablespoons pulverized coffee

2 tablespoons sugar
2 teaspoons ground ginger

Place all the ingredients in a pot and bring to a boil; then remove from the heat. Return to the heat and again bring to a boil; then repeat another two times, before serving in demitasse cups.

Grape Drink

Morocco

Makes 1 quart

1 quart grape juice
2 tablespoons sugar

2 tablespoons orange blossom water (*mazahar*)
1 teaspoon cinnamon

Thoroughly mix all the ingredients; then refrigerate before serving.

Lemon Tea

Kuwait

6 cups water
2 unpeeled lemons, washed and
    quartered

5 tablespoons sugar
1 tablespoon orange blossom water
    (*mazahar*)

Place the water and lemons in a pot and bring to a boil; then cover and boil over medium heat for 20 minutes. Strain into a teapot, and stir in the sugar and *mazahar*; then bring to a boil and serve.

Mint Tea
Atay bi-Na'na'
Morocco and North Africa

Serves 4

The preparation of *atay* is considered an art by the Moroccans. It is traditionally served in a richly engraved silver pot, and poured from a great height into ornamented glasses. *Atay* is Morocco's most popular drink. It is consumed at all times of the day by all types of people. Whether served in a humble café, an elaborate restaurant, or in the home, this drink is the refreshment most loved by the Moroccans and the rest of the peoples of North Africa.

boiling water
1$\frac{1}{2}$ tablespoons green tea
5 to 6 oz sugar cubes

$\frac{1}{2}$ cup of fresh mint leaves with stalks (dried mint leaves are not as good, but can be used if fresh mint is not available)

Rinse out a 3-cup metal teapot with hot water; then add the tea. Pour in $\frac{1}{2}$ cup boiling water, swish around in the pot quickly and discard the water, making sure not to discard the tea. This rinse removes the bitterness from the tea.

Stuff the mint leaves with their stalks in the pot and add the sugar. Fill the pot with boiling water and let steep for 5 minutes, checking occasionally to be sure the mint doesn't rise above the water. Stir and taste, adding sugar if necessary.

Traditionally, the tea is served in small glasses set in silver holders, but demitasse cups or standard cups will do.

Note: For second helpings, leave the mint and the tea in the pot, add a teaspoon of tea, several mint leaves, and some sugar cubes and fill again with boiling water. When the mint rises to the surface, the tea is ready. Stir and taste for sugar; then serve. The same process is repeated for the third pot. In Morocco, custom requires that three helpings be offered and three helpings be accepted.

If green tea is not available, use an Indian tea. You may also serve the tea Western style by omitting the sugar, and allowing each person to sugar his or her own cup to taste.

Orange Juice Drink

Morocco

Makes 1 quart

1 quart orange juice
4 tablespoons sugar

2 tablespoons orange blossom water
(*mazahar*)

Thoroughly mix all the ingredients; then refrigerate before serving.

Yogurt Drink

Iraq

A very refreshing drink during the hot summer months.

2 cups yogurt
4 cups water

$\frac{1}{2}$ teaspoon salt

Thoroughly mix all the ingredients and refrigerate for at least two hours; then stir and serve. Always stir just before serving.

Where to Find Ingredients

Arizona

Hajji Baba Middle
 Eastern Food
1513 East Apache
Tempe, AZ 85281

California

Al-Baraka Market
4135 Spulveda Blvd.
Culver City, CA 90230

Al-Jibani Halal Market
23385 Golden Springs
 Drive
Diamond Bar, CA 91765

Avocado Food Market
852 Avocado Avenue
El Cajon, CA 92020

Fairuz Middle Eastern
 Grocery
3306 N. Garey at Foothill
Pomona, CA 91767

Fresno Deli
2450 E. Gettysburg
 Ave.
Fresno, CA 93726

International Groceries
3548 Ashford Street
San Diego, CA 92111

K & C Importing
2771 West Pico Blvd.
Los Angeles, CA 90006

Levant International
9421 Alondra Blvd.
Bellflower, CA 90706

Marhaba Supermarket
10932 East Emperial Hwy.
Norwalk, CA

M & J Market & Deli
12924 Vanowen St.
North Hollywood, CA
 91605

Middle East Food
26 Washington Street
Santa Clara, CA 95050

Near East Foods
4595 El Cajon Blvd.
San Diego, CA 92115

P & J Deli Market
754 N. Lake Avenue
Pasadena Lake Center
 Pasadena CA

Samiramis Importing Co.
2990 Mission Street
San Francisco, CA 94110

Sunflower Grocery
20774 E. Arrow Hwy.
Covina, CA 91724

Sweis International
6809 Hazeltine Avenue
Van Nuys, CA 91405

Colorado

International Market
2020 South Parker Road
Denver, CO 80231

Middle East Market
2254 S. Colorado Blvd.
Denver, CO 80222

Connecticut

Nouzaim Middle Eastern
 Bakery
1650 East Main Street
Waterbury, CT 06705

Shallah's Middle Eastern
 Importing Co.
290 White Street
Danbury, CT 06810

Florida

Ali Baba Food, Inc.
2901 West Oakland
 Park Blvd.
Fort Lauderdale, FL
 33311

Damascus Grocery
5721 Hollywood Blvd.
Hollywood, FL 33021

Sahara Mediterranean
 Food Mart
3570 N. State Road 7
Lauderdale Lakes, FL
 33319

Georgia

Leon International
4000-A Pleasantdale
 Road, NE
Atlanta, GA 30340

Middle Eastern Groc.
22–50 Cobb Parkway
Smyrna, GA 30080

Illinois

Holy Land Grocery
4806–8 N. Kedzie Ave.
Chicago, IL 60625

Middle Eastern Bakery
1512 W. Foster Avenue
Chicago, IL 60640

Maryland

Dokan Deli
7921 Old Georgetown
    Road
Bethesda, MD 20814

Yekta Deli
1488 Rockville Pike
Rockville, MD 20800

Massachusetts

Lebanese Grocery
High Point Shopping
    Center
4640 Washington St.
Roslindale, MA 02131

Near East Baking Co.
5268 Washington
West Roxbury, MA
    02132

Syrian Grocery
270 Shawmut Avenue
Boston, MA 02118

New York

Al-Asmar
202 Atlantic Avenue
Brooklyn, NY 11201

Malko
174 Atlantic Avenue
Brooklyn, NY 11201

Nablus Grocery
456 S. Broadway
Yonkers, NY 10705

Nadar Imports
One East 28th Street
New York, NY 10016

Oriental Grocery
170–172 Atlantic Ave.
Brooklyn, NY 11201

Sahadi Importing Co.
187 Atlantic Avenue
Brooklyn, NY 11201

Sunflower Store
97–22 Queens Blvd.
Rego Park, NY 11374

The Family Store
69–05 3rd Avenue
Brooklyn, NY 11209

North Carolina

The Middle East Deli
4508 E. Independence
    Blvd. # 111
Charlotte, NC 28205

Nur, Inc.
223 Avent Ferry Road
Raleigh, NC 27606

Ohio

Gus's Middle Eastern
    Bakery
308 East South Street
Akron, OH 44311

Holy Land Imports
12831 Lorain Avenue
Cleveland, OH 44111

Middle East Foods
19–57 West 25th St.
Cleveland, OH 44113

Sinbad Food Imports
2620 N. High Street
Columbus, OH 43202

Oklahoma

Mediterranean Imports
36–27 North MacArthur
Oklahoma City, OK
    73122

Michigan

The Arabic Town
16511 Woodward
Highland Park, MI
    48203

Minnesota

Cindybad Bakery & Deli
1923 Central Avenue, NE
Minneapolis, MN 55418

Missouri

Campus Eastern Foods
408 Locust Street # B
Columbia, MO 65201

New Jersey

Al-Khayyam
7723 Bergenline Ave.
North Bergen, NJ 07047

Arabic Town
63–10 Bergenline Avenue
North Bergen, NJ 07093

Fattal's Syrian Bakery
977 Main Street
Paterson, NJ 07503

M & N Grocery
28–01 Kennedy Blvd.
Jersey City, NJ 07306

Nouri's Syrian Bakery
983–989 Main Street
Paterson, NJ 07503

Sahara Fine Food
242 S. Summit Avenue
Hackensack, NJ 07601

Pennsylvania

Bitar's
947 Federal Street
Philadelphia, PA 19147

Makhoul's Corner Store
448 North 2nd Street
Allentown, PA 18102

Salim's Middle Eastern
   Food Store
47–05 Center Avenue
Pittsburgh, PA 15213

South Carolina

Mediterranean Grocery
1421 Laurens Road
Greenville, SC 29607

Texas

Droubi's Bakery & Grocery
7333 Hillcroft
Houston, TX 77081

Jerusalem Grocery
201 E. Main
Richardson, TX 75081

Phoenicia Bakery & Deli
2912 S. Lamar
Austin, TX 78704

Rana Food Store
1623 W. Arkansas Lane
Arlington, TX 76013

Worldwide Foods
2203 Greenville Avenue
Dallas, TX 75206

Virginia

Aphrodite Greek Imports
5886 Leesburg Pike
Falls Church, VA
   22041

Halalco
108 E. Fairfax Street
Falls Church, VA
   22046

Mediterranean Bakery
374 S. Picket Street
Alexandria, VA 22304

Canada

Abir Foods, Inc.
1272 A Eglinton Ave. E.
Mississauga, Ontario
Canada L4W 1K8

Byblos Mini Mart
2667 Islington Ave.
Rexdale, Ontario
Canada M9V 2X6

Jerusalem Supermarket
3355 Hurontario St. #8
Mississauga, Ontario
Canada L5A 2H3

Nasr Foods
1996 Lawrence Ave. E.
Scarborough, Ontario
Canada M1R 221

Marché Adonis
9590 de l'Acadie
Montréal, Québec
Canada H4N 1L8

Supermarché Alchallal
475 Côté Vertu
Saint-Laurent, Québec
Canada H4L 1X7

Provisions Byblos
175 Côté Vertu
Saint-Laurent, Québec
Canada H4N 1C8

Marché Suidan
710 Boul. Labelle
Chomedy, Laval,
Québec
Canada H7V 2T9

Mid East Food Centre
1010 Belfast Rd.
Ottawa, Ontario
Canada K1G 4A2

Lockwood Farm Mkt.
699 Wilkins St.
London, Ontario
Canada N6C 5C8

Phoenicia Foods Ltd.
2594 Agricola
Halifax, Nova Scotia
Canada B3K 4C6

Rosslyn Food Market
11316 134th Ave.
Edmonton, Alberta
Canada T5E 1K5

Elmasu Food Imports
3477 Commercial St.
Vancouver, British
Columbia V5N 4E8

Index

Index of Recipes and Ingredients in Arabic

Metric Conversion Chart

	U.S. Measures	Metric Equivalents
LENGTH	1 inch	2.54 centimeters
		(25 millimeters)
	12 inches	30 centimeters
	(1 foot)	
VOLUME	1 teaspoon	5 milliliters
	1 tablespoon	15 milliliters
	(3 teaspoons)	
	1 cup	236 milliliters
	(16 tablespoons)	(about 1/4 liter)
	1 quart	1 scant liter
	(4 cups or 2 pints)	
	1 gallon	3.78 liters
	(4 quarts)	
	1 pint	0.47 liter
	(16 fluid ounces)	
WEIGHT	1 ounce	28.35 grams
	1 pound	
	(16 ounces)	454 grams
		(0.454 kilogram)

	Fahrenheit	Centrigrade
OVEN TEMPERATURES	212°F	100°C
	225°F	107°C
	250°F	121°C
	275°F	135°C
	300°F	149°C
	325°F	163°C
	350°F	177°C
	375°F	191°C
	400°F	204°C
	425°F	218°C
	450°F	232°C
	475°F	246°C
	500°F	260°C